GEORGE MACDONALD FRASER

George MacDonald Fraser was born in Carlisle, England on April 2, 1925, and was educated at Carlisle Grammar School and Glasgow Academy. He entered the military in 1943, serving for four years with first the Border Regiment and then the Gordon Highlanders. In 1947 he began a twenty-two-year career on newspapers in Britain and Canada, ending as deputy editor of the *Glasgow Herald* from 1964 to 1969.

Mr. Fraser is best known as the author of the acclaimed "Flashman" novels, the first of which was published in 1969 *(Flashman),* and the most recent in 1999 *(Flashman and the Tiger).*

He has also written three collections of stories about Private "Piltdown" McAuslan: *The General Danced at Dawn* (1970), *McAuslan in the Rough* (1974), and *The Sheikh and the Dustbin* (1988). The three are brought together in an omnibus COMMON READER EDITION, under the title *McAuslan Entire.* His other novels are: *Mr. American* (1980), *The Pyrates* (1984), *Black Ajax* (1988), and *The Candlemass Road* (1993).

His other work includes several screenplays, most notably *The Three Musketeers* (1973), *The Four Musketeers* (1975), and the James Bond film *Octopussy* (1983), as well as three volumes of nonfiction: *The Steel Bonnets* (1971), *The Hollywood History of the World* (1988), and *Quartered Safe Out Here* (1992). About the latter, John Keegan has said: "There is no doubt that it is one of the great personal memoirs of the Second World War."

In 1999, Mr. Fraser was awarded an OBE by Queen Elizabeth II. He lives with his wife on the Isle of Man.

By George MacDonald Fraser in COMMON READER EDITIONS:
McAuslan Entire • The Steel Bonnets
The Candlemass Road • Quartered Safe Out Here
The Pyrates

COMMON READER EDITIONS with Introductions by George MacDonald Fraser:
Captain Blood, by Rafael Sabatini
The White Company & Sir Nigel, by Sir Arthur Conan Doyle

By the same author in
COMMON READER EDITIONS:

The Steel Bonnets
McAuslan Entire
The Candlemass Road
The Pyrates

QUARTERED
SAFE
OUT HERE

A Recollection of the War in Burma

GEORGE MACDONALD
FRASER

A COMMON READER EDITION
THE AKADINE PRESS
2001

Quartered Safe Out Here: A Recollection of the War in Burma

A COMMON READER EDITION published 2001
by The Akadine Press, Inc., by arrangement with the author.

Copyright © 1992 by George MacDonald Fraser
Epilogue copyright © 2000 by George MacDonald Fraser

First published in 1992 by
Harvill, an imprint of HarperCollins*Publishers*.

A COMMON READER EDITION and fountain colophon are trademarks
of The Akadine Press, Inc.

ISBN 1-58579-024-9

10 9 8 7 6 5 4 3 2 1

FOR JACK, ANDREW, HARRY, AND TOM,
SOME DAY,
THE TALE OF A GRANDFATHER

You may talk o' gin and beer
When you're quartered safe out here,
An' you're sent to penny fights an' Aldershot it,
But when it comes to slaughter
You will do your work on water
An' you'll lick the bloomin' boots of 'im that's got it.

RUDYARD KIPLING, *Gunga Din*

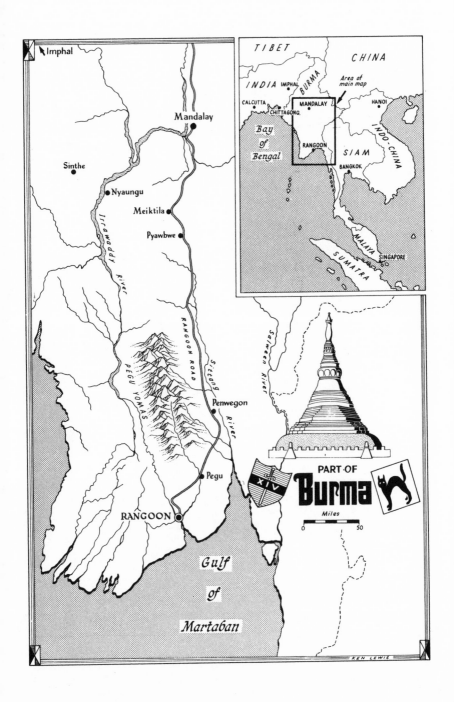

INTRODUCTION

It is satisfying, and at the same time slightly eerie, to read in an official military history of an action in which you took part, even as a very minor and bewildered participant. A coloured picture of men and guns and violent movement comes between the eye and the printed page; smells return to the nostrils, of dusty heat and oil and cordite smoke, and you hear again the rattle of small arms and crash of explosions, the startled oaths and the yells of command. And if the comparison is a humbling one, it is worth making if only to show how dehumanised military history has to be.

By rights each official work should have a companion volume in which the lowliest actor gives his version (like Sydenham Poyntz for the Thirty Years' War or Rifleman Harris in the Peninsula); it would at least give posterity a sense of perspective.

For example, on page 287 of *The War Against Japan: volume IV (The Reconquest of Burma)*, it is briefly stated that "a second series of raids began . . . and — Regiment suffered 141 casualties and lost one of its supporting tanks . . ."

That tank burned for hours, and when night came down it attracted Japanese in numbers. We lay off in the darkness with our safety catches on and grenades to hand, watching and keeping desperately quiet. The Japs milled around in the firelight like small clockwork dolls, but our mixed group of British, Gurkhas, and Probyn's Horse remained undetected, although how the enemy failed to overhear the fight that broke out between a Sikh and a man from Carlisle (someone alleged that a water chaggle had been stolen, and the night was briefly disturbed by oaths in Punjabi and a snarl of "Give ower, ye bearded booger!") remains a mystery. It was a long night; perhaps memory makes it longer.

Or there is Appendix 20, an account of Deception Plan "Cloak", whereby General Slim deceived the Japanese by a fake crossing of the Irrawaddy. He confused Nine Section, too; we dug in at no fewer than three different positions in as many hours, Grandarse lost his upper dentures on a sandbank, little Nixon disturbed a nest of black scorpions in the dark, we dug in hurriedly in a fourth position, and the general feeling was that the blame for the whole operation lay at the door of, first, Winston Churchill, secondly, the royal family, and thirdly (for some unimaginable reason) Vera Lynn. It should be understood that we did not know that "Cloak" had worked brilliantly; we were footsore, hungry, forbidden to light fires, and on hundred per cent stand-to – even although, as Grandarse, articulating with difficulty, pointed out, there wasn't a Jap within miles.

It is not facetious to recall these undertones of war. With all military histories it is necessary to remember that war is not a matter of maps with red and blue arrows and oblongs, but of weary, thirsty men with sore feet and aching shoulders wondering where they are, and when the historian writes:

"17th Division closed in on Pyawbwe from all directions"

that this involved, inter alia, the advance of long green lines of bush-hatted men, ducking but not breaking stride as the low-angle shells burst among them, and Sergeant Hutton muttering: "Ah knew we'd git the shit – if we'd been lead platoon, or at back, we'd ha' bin reet, but we 'ad to be in't bloody middle! Keep spread oot!", and a corporal with a bleeding furrow across his temple propped against a bank shouting: "Ga'n git 'em, marras!" and starting to sing "John Peel", and little Nixon making his usual philosophic remark that we'd all git killed and he didn't want to die Tojo's way, and someone falling down a well and having to be pulled out, and it ended with a hectic charge to a wrecked railway line, and we caught them in the open on the other side, and I was kneeling, sodden and steaming, with little Nick beside me shooting and humming under his breath and remarking: "Ye're firin' low an' left, Jock – that's it ... git that booger, he's nobbut wounded!"

Eleven hundred Japanese died in that battle; the official history records the fact, but doesn't tell you how.

I wrote the above, or something like it, as a book review twenty-five years ago, which was twenty years after it happened. It is ancient history now, and war, and attitudes to war, have changed so much that you may wonder if it is worth returning to, so late in the day. But I think it is those changes, really, that make it worth while. After all, if mankind is lucky, it may be that the end of the Burma campaign was the last great battle in the last great war; and even if it wasn't, it may still be worth remembering from an ordinary foot-soldier's point of view, for it is a story of an army the like of which had not been seen (in Churchill's words) since Xerxes crossed the Hellespont – a huge foreign legion of what Attlee called "the scrapings of the barrel" from half the nations under the sun, fighting under one of the great captains in mountain, jungle, and dry plain, in hot sun and drenching monsoon, and inflicting on one of the great warrior races its most crushing defeat.

That is my reason for writing not a history, for that has been done better than I could do it, or even a coherent detailed narrative, for I haven't got that kind of memory, but simply what I know and remember of the Burma war.

Looking back over sixty-odd years, life is like a piece of string with knots in it, the knots being those moments that live in the mind forever, and the intervals being hazy, half-recalled times when I have a fair idea of what was happening, in a general way, but cannot be sure of dates or places or even the exact order in which events took place. I suspect it is the same with most folk, although I am often astonished (and suspicious, being an old newspaperman) at the orderliness with which some can trace a continuous thread of recollection. In my case, there are coloured strips of film at each knot of memory, and in between many rather grainy sequences which can be made out only with difficulty, and in some cases the print is spoiled or even undeveloped.

To give an example: I have the most vivid recollection of my first encounter with an angry Japanese, and the immediately preceding and succeeding events – but I have only the vaguest idea of where and when that momentous encounter took place. I do not know what day General Slim visited us when we were holding Meiktila, or whether the lake shore on which he stood was the northern or southern one, but I see him clear, with that robber-baron face under the Gurkha hat, and his carbine slung, looking like a rather scruffy private with a general's tabs – which of course is what he was. I don't know from which point of the compass we attacked Pyawbwe, because it didn't matter to me, but I know what happened there. I could not come within weeks of naming the day when our canoe foundered in a tributary of the Sittang, which was also the day we picked up the section's first Jap prisoner, and Forster stole his watch. I don't even know where I was on VJ Day – and if it seems remarkable that I am unaware of these things, I must emphasise that at private soldier level you frequently have no idea where you are, or precisely how you got there, let alone why.

Had I been an officer my memories would be very different. I discovered this a year or two later, as a subaltern in a Highland regiment in the Middle East: the whole chronology of that time is clear and connected, possibly because an officer's concerns cannot be the selfish ones of a private soldier, who need not look beyond himself and his mates; an officer, even a subaltern, must at least know where he is and have a broader picture of what is happening. Well, more or less.

Certain matters have become clearer to me in the course of writing, because I have had recourse to written histories of the war. I had a rough idea, when we attacked the place I call the temple wood, and ran into rifle and machine gun fire which took out a third of the section in a matter of seconds, why we were doing it, but now I understand the overall plan of which that attack was a small part. I remember vividly the free-for-all battle when we finally got into the wood, but only now do I learn that during it we killed 136 Japanese. I understand at last the strategic implications of the monsoon's breaking two weeks early, but my chief memory of the beginning of that monumental deluge is of a giant centipede emerging, all fifteen scaly inches of it, from the folds of a tent we were trying to erect. That was the time, the histories tell me, when thousands from the shattered Japanese divisions were trying to escape east from the Pegu Yomas across the Sittang, giving rise to the Battle of the Rangoon Road: that was Slim's strategic problem; our tactical one was that the tent canvas was so rotten it fell apart, and we slept in the open in six inches of warmish water, with Grandarse beaming contentedly up at the downpour, remarking: "Aye, grand growin' weather."

A strange trait of the human memory – of mine, at any rate – is that it is no respecter of the great and important; the most utter trivia becomes as embedded in the mind as matters of life and death. It is natural enough that I should have an indelible image of Long John frowning at his bayonet which was bent almost double after he had pulled it out of a Japanese on the night when they got inside our position and all hell broke loose in the dark; or remember the sick feeling in my throat when, as the section scout, I found myself advancing alone, safety catch off and one up the spout, across a hundred yards of open ground to a silent screen of palm and thicket concealing a village where there might, or might not be, a Japanese position. There wasn't, as it happened, but I remember every step, and the fact that I got no comfort at all from mentally reciting Browning's "Prospice" as I walked on eggshells wishing to God I'd passed Lower Latin and got into university in 1943. But why should I remember just as plainly that a cigarette smoked during an ambush on the Sittang was a brand called Panama, or hear so clearly Bing Crosby singing "The Wedding Song of Reynaldo" on the company set in a basha on the Rangoon road, or be able to see the jungle sore on the wrist of a comrade as he rummaged in his housewife for a needle when I can't even recall his face, or have near total recollection of Madame Dubarry's name cropping up in the section's conversation, and her imagined charms being compared (unfavourably) to those of Susanna Foster, the film star?

I mention these things to explain, not to excuse, the random nature of what follows – a young soldier's recollections of one small part (and mine was a very small part, for my service did not compare in length or hardship to my comrades') of one campaign in a war that is already fading into the shadows. Many officers have written about Burma, but not many private soldiers, I think; that is one reason for doing it. Another is to make some kind of memorial to Nixon and Grandarse and Hutton and Long John and Parker and Forster and Tich and Gale and the Duke, and all the rest of those matchless men whose grimy brown faces I can see, and whose Northern voices I can hear, as though it were yesterday, and not half a century on. I suppose they'd look ordinary enough to the world, but they still seem matchless to me, and I want to set down, before night, how they went to war, how they spoke and thought, how they were armed and dressed, how they fought and lived and died, and how they beat the living daylights out of Jap.

I have not used their real names (except for one officer's nickname) because while some of the conversation quoted is word for word, most of it obviously is not, although it is entirely faithful in gist, subject and style. Also, some details might cause distress to relatives or friends of those who died; for this reason I have shifted one incident out of chronological order. The rest is as I remember it, and if I have erred in matters which were beyond my ken, and of which I have had to write at second hand, or my memory has played me false in details like, say, aircraft markings, weapon calibres, or location descriptions, I apologise. I have checked as best I can, and must record my thanks to Lieutenant-Colonel John Petty, M.B.E., M.C., formerly officer commanding B Company, 9th Battalion The Border Regiment, 17th Indian Division, for reading the manuscript and correcting me on a number of factual details.

There is a third reason for writing: to illustrate, if I can, the difference between "then" and "now", and to assure a later generation that much modern wisdom, applied in retrospect to the Second World War, is not to be trusted. Attitudes to war and fighting have, as I said earlier, changed considerably, and what is thought now, and held to be universal truth, was not thought then, or true of that time. Myth, revisionist history, fashionable ideas and reactions, social change, and the cinema and television, have distorted a good deal over the past half-century. So I shall try to set it straight (or what seems straight to me, an eye-witness) in small and possibly unimportant matters of fact as well as in wider aspects.

Just to give three examples, the first trivial, the others rather more important:

I have read, in an essay by a respected military journalist, that the weapon known as the Piat (projector, infantry, anti-tank), while then in existence, was never used in Burma. Well, I carried the bloody thing, and fired it five times, with startling results.

Secondly, a couple of years ago I read a review of a book about "Understanding and Behaviour in the Second World War". The book, I believe, was written by an ex-combattant, and according to the review it concentrated on "the rationalisations and euphemisms people needed to deal with an unacceptable reality". I quote the review in part:

> In chapters such as Chickenshit: An Anatomy, High-mindedness, and Typecasting, he underlines the lasting damage the war inflicted on "intelligence, honesty, complexity, ambiguity and irony." The frustration and disgust of the soldiers who knew that, for the benefit of those at home, their experience was being "systematically sanitised, Norman Rockwellised, not to mention Disneyfied" is documented, as are the stupidity and sadism that were represented by the media as tactical brilliance and noble courage.

Now, I haven't read the book, so I can comment only on what I read in the review, and I don't know if the reviewer served in, or was even an adult at the time of the war. Nor do I know whether the book is largely based on American experience or whether, as the review seems to suggest, it applies equally to Britain. If it does, then I am bound to say that the fifth word of the quoted passage is too kind a description of the rest of the paragraph.

But to start with, anyone who writes of "unacceptable reality" simply does not know what he is talking about; the reality of the Second World War was acceptable and accepted, and no "rationalisations and euphemisms" were required. This may be hard for a modern reviewer to understand; he may not realize that the rhetoric and propaganda of newspapers, broadcasts, and newsreels were recognised as such, at the time, both in the front line and at home. Of course media and government felt obliged to present the war in as favourable terms as possible, but that was understood, and nobody was fooled, and no softening was "needed" by the public in the condescending sense that the review suggests. The British people were not stupid; they had been to war before, and knew all about its realities at first hand.

It is difficult for later generations to understand this; they have a tendency to envisage themselves in the 1940s, and imagine their own reactions, and make the fatal mistake of thinking that the outlook was the same then. They cannot see that they have been conditioned by the past forty years into a new philosophic tradition, requiring new explanations; they fail to realise that there is a veil between them and the 1940s. They want to see the last war in *their* terms; they want it to conform to *their* notions. Well, it won't.

To continue. Whatever damage the war inflicted on intelligence, honesty, etc., cannot be measured, let alone proved; it is a matter of opinion. I doubt if it had any special effect on anyone's intelligence or honesty; how you can inflict damage on complexity, ambiguity, and irony, is not clear to me or, I suggest, to anyone who prefers plain English to jargon. Obviously the war influenced people's thinking permanently, but to call such shaping of the mind "lasting damage" is fatuous. One might as well say that forty years of comparative peace have inflicted "lasting damage" on modern intelligence, and adduce modern theories about the 1940s as proof.

But the last sentence of the quoted paragraph is the real beauty. I have a fairly wide acquaintance among my generation, embracing most of the British campaigns of the war, and I have yet to meet anyone who felt "frustration and disgust" about the way his experience was presented to the public. To speak of sanitisation, Norman Rockwell, and Disney in this context is to employ cheap emotional cliché; it betrays the kind of blinkered mind which cannot appreciate that a Norman Rockwell idealisation (since his name has been dragged in) is not necessarily false for being an ideal, or for failing to satisfy a revisionist's misconception of the truth. If you want to believe that soldiers felt "frustration and disgust" you will no doubt find some to agree with you, if you try hard enough, but my own experience suggests that, in Britain at least, they would be a small minority. As to stupidity and sadism: yes, this soldier saw plenty of one and a little of the other, but never knew them to be represented as tactical brilliance or noble courage. No doubt convenient examples could be provided, but it would be extremely unwise to draw a general conclusion from them.

The review goes on to say that "what, in time of war, was seen as necessary to uphold the morale of soldier and civilian alike has persisted for almost fifty years as a method of determining what should be accepted as reality". So far as that has a meaning, it appears to be that misrepresentation of war was necessary at the time, and has continued until now, when presumably some omniscient revisionist has seen through the sham. Well, such a conclusion is false, and insulting. It fails to see that morale, far from being inspired by policy, comes from within, and is nourished by friends, family, and example. Government and media may reflect that – as Churchill did – but they cannot create it. Perhaps no one can understand that who was not alive and aware in Britain during the war, or experienced the Blitz, or was torpedoed, or confronted death and mortal peril at point-blank.

There is, for some reason which I don't understand, a bitter desire in some to undermine what they call the "myths" of the Second World War. Most of the myths are true, but they don't want to believe that. It may be a natural reaction to having the war rammed down their throats by my generation; it may have its roots in subconscious envy; it may even spring from a reluctance to recognise that today's safety and comfort were bought fifty years ago by means which today's intelligentsia find unacceptable, and from which they wish to distance themselves. I cannot say – but I do know that the review I have quoted is typical in presenting a view which is false. It is also dangerous because it may be taken as true by the uninformed or thoughtless, since it fits fashionable prejudice. And that is how history is distorted. You cannot, you must not, judge the past by the present; you must try to see it in its own terms and values, if you are to have any inkling of it. You may not like what you see, but do not on that account fall into the error of trying to adjust it to suit your own vision of what it ought to have been.

Thirdly, it is now widely held (or at least it has been widely stated) that the dropping of atomic bombs was unnecessary because the Japanese were ready to give in. I shall have something to say of that bombing later – and not entirely, perhaps, what you might think – but for the moment I shall say only that I wish those who hold that view had been present to explain the position to the little bastard who came howling out of a thicket near the Sittang, full of spite and fury, in that first week of August. He was half-starved and near naked, and his only weapon was a bamboo stake, but he was in no mood to surrender.

Finally, if any young soldiers of today should chance to read this book, they may understand that while the face of war may alter, some things have not changed since Joshua stood before Jericho and Xenophon marched to the sea. May they come safe to bedtime, and all well.

AUTHOR'S NOTE

The dialects of Cumberland are among the purest and, to the outsider, least comprehensible in the English-speaking world. Rendering them phonetically is difficult, but I have tried because that is the way my comrades talked, and to translate their conversation into normal English would be to change the characters of the speakers out of recognition; they were the way they spoke: tough, strong, forthright, and frequently aggressive. But while I hope I have conveyed their accent, I have to rely on meaning and context to suggest the style in which their speech was delivered. For example, the Cumbrian voice is well suited to derision; everyone knows the common English expression of disbelief, "Get away!" and the equally familiar North Country "Give over!", meaning "Stop it", but as rendered by the Cumbrian "Girraweh!" and "Give ower!" have respectively a snarling contempt and a violence which have to be heard. At its heaviest, the accent is a harsh, rasping growl, and it is this as much as the occasionally archaic vocabulary which baffles the foreigner. Just to give one quick example of pure Cumbrian, I give the translation of:

"Have you seen a donkey jump over a gate?" which is

"Est seen a coody loup ower a yett?"

That sentence, in Cumbrian, illustrates one of the most distinctive features of the county's speech—the occasional use of the second person singular: "Est" or "Esta" is "Hast thou". I emphasise occasional use; the Cumbrian, especially the countryman, will use "thou" (pronounced "thoo" or "tha") and "you" or "ye" indiscriminately. "You will" in Carlisle may be spoken as "you'll" or "ye'll", but out on the fellside it is liable to be "tha'lt" ("thou wilt"). Similarly, his assent may be "yes", "yiss", or "aye"; he alternates "well" and "weel"; "go" may be "gaw", "gan", or "ga"; he may say "how" perfectly normally, but he may also say "'oo". The list is endless: "don't" is usually "doan't" or "dawn't", but occasionally it is "divvn't"—and don't (or divvn't) ask me why.

I have said the dialect is pure, because it is both ancient and grammatical; Chaucer might well understand a modern Cumbrian better than he would a modern Londoner. But it has its antique ungrammatical lapses, too – "Ah's" ("I is") and "Thoo's" ("Thou is") are examples to balance against the purity of "Th'art" ("Thou art") and "looksta" and "sista" ("lookest thou" and "seest thou").

All of which may convince the uninitiated that my characters might as well be speaking Turkish; in fact, I don't think their speech will be too difficult to understand, and where I think it may be I have appended footnote translations. The glossary at the end consists largely of Hindustani words and slang expressions current in the British Army fifty years ago.

G.M.F.

QUARTERED SAFE OUT HERE

THE FIRST TIME I SMELT JAP was in a deep dry-river bed in the Dry Belt, somewhere near Meiktila. I can no more describe the smell than I could describe a colour, but it was heavy and pungent and compounded of stale cooked rice and sweat and human waste and . . . Jap. Quite unlike the clean acrid wood-smoke of an Indian village or the rather exotic and faintly decayed odour of the bashas* in which the Burmese lived – and certainly nothing like the cooking smells of the Baluch hillmen and Gurkhas of our brigade, or our own British aromas. It was outside my experience of Oriental stenches – so how did I know it was Jap? Because we were deep inside enemy-held territory, and who else would have dug the three bunkers facing me in the high bank, as I stood, feeling extremely lonely, with a gallon tin of fruit balanced precariously on one shoulder and my rifle at the trail in my other hand?

I had never seen a live Japanese at this time. Dead ones beyond counting, corpses sprawled by the roadside, among the huts and bashas of abandoned villages, in slit-trenches and fox-holes, all the way, it seemed, from Imphal south to the Irrawaddy. They were what was left of the great army that had been set to invade India the previous year, the climax of that apparently irresistible tide that had swept across China, Malaya, and the Pacific Islands; it broke on the twin rocks of Imphal and Kohima, where Four-teenth Army had stopped it and driven it back from the gates of India. (I imagine that every teenager today has heard of Stalingrad and Alamein and D-Day, but I wonder how many know the name of Imphal, that "Flower on Lofty Heights" where Japan suffered the greatest catastrophe in its military history? There's no reason why they should; it was a long way away.) While I was still a

* native houses, large huts

3

recruit, training in Britain, this battalion had fought in that terrible battle of the boxes,* and their talk was still of Kennedy Peak and Tiddim and the Silchar track, and "duffys" – the curious name for what the Americans now call fire-fights – in the jungle and on the khuds† of Assam. There they had fought Jap literally to a standstill, and now we were on the road south, with Burma to be retaken. We had said goodbye to the mules which had been the only possible vehicles in that fearful country; trucks had brought us to the Irrawady and beyond, courtesy of East African drivers whose one notion of convoy discipline had been to get to the front and stay there, screaming with laughter as they skidded round hairpins on mountain roads with cliff on one side and a sheer drop of hundreds of feet on the other. The driver would hunch over his wheel, giggling, while his mate hung out on the other side shrieking his slogan "Whoa! Bus!‡ Go! Stop! Fakoff!" at defeated opponents. They were, incidentally, the finest drivers I have ever seen, enormous jungle-wallahs in greatcoats and vast ammunition boots, with tribal cuts on their beaming black faces; they wouldn't last thirty seconds in a driving test, not even in Bangkok, but at motoring with two wheels in thin air they were impressive.

They put us where Slim wanted us to be, south of the river, in that strange land known as the Dry Belt. People think of Burma as one great jungle, but in its centre there are large tracts which are almost desert; stony, sun-baked plain dotted with jungly patches and paddy-fields and criss-crossed by nullahs§ and river beds which, outside the summer monsoon, are bone dry. This was where Slim wanted to catch Jap in the open, by pretending to make his main drive at Mandalay, to the east, while we, the 17th Division, crossed the river farther west, making for Meiktila, eighty miles below Mandalay, in Jap country. This had been explained to us by our divisional commander, a kindly, hook-nosed Glasgow graduate called Cowan and nicknamed "Punch"; we would take Meiktila with a fast thrust, hold it against the

* Box = a defensible position, containing anything from thousands of men to platoon boxes of 30 men or fewer
† jungle hills
‡ bus = finished
§ gullies, dry watercourses

4

surrounding Japanese forces, and wait for 5th Division (tastefully known, from their red disc insignia, as the Flaming Arseholes) to fight through to our relief.

"We are the anvil," Punch had said gently, "and they are the hammer."

"An' they won't be the only fookin' 'ammer," little Nixon had observed. "Bloody great Jap Imperial Guardsmen – aye, White Tigers, runnin' all ower the shop, shoutin' 'Banzai!' Aye, weel, we'll all get killed."

So much for the broad picture. At one point it narrowed down to our platoon, making a sweep across a huge, dusty plain, looking for Japanese positions; it was not expected that we would find any. We were in extended line, twenty yards apart, and I was on the extreme left flank; a deep nullah was opening up to my left, forcing me to close on the next man, who was little Nixon.

"Keep yer bloody distance, Jock!" bawled Sergeant Hutton, from his station right and rear, so I obediently scrambled down the side of the nullah, dropping the tin of fruit en route and missing my footing, so that I rolled the last fifteen feet and ended up winded in the nullah bottom.

It seemed to run fairly straight, and as long as it did I would be moving parallel with the rest of the platoon, now hidden from sight by the steep nullah side. So I shouldered the fruit tin again and set off along the nullah, with that awkward burden digging into my shoulder. It had been part of the big pack of compo rations which was the section's food for the day and which had been divided among us at daybreak, to be eaten that night when we dug in. I had suggested opening it when we tiffined on the march, but Grandarse and Forster had said no, it would make a grand pudding at supper. So I'd cursed those Epicureans through the long hot afternoon, wondering if P. C. Wren had ever carried a gallon of fruit in the Foreign Legion, and muttering "Boots, boots, boots, boots", to myself – not that it had been much of a march; ten or twelve miles, maybe, not enough to be foot-sore. But the tin was getting heavier by the minute as I trudged up the nullah, and I was going to have a hell of a job climbing the bank with it, as I would have to do in a minute, for the nullah was starting to tend left, carrying me away from the section's line of march.

I stopped for a swig of chlorinated water from the canvas chaggle slung on my right shoulder, and took stock. There wasn't a breath of air in the nullah – and not a sound, either. I scanned the twenty-foot red banks, looking for a place to scramble up. There wasn't one; I would have to carry on, hoping to find one soon – either that or retrace my steps to the spot where I'd climbed down, which would leave me a long way behind the section, with night not far off. I couldn't see the sun, but it had been dipping to the horizon when last seen, and I'd no wish to be traipsing about in the dark, getting shot by one side or the other. I heaved the tin to a less painful position, and started to walk quickly up the nullah – and it was just then that I saw the bunkers.

Usually a bunker is a large hole in the ground, roofed with timber or bamboo and covered with sandbags or hard-packed earth, with firing slits at ground level. These were different: three dark doorways about ten yards apart, cut in the side of the nullah, with man-made caves within. Jap bunkers, without a doubt . . . empty? Or not?

They were on the right side of the nullah, and on the plain above and beyond, the rest of the section would be moving forward – they might be a quarter of a mile away by now, or still level with where I stood; I couldn't tell. Ideally, I should have climbed out and alerted them, but the banks were sheer. If I shouted, and brought them down into the nullah, and the bunkers were old and long abandoned, a lot of thanks I'd get – and if there *were* Japs in the bunkers, and I shouted . . . quite. Or I could pass quickly by on the other side, leaving them unexamined, and find some spot ahead to climb up and rejoin the lads . . . No, you can't do that – but you're a very keen young soldier if you don't *think* about it.

I've never felt lonelier. Suddenly it was cold in the nullah, and the sun had sunk so low that there wasn't a shadow. Five minutes earlier I had been sweating hot; now I was trickling ice. I stood hesitant, looking at those three long black slits in the bank, wondering what to do . . .

It was then I smelt Jap, rank and nasty. The question was, did it come from Jap *in situ,* or had he just left his stink behind him? Was he lurking within, wondering who was outside throwing tins of fruit about, or was he long gone to the south'ard? If he was present, was he as scared as I was? No, he couldn't be.

The lunatic thought crossed my mind that the best way of finding out was to heave one of my two grenades into the nearest doorway and hit the deck, finger on trigger, waiting to see what emerged. And bloody clever I'd look when the section came running to the scene and found me bombing empty bunkers – I was a very young soldier then, you understand, and sensitive; I had no wish to be looked at askance by veterans of Oyster Box and K.P.* (Three months later I'd have heaved in both grenades *and* the tin of fruit, and anything else handy; better to be laughed at than dead – and I wouldn't have been laughed at.)

Anyway, hesitation was pointless. I couldn't leave the bunkers uninvestigated; I couldn't tell young Gale, our platoon commander, that I'd been too terrified; I couldn't leave them unreported. It was that simple; anyway, they *looked* empty.

I lowered the fruit tin carefully to the ground, pushed the safety catch forward on my rifle, made sure my kukri was loose in its sheath, touched the hilt of the dirk in my small pack for luck, and moved delicately towards the nearest entrance, hugging the nullah side. I waited, listening; not a sound, just that hellish smell. I edged closer, and saw where most of it was coming from.

Just inside the doorway, where an unwary foot would tread on it, was a *punji,* which is a sharpened stake set in the ground point upwards, that point usually being smeared with something nice and rotten, guaranteed to purify the victim's bloodstream. Some *punjis* are elaborate cantilevered affairs set to swing out of a darkened bunker and impale you; I had even heard of a crossbow variety, triggered by touching a taut cord. This was a conventional one, decorated with excrement by the look of it. But how old was it? (The things one does for a living: trying to determine the age of Jap crap, for eighteen rupees a week.)

Old or new, it didn't suggest anyone in residence. I took a huge breath and slipped inside, dropping to one knee – and there wasn't a thing to be seen but dim earth walls and a couple of Jap mess-tins, still half full of rice. I crouched there, wet with fear and relief,

* Kennedy Peak

QUARTERED SAFE OUT HERE

keeping my trembling finger well away from the trigger. I'd willingly have stayed there permanently, recovering, but it would be dark soon, so, carefully avoiding the *punji* (modern war is a pretty Stone Age business, when you think about it), I stepped outside again.

The second bunker looked much more promising. The earth on one side of the doorway had fallen in, and the dead fire in its entrance was days old. There seemed to be rubbish piled within, and the whole thing had an ancient, neglected look, so I passed it by and cautiously approached Number 3. Its doorway was so wide that I could see in to the back of the little cavern. I tossed a stone in, listening, and then nipped inside – empty, bare walls, and nothing but a crumpled Kooa* packet in one corner.

I came out of that bunker feeling pretty heroic, and was retrieving my fruit tin when it occurred to me that I *ought* to go into the second one, too, just to make a job of it. And I was moving towards it when I heard a faint, distant whistle from over the top of the bank – little Nixon, for certain, wondering where his wandering boy had got to. I ran up the nullah, and found a crack in its side only about twenty yards farther on. I scrambled up, heaving the tin ahead of me, clawing my way over the lip to find Nick standing about ten yards off, and Sergeant Hutton hastening towards me with blood in his eye.

"Where the hell 'ave you been?" he blared. "Wanderin' aboot like a bloody lost soul, what d'ye think yer on?"

"There were bunkers," I began, but before I could get out another word Nick had shouted "Doon, Jock!" and whipped up his rifle.

How I managed it I have no idea, but I know my feet left the ground and I hit the deck facing back the way I had come. Whatever Nick had seen was in that direction, and I wanted to get a good look at it – I suppose it was instinct and training combined, for I was scrabbling my rifle forward as I fell and turned together. And I can see him now, and he doesn't improve with age.

Five yards away, not far from where the bunkers must have

---

* A brand of Chinese cigarettes, presumably looted by the Japanese. We smoked captured supplies of them; they weren't bad.

been, a Jap was looking towards us. Half his naked torso was visible over the lip of the bank – how the hell he had climbed up there, God knows – and he was in the act of raising a large dark object, about a foot across, holding it above his head. I had a glimpse of a contorted yellow face before Nick's rifle cracked behind me, three quick shots, and I'd got off one of my own when there was a deafening explosion and I was blinded by an enormous flash as the edge of the nullah dissolved in a cloud of dust and smoke. I rolled away, deafened, and then debris came raining down – earth and stones and bits of Jap, and when I could see again there was a great yawning bite out of the lip of the nullah, and the smoke and dust was clearing above it.

"Git doon!" snapped Hutton, as I started to rise. Suddenly, as if by magic, the section were there behind me, on the deck or kneeling, every rifle covering the lip, and Hutton walked forward and looked into the nullah.

"Fook me," he said. "Land mine. Fook me. Y'awreet, Jock?"

I said I was.

"Wheer th'ell did 'e coom frae? The booger!"

I told him, no doubt incoherently, about the bunkers: that I'd checked two and been on the way to the third when Nick had whistled. "It looked empty," I said.

"Well, it bloody well wasn't, was it?" he shouted, and I realised he was not only angry, but shaken. "Duke, giddoon theer an' 'ev a dekko! Rest o' you, git back in extended line – move!"

Nick was recharging his magazine. I realised that I was trembling. "Land mine?" I said. "Did you hit it?"

"Nivver," said he. "Ah hit him, though. Naw, he would have it wired. Suicide squad, waitin' to blaw oop anyone that cam' near 'im." He grinned at me. "Might ha' bin thee, Jock boy. Ye shoulda give us a shout, man."

I explained why I hadn't, and he shook his head. "Nivver ga in on yer own, son. That's 'ow ye finish up dyin' Tojo's way. Ye wanna die yer own fookin' way."

"Git fell in, you two!" It was Hutton again. "Standin' aboot natterin' wid yer thumbs in yer bums an' yer minds in neutral! Awreet, Duke? Ad-vance! Coom on, it'll be bloody dark in a minute!"

9

That evening, when we had dug in and were sitting round the fire eating our Maconochie's, Hutton, who had been talking apart with the Duke, called me over. He was jotting in his notebook.

"Three boonkers, reet?" he said. "What was in the two ye looked in?"

"Nothing, sarn't. Well, there was a *punji* in one, and a couple of Jap mess tins. Nothing at all in t'other."

"Nowt at a'?"

"No . . . well, nothing but a Kooa packet over in a corner. Empty."

He didn't glance up from his notes, but his glance flicked sideways for a second, and out of the tail of my eye I caught the Duke's almost imperceptible nod. Hutton finished writing, and when he looked up I'll swear there was relief in the battered face. It took me a moment to understand why.

"Awreet, Jock." Then suddenly he was angry again. "Nivver – nivver go in a boonker by yersel!" He stabbed me in the chest. "Mallum?† Git yer mucker to cover you, or git me! Ye're not fookin' Gary Cooper!" Irrelevantly, it seemed to me, he added: "Fookin' Scotsmen!" He feinted a jab at my chin. "Reet, son, fall oot."

By this time the gastronomes round the fire were clamouring for their dessert. Grandarse produced a can of condensed milk which he punctured with a pig-sticker bayonet, while Corporal Little set to work on my gallon tin with his jack-knife.

Grandarse, mess-tin in hand, smacked his lips. "By Christ, eh! Peaches an' Nessles, w'at? Aye, that'll joost aboot do!"

"Might be pears," suggested the Duke.

"Or pineapple," I said.

"Ah don't give a fook w'at it is," said Grandarse, Penrith's answer to Lucullus. "Eh, tho', mebbe it's fruit salad!"

It wasn't. It was carrots, in brine. Inevitably, since I'd been carrying the tin, they blamed me.

---

* Tinned stewed steak, and very good
† understand?

BACK IN BLIGHTY, or even out of the line, a soldier's first loyalty was to his regiment, and even the most cynical reluctant conscript was conscious of belonging to something special. If he came from the regimental area, the tie was all the stronger; he could call himself a Devon, an Argyll, a Gloucester, or a Middlesex, and take some pride in belonging to the Bloody Eleventh, the Thin Red Line, the Back-to-Backs, or the Diehards, as those regiments were nicknamed; he would probably know how they got them. And regimental pride would stay with him, as I'm sure it does still, even after amalgamation has played havoc with the old territorial system.

On active service, in my experience, the loyalty, or perhaps I should call it dependence, narrowed down to the infantry section of ten. Each battalion normally had four rifle companies (apart from headquarter and perhaps support companies for transport and 3-inch mortars); each company was split into three platoons, each commanded by a lieutenant and sergeant; and each platoon into three sections. In parade-ground theory, a section consisted of ten men (corporal, lance-corporal, Bren gunner, and seven riflemen, one of whom was the Bren gunner's "number two"), but in practice the strength was more likely to be about eight; six was the operational minimum.* But whatever its strength, the section was the essential unit, operating as a team; of course on platoon operations it acted in concert with the two other sections; and half-company, company, and battalion actions were common also; but whatever the size of the action it was the section that mattered to the private soldier. It was his military family; those seven or

---

* Credit for the invention of the ten-man section belongs to that great military organiser, Genghiz Khan. The Romans, despite their decimal system, used the eight-man section, of which there were ten to a century (which consisted, perversely, of 80, not 100, men).

eight other men were his constant companions, waking, sleeping, standing guard, eating, digging, patrolling, marching, and fighting, and he got to know them better, perhaps, than anyone in his whole life except his wife, parents, and children. He counted on them, and they on him.

Within the section he would have his own immediate comrade, his "mucker", known in some units as oppos or mates. Our own battalion was predominantly Cumbrian, and the men from the west coast called each other "marrow",* pronounced marra. I had three muckers in the course of the campaign, as a result of death and promotion. There was nothing official about the mucker arrangement, it just happened of necessity and mutual consent, and is certainly as old as war itself.

My first mucker was the section leader, Corporal Little – no doubt because at nineteen I was the youngest and least experienced man in the section. He was a Cumbrian by birth and race, which is to say he was the descendant of one of the hardest breeds of men in Britain, with warfare (if not soldiering) bred into him from the distant past. Like their enemies on the Scottish side of the frontier, the Cumbrians of old lived by raid, cattle theft, extortion, and murder; in war they were England's vanguard, and in peace her most unruly and bloody nuisance. They hadn't changed much in four centuries, either; the expertise in irregular warfare, to say nothing of the old reiver spirit of "nothing too hot or too heavy", was strong in the battalion; their names (and nicknames) are to be found in the bills of warden courts four centuries ago, opposite charges of slaughter, spoil, ambush, and arson, and if you could have seen Nine Section, honestly, you wouldn't have been a bit surprised. To all of which must be added the virtues of endurance, courage, and deep tribal loyalty; they were, as the chronicler said of their forefathers, "a martial kind of men".

Little, known inevitably as "Tich" (just as I, the only Scot, was "Jock"), was typical – lean, dark, wiry, speaking seldom and then usually in the harsh derisive fashion of the Border. An outsider would have found him wary and decidedly bleak, and marked him

---

* companion, partner

as a dangerous customer, which he was; he was also remarkably kind and, when least expected, as gentle as a nurse.

Nixon was small, sprightly, and wicked, with a drooping gun-fighter moustache and his own line of cheerful pessimism. His parrot-cry of "You'll all get killed" was rendered in the wail of a mueddin at prayer, and one thing no one doubted: whoever got killed, it wouldn't be Nick. That is not a criticism: no one took a greater share of rough work and risk; it was just that he had survivor written all over him. There are such men; they seem to have an Achilles-immunity. In Nick's case it probably came of long and very active service, for he had been continuously at war for six years; he was cool and wise and never ruffled.

Grandarse, as his name implies, was on Falstaffian lines; I had slept on the lower bunk of a double-decked cot at Ranchi with his ponderous bulk creaking the lashings just overhead, and prayed nightly that they didn't break. He was red and hearty and given to rich oaths; as a wrestler – and the wrestlers of Cumberland have no peers anywhere – he could hold his own against Sergeant Bellas of Gilsland, who had won Grasmere before the war*. In civilian life Grandarse was a forester, and had spent his spare time rescuing climbers in the Lake mountains, "an' nivver got a bloody penny for it, the boogers!"

Forster was a fly man who never had a cigarette to his name. "W'ee's smeukin'?"†, in an aggressive wheedle, was his watchword, generally responded to with "Iveryone but thee". He was crafty, foul-mouthed, ignorant, and dishonest; sufficient to say that in a battalion of expert scroungers, Forster was gifted beyond the ordinary; there are Burmese villages which must be wondering still where their pigs and chickens went to in '45.

---

* Cumberland wrestling, one of the most scientific forms of close combat, is thought to be of Viking origin, although many of its holds are to be seen on ancient friezes. Although little known outside Cumberland and Westmorland, it attained an international reputation early in the century when, under the patronage of Lord Lonsdale, a team of four Cumbrians met and defeated in Paris a quartet of champions from Europe, Turkey, the U.S.A., and Japan. There are annual world championships at light, middle, and heavyweight, but the ultimate ambition is to "win Grasmere"; that is, the prize at the summer sports held at Grasmere, Westmorland.

† "Who's smoking?"

Steele was a Carlisle boy, tough and combative and noisy, but something of a mate of mine, even if he did use the word "Scotch" to me with occasional undue emphasis; once he added "bastard" to it (there was no race relations legislation in those happy days), and I responded with a fist; we battered each other furiously until Corporal Little, who was half our size, flew at us with a savagery that took us aback; he knocked me down and half-strangled Steele before dragging us face to face. "Noo shek 'ands! Shek 'ands! By Christ, ye will! Barmy boogers, ye'll 'ev enoof fightin' wid Jap, nivver mind each other! Ga on – shek 'ands!" Confronted by that raging lightweight, we shook hands, with a fairly ill grace, which was not lost on him. Then, being a skilled man manager, he put us on guard, together.

Stanley was large and fair and quiet, and had the unusual ability of sleeping on his feet, which was a genuine torment to him when he had to stand stag.* He had been a cinema projectionist, and for sheer cold courage I never saw his like, as I shall tell later. He might have had a decoration, but his heroism manifested itself in a lonely place, by night, and no one in authority ever knew about it.

Wedge was a Midlander, and said "Ace, king, quine," among other vocal peculiarities, like "waiter" for "water". Being used to carry saggars† in the Potteries, he would bear his big pack and other impedimenta on his head when necessary, leaving his hands free for other burdens. When we were cut off in Meiktila he developed an obsession about the 5th Division, who were to be the "hammer" to our "anvil". "Wheer's 5th Div, then?" was his stock question at the section O-group (the little conference which took place each evening, when the corporal passed on news and orders from the platoon commander). No one could tell him, and he would lapse into gloomy silence. He was deeply religious, and eager for education because, he told me, "Ah want to improve meself. Ah want a trade efter t'war, not carryin' bloody saggars. A reet trade, Jock – Ah dunno what, though; Ah'll 'ave to see." Once, I remember, when we were on stag together, he told me

---

* guard, sentry-go, usually at night
† pottery cases carried piled on the head

how much he had enjoyed the pirate movie, *The Black Swan*, and I told him something of Morgan's buccaneers and their exploits; from that moment he seemed to regard me as a latter-day Macaulay and pestered me for historical information, and since I am God's own history bore, he got plenty, and his gratitude was touching. I doubt if it helped him to get a trade, but you never know.

The Duke, whose surname I have forgotten, if I ever knew it, was so called from his refined public school accent. He was tall and lethargic and swarthy as a gypsy, with a slow smile and a manner which grew more supercilious in proportion to the rank of whomever he was addressing; he was almost humble to Corporal Little, but I have heard him talk – with studied courtesy, mind you – to a brigadier as though the man were the veriest trash. He got away with it, too. The rumour ran that he was related to the royal family, but informed opinion was against this: Grandarse had seen him in the shower at Ranchi and had detected no sign of a birthmark.

Parker I have left to the last because he was easily the most interesting, a dapper, barrel-chested Cockney who was that rare bird, a professional soldier of fortune. He was in his forties, and had been in one uniform or another since boyhood, having just got into the tail of the First World War before serving as a mercenary in China in the 'twenties, in what capacity I never discovered, and thereafter in South America, the Spanish Civil War (from a pungent comment on the International Brigade I deduced that he had been with the Nationalists), and China again in the late 'thirties. He re-enlisted in 1939, came out at Dunkirk, and had been with Eighth Army before being posted east. He was a brisk and leathery old soldier, as brash and opinionated as only a Londoner can be, but only rarely did you see the unusual man behind the Cockney banter.

I first noticed him on the dusty long haul by troop-train across India, when the rest of us slept on the floor or the cramped wooden seats, while Parker improvised himself a hammock with his groundsheet and lengths of signal cable. But I didn't speak to him until the end of a marathon game of nine-card brag in which I had amassed the astonishing sum of 800 rupees (about £60, which was money then). I'm no card-player, let alone a gambler, but the priles* kept coming for once, and I was just wondering how to quit in the face of the chagrined opposition, which included various blue chins and hairy chests of Australian, American, and mixed origin, when Parker, who had been watching but not playing, leaned over, picked up my winnings, and stuck them inside his shirt.

"That's yer lot, gents," he said cheerfully. "E's out."

There were menacing growls, and a large individual with a face like Ayers Rock rose and demanded who said so.

"I bleedin' do," said Parker. "I'm 'is uncle, an' you've 'ad a fair shot, so you can brag yer bollocks off all the way to Cal† – by yerselves. E's out, see?" To me he simply said: "Better let me look arter it." Which he did, all the way to Ranchi, where he escorted me to the paymaster to see it deposited. I won't say I didn't watch him with some anxiety during the last days of the journey, but I never even thought of asking for my money: some people are fit to look after a small fortune east of Suez, and some aren't.

One result of his mother hen behaviour was that I learned something of his background. He was an orphan, and the proceeds of twenty years' free lancing had put his younger brother through medicine; this emerged when I offered him a cut of my winnings for his good offices as banker; he didn't need it, he said, and out came the photographs of his kid brother in his M.B. gown, and in hospital groups; Parker's pride was something to see. "E'll go in the R.A.M.C. shortly, I 'spect; 'e'll be an officer then. An' arterwards, 'e can put up his brass plate an' settle dahn, get married 'an 'ave kids, make me a real uncle. 'E's done bloody well for a Millwall sparrow, 'as Arthur. Mind you, he allus was bright, top o' the class, not like me; I lef' school when I was nine an' never looked back. Yerss, I'm prahd of 'im, orlright." He must have realised that he was running on, for he grinned sheepishly and put the photos away, remarking jauntily that a medico in the family allus came 'andy, didn't it, case you got a dose o' clap.

---

* three of a kind, e.g. three aces
† Calcutta

I said my parents had wanted me to be a doctor, and he gave me a hard stare.

"You didn't make it? Why not?"

"Not clever enough, I suppose. Didn't get into university."

"Too bloody lazy, more like. Idle little sod."

"Well, I didn't want to be a doctor! I wanted to get into the Army, try for a commission."

"Did you, now? Stupid git. Well, 'ave you applied?"

"Yep. Selection board turned me down. I've been busted from lance-jack a couple of times, too."

"Christ, some mothers don't 'alf 'ave 'em! An educated sod like you – I seen you doin' bleedin' crosswords." He cackled and shook his head. "Well, I shall just 'ave to kick you up the arse, young Jock, I can see that. Ne' mind – with my permish you'll get a commish!" He liked the sound of that, and it became a private slogan whenever the going got uncomfortable: if I was sodden through, or was marching on my chin-strap, as the saying was, or bone-tired after digging or standing to all night, and even when we went in under the guns at Pyawbwe, Parker's raucous cry would be heard: "Bash on, Jock – wiv my permish you'll get a commish!" It was as regular as Nick's "You'll all get killed!" and just about as encouraging.

That was the section, and if they sound like a typical cast for a Gainsborough war movie, and I am suspected of having used clichés of character, I cannot help it. Every word about them is as true as I can make it. War is like that, full of clichés, and of many incidents and speeches that you couldn't get away with in fiction. Later I shall describe how a comrade of mine, on being shot in the leg, rolled on the ground shouting: "They got me! The dirty rats, they got me!" I would not use it in a screenplay – and I know what the director and actor would say if I did. But it happened, word for word, nature imitating art.

I have said that was the section, but obviously it changed. We took casualties, and new men came in, and some of them became casualties, and reorganisations took place, often in haste during an action – I suppose as many as twenty men, perhaps even more, served in the section in six months, but the nine I have described are the ones I remember best. Eventually I left the section, and found myself in the last stages of the war among unfamiliar faces. But up to Meiktila we were all together, and whatever I learned I learned from them.

BECAUSE I DISLIKE BOOKS which bewilder me by taking for granted technical details which I don't know, and also for the record, I shall say how we were dressed and armed. Burma was a barebones war; in many ways we were like soldiers of the last century in that our arms and equipment were of the simplest; it was so because it was largely a close-contact, hand-to-hand war in which, while tanks and aircraft and artillery played an important part, it was first and foremost an infantryman's business, and actions tended to be on a small scale compared with the battles in Europe. By today's standards we were sparsely equipped. Thank God.

The uniform was all dark green; even underpants, vests, and socks had gone into the big dye vat at Ranchi; watch-straps had to be green or khaki. You had two shirts, two pairs of trousers, puttees (a better protection than anklets against leeches and other crawlies), and boots – British-made, if you were lucky, rather than the clumsier Indian pattern; later we sometimes wore captured Jap jungle boots, with their thick crepe soles. A few – Parker, for one – dispensed with socks and filled their boots with tallow, claiming that it prevented blisters. It was also messy, and stank. I tried it – once.

Fourteenth Army's distinguishing feature was the bush-hat, that magnificent Australian headgear with the rakish broad brim which shielded against rain and sun and was ideal for scooping water out of wells. In some ways it was a freak, in the steel-helmeted twentieth century, and it may have cost some lives under shell-fire, but we wouldn't have swapped it. It looked good, it felt good; if you'd been able to boil water in it you wouldn't have needed a hotel. Everyone carried a razor-blade tucked into the band, in case you were captured, in which event you might, presumably, cut your bonds, or decapitate your jailer by stages, or if the worst came to the worst and you were interrogated by Marshal Tojo in person, present a smart and soldierly appearance.

Equipment consisted of the standard web belt; cross-braces; pouches worn brassière fashion; small pack containing two mess-tins, *pialla* (enamelled mug), knife, fork, and spoon, housewife with needle and thread, water purification pills, mepacrin (to ward off malaria, which it didn't), and any personal effects you felt like carrying, plus your rations; a pint water-bottle; entrenching tool, a steel mattock head with a detachable handle; and a log-line, a five-yard coil of thin rope. The last three items hung from the belt behind. A small trouser pocket contained a field dressing, but everyone scrounged a spare one because the gauze made a splendid sweat-rag-cum-neckerchief.

Weaponry was equally simple. There were a few tommy guns (but none of the hated Stens, the plumber's nightmare) in the company, but the standard arm was the most beautiful firearm ever invented, the famous short Lee Enfield, either of the old pattern with the flat backsight and long sword bayonet, or the Mark IV with the pig-sticker, a nine-inch spike with no cutting edge. The old pattern, which I carried, was the great rifle of the First World War, which the Old Contemptibles used with such speed and skill that the enemy often believed they were facing automatic weapons, and one German general told of how his division had been "shot flat" by its disciplined fire. It held ten rounds with its magazine charged, and another up the spout, had an extreme range of close to a mile, and in capable hands was deadly accurate up to four hundred yards. I'm no Davy Crockett, but I could hit three falling plates (about ten inches square) out of five at two hundred, and I was graded only a first-class shot, not a marksman. The Lee Enfield, cased in wood from butt to muzzle, could stand up to any rough treatment, and it never jammed. "She's your wife," as the musketry instructors used to say. "Treat her right and she'll give you full satisfaction." And she did, thirty years old as she was; treating her right consisted of keeping her "clean, bright, and slightly oiled" with the pullthrough and oil bottle in her butt trap, and boiling her out after heavy firing. She's a museum piece now, but I see her still on T.V. newsreels, in the hands of hairy, outlandish men like the Mujahedeen of Afghanistan and capable-looking gentry in North Africa, and I have a feeling that she will be loosing off her ten rounds rapid when the Kalashnikovs and Armalites are forgotten. That's the old reactionary talking: no doubt Agincourt die-hards said the same of the long bow.

Nowadays the automatic rifle, and concentrated firepower, are the thing, spraying rounds all over the place – which must give rise to hideous supply problems, I imagine. We had it drummed into us that each round cost threepence; "one bullet, one Jap" was proverbial, if obviously impractical. I know I sound like a dino-saur, but I doubt if the standard of marksmanship is what it was – it can't be, except at short range – and I wonder what happens if, say, a bridge has to be blown from a distance, because there's no fuse, and someone has to hit a gun-cotton primer the size of a 10p piece at two hundred yards? (A Sapper lieutenant did that in Burma, with a Lee Enfield, one shot.) Possibly such problems don't arise in modern high-tech war, or perhaps they just plaster the bloody thing with automatic fire, and hope. But I digress. We carried fifty round apiece, in a canvas bandolier draped over the buttocks.

Apart from the bayonet, the other essential sidearm was the kukri, the curved short sword of the Gurkha, slung behind the right hip. Mine cost me ten rupees, and some swine pinched it near Rangoon. The alternative was the *dah*, a long, broad-bladed machete.

In one pouch you carried two armed 36 grenades (Mills bombs), and these posed a problem. A grenade has a split pin holding in place an arm which, when the pin is withdrawn, releases a plunger which causes havoc with a fulminate of mercury detonator; depending on the internal fuse, you then have five or seven seconds to get rid of the thing, or good night, sweet prince. The cast iron casing is split into segments like a chocolate bar, and on explosion these segments (plus the base plug) will take care of anything within five yards, give or take. The question is, do you when given grenades to carry render them safe by hammering the split ends of the pin apart, or, bearing in mind that an angry Jap is not going to stand around while you un-hammer them, do you leave the pins so that they can slip out easily? The thought that Grandarse, who would make a bullock look security-conscious, is snoring beside you with his pins loose, is no inducement to untroubled sleep. In practice you just left them extractable with a sharp tug – and if Victor McLaglen, who is to be seen in old movies yanking the pins out with his teeth, ever tried it during his own army service, his incisors must still be in Mesopotamia. You do it with your finger or thumb.

There was another type of grenade, the plastic 77, which was a smoke bomb. It also sprayed phosphorus about, and was used in clearing bunkers.

In the other pouch were two Bren gun magazines, holding between 25 and 30 rounds, for the section's light machine-gun; rifle and Bren ammunition being identical. The Bren gunner normally fired from a lying position with his number two alongside to change magazines if required and turn the "immediate action" plug when the gun jammed, as it could when over-heated. It was a good gun, but needed intelligent handling, for when held firm it was accurate enough to punch a hole in a brick wall with a single magazine, and to get a good spread the gunner had to fan it about judiciously. It could also be fired from the hip, given a firm stance, for without one it would put you on your back.

Any other weapons were a matter of personal choice. Most of the section carried long-bladed flick-knives, bought in Indian bazaars; my own knife was something like a Commando dirk, worn with the butt protruding from the small pack, behind the right shoulder. The only other personal items were the rubber-ised ground-sheet, folded inside the top of the small pack (later we were issued with waterproof monsoon capes), a blanket, and a canvas water chaggle, carried only if you were marching some distance – and only those who have been really dry know that there is no drink like chaggle water, brackish, chlorinated, with a fine earthy silt at the bottom, pure Gunga Din juice. We hated it and would have sold our souls for it. And I should mention the pale green masks, with eye-slits à la Dick Turpin, worn only if you were travelling by truck through dusty country; they were not for concealment. Camouflage paint was unknown, nor did we ever black up, presumably because sun and dirt made it unnecessary.

We were not bearded; that was a Chindit* fashion. I grew a beard at the end of the campaign, when I was away from the battalion, but that was sheer laziness (and swank), and I got rid of it after a few weeks.

So there we were, nine or ten men with a thousand rounds of .303 and twenty grenades among us, and if my list has been a long one it still describes one of the most lightly armed and least encumbered foot soldiers since the introduction of firearms in war. It was gear designed for fast, easy movement by the lightest of light infantry – and I wonder why it has gone out of fashion.

The question is prompted by what I see on television of the Army today. To my eye the loose camouflage blouse is ugly, clumsy, and ill-fitting compared to our tight shirt and trousers; it might have been designed to catch on snags and hinder its wearer, and as if that wasn't enough, the poor infantryman is festooned with more kit than would start a Q.M. store. I'm sure it's all necessary; I just can't think what for. I don't like the helmet, and suspect it cramps head movement. Very well, I'm old-fashioned and ignorant, but I hold that a streamlined soldier is better off than one who looks as though he has been loosely tied in the middle, and I'd hate to try to crawl through a hedge or swim a river in that lot. Perhaps if those who design the Army's equipment had to do either of those things, they'd come up with something better.

---

* There were six brigades of Special Force (Chindits) in Fourteenth Army, operating behind enemy lines in 1943–4, under the celebrated Orde Wingate. They took heavy casualties, and by the last year of the war few specialist units of this kind were being employed: there was certainly a strong feeling, said to be shared by Slim himself, that well-trained infantry could do anything that so-called elite or special troops could do, and that it was a waste of time and manpower to train units for particular tasks.

It was said of the Chindits at the time that, whatever the strategic value of their operations, they had performed a valuable service by proving that the Japanese were not invincible. With all respect to Special Force, whose contribution was second to none in Burma, this is not true. So far as the Japanese did have a reputation as military supermen, especially in jungle, this was exploded in the Imphal-Kohima campaign where they suffered the worst defeat in Japan's history.

I am in no position to say how the Japanese were viewed before that decisive battle, but I do know that after it Fourteenth Army had no illusions about Japanese superiority, either en masse or as individuals; their heroism was acknowledged, but no one regarded them as better or more skilful soldiers.

I suppose our war was different. A military historian has written that Fourteenth Army was stripped to the belt, and certainly it took makeshift and improvisation for granted, and relied, when it had to, on what it could carry and what was dropped to it from the air. While you were with your trucks, you were part of a mechanised force, transport, tanks, artillery and all; there was a company cookhouse (dispensing bully stew and boiled eggs, mostly) and a regular water truck, and an M.O. and padre, the regimental police and familiar Army organisation, and perhaps even a Church of Scotland or Salvation Army mobile canteen – I can see it now, a jungle clearing and two smiling douce old ladies from Fife, with their battered tea-urn and tray of currant scones. "Mai guidness, Ennie, we're running out of sangwidges! Did I not say we needed anither tin of spem? Dearie me! More tea, boys?" And afterwards they would rattle off in their truck ("*Furst* gear, Ennie – and don't rev the motor, woman! Oh, mai, take a hemmer to it! Bay-bay, boys!") beaming and waving and adjusting their hair-pins, with Jap just up the road. There are heroines; I've seen them.

That was with the battalion, but there was no doubt that those long desperate months in the khuds and jungle (before my time) had bred in Nine Section an aptitude for something closer to guerrilla warfare. When the trucks had been left behind, and the battalion had faded into the distance, things were different: the long patrol, the independent operation at platoon or section level, the scout to an outlying village or just to a map reference, the lying-up perhaps in a ruined temple at what seemed the back of beyond, the feeling of being part of a reiver foray – the section seemed somehow easier, if not happier, at that kind of work; you felt that if the Army had vanished, and they had been left alone in that wild country halfway to China, they would have damned the government, had a smoke, and carried on regardless, picking up this and that on their way back to India.

I must emphasise that the platoon, much less the section, didn't operate independently very often, and only in the later stage of the campaign when the nature of the war had changed from a pursuit in divisional strength to a more confused and piecemeal operation whose object was the final demolition of the beaten Japanese armies. By then they were scattered and disorganised, often into quite small parties, so it was no longer a question of a general advance by Fourteenth Army with set-piece battles, but of road-blocks and ambushes and patrolling on a smaller scale. Those were the conditions in which the section might find itself briefly on its own, and the occasions (mercifully few) which are large in my memory are those on which, having attained the dizzy height of lance-corporal, I had nervous charge of seven or eight old sweats watching with interest to see what the young idiot would do next. To me, each decision was momentous, whether it was to kip down in a village for the night, or turn for home, or to ford a milk-white river with snake-like shapes writhing in its depths, or to allow the section to accept rice-cakes from an evil-looking headman who was so greasily friendly I was convinced he was a Jap collaborator – he wasn't, as it turned out, nor did his rice-cakes con-tain ground-glass. Small stuff, I know, but it seemed very big stuff then.

I might have found decisions easier if the others hadn't kept reminding me, with gloating obscenity, that I wasn't old enough to vote at the forthcoming General Election. It was a reminder that I had not been trained for authority in eccentric warfare. The young soldiers' battalion had given excellent military instruction, but no guidance on what to do if, on a long patrol, we found a group of obvious Indians in their underwear holed up in a *chaung** (they were "Jifs" – deserters to the Japanese "Indian National Army"); or if the section lunatic decided to shoot a vulture in open paddy, thereby alerting any Japs who might be within earshot; or how to cope with a seasoned veteran who, in a lonely basha at night, swore that there were Japanese outside, hundreds of them but only eighteen inches tall, and led by his Member of Parliament, Sir Walter Womersley, Minister of Pensions. He was the only case (the veteran, not Womersley) that I ever encountered of what is now called, I believe, post-battle trauma; I'm sure it would need psychiatric reports and counselling by social workers nowadays, but the section simply advised him to take his kukri to them – which he did, cleaving the air and crying: "Pensions, you old

* River gully

25

bastard!" before going back to sleep. He was entirely normal for the rest of the campaign.

What I had been trained for was to be an obedient cog in the great highly-disciplined machine that was launched into Europe on D-Day. That would at least have been in civilised countryside, among familiar faces and recognisable environment, close to home and the main war effort, in a campaign whose essentials had been foreseen by my instructors. The perils and discomforts would have been no less, probably, but they would not have been unexpected. It is disconcerting to find yourself soldiering in an exotic Oriental country which is medieval in outlook, against a barbarian enemy given to burying prisoners up to the neck or hanging them by the heels for bayonet practice, among a friendly population who would rather turn dacoit than not, where you could get your dinner off a tree, be eaten alive by mosquitos and leeches, buy hand-made cheroots from the most beautiful girls in the world (with granny watching, puffing her bidi* and rolling the tobacco leaf on her scrawny thigh), wake in the morning to find your carelessly neglected mess-tin occupied by a spider the size of a soup-plate, watch your skin go white and puffy in ceaseless rain the like of which no Westerner can imagine for sheer noise and volume, gape in wonder at huge gilded pagodas silent in the wilderness, and find yourself taken aback at the sight of a domestic water-tap, because you haven't seen such a thing for months.

It seemed a terribly old-fashioned kind of war, far closer to the campaign my great-uncle fought when he went with Roberts to Kandahar (he's buried somewhere in Afghanistan; I wore his ring in Burma) than to what was happening in Europe. Compared to that, or the electronic campaigns of today, it looks downright primitive. (Not that the electronic campaigns won't be primitive enough, when the barrage lifts and the infantry start walking.)

If it seemed somehow to be a long way back in time, it was also a very long way from home, and had taken a lot of hot, weary travelling to get to. It was a far corner of the world, and even although a letter written in Carlisle on Sunday could be in your hands in a *chaung* by the Sittang on Thursday, when you opened

* native cheroot

the blue air-mail form and saw the well-remembered writing, you had the feeling that it came from another planet. That's not a complaint, or an attempt to suggest special hardship; our campaign, or at least what I saw of it (Imphal and the northern khuds being something else) was probably no harder than any other. But you did feel the isolation, the sense of back of beyond. Perhaps that came, in part, from being called "the Forgotten Army" – a colourful newspaper phrase which we bandied about with derision*; we were not forgotten by those who mattered, our families and our county. But we knew only too well that we were a distant side-show, that our war was small in the public mind beside the great events of France and Germany.

Oh, God, I'll never forget the morning when we were sent out to lay ambushes, which entailed first an attack on a village believed to be Jap-held. We were lined up for a company advance, and were waiting in the sunlight, dumping our small packs and fixing bayonets, and Hutton and Long John were moving among us reminding us quietly to see that our magazines were charged and that everyone was right and ready, and Nixon was no doubt observing that we'd all get killed, and someone, I know, was muttering the old nonsense "Sister Anna will carry the banner, Sister Kate will carry the plate, Sister Maria right marker, Salvation Army, by the left – charge!" when a solitary Spitfire came roaring out of nowhere and Victory-rolled above us. We didn't get it; on the rare occasions when we had air support the Victory roll came after the fight, not before. While we were wondering, an officer – he must have been a new arrival, and a right clown – ran out in front of the company and shouted, with enthusiasm: "Men! The war in Europe is over!"

There was a long silence, while we digested this, and looked through the heat haze to the village where Jap might be waiting,

* According to my regimental magazine, the phrase "Forgotten Army" may have originated in an article by Stuart Emery of the *News Chronicle* who visited Fourteenth Army as a war correspondent in 1943; indeed, he seems to have applied the term "forgotten men" to the very battalion of which I am writing, for although he could not identify it by name, for security reasons, he did give its nickname: the "White Gurkhas". He, in turn, may have been inspired by the song "My Forgotten Man", sung by Joan Blondell in the film *Gold Diggers of 1933*, which refers to American ex-servicemen of the Great War.

and I'm not sure that the officer wasn't waving his hat and shouting hip, hooray. The silence continued, and then someone laughed, and it ran down the extended line in a great torrent of mirth, punctuated by cries of "Git the boogers oot 'ere!" and "Ev ye told Tojo, like?" and "Hey, son, is it awreet if we a' gan yam?"* Well, he must have been new, and yet to get his priorities right, but it was an interesting pointer.

But if we resented, and took perverse pleasure in moaning (as only Cumbrians can) about our relative unimportance, there was a hidden satisfaction in it, too. Set a man apart and he will start to feel special. We did; we knew we were different, and that there were no soldiers quite like us anywhere. Partly it sprang from the nature of our war. How can I put it? We were freer, and our own masters in a way which is commonly denied to infantry; we were a long way from the world of battle-dress serge and tin hats and the huge mechanised war juggernauts and the waves of bombers and artillery. When Slim stood under the trees at Meiktila and told us: "Rangoon is where the big boats sail from", the idea that we might one day get on one of those boats and sail halfway round the world to home might seem unreal, but it was a reminder that we were unique (and I don't give a dam who knows it). We were Fourteenth Army, the final echo of Kipling's world, the very last British soldiers in the old imperial tradition. I don't say we were happy to be in Burma, because we weren't, but we knew that Slim was right when he said: "Some day, you'll be proud to say, 'I was there'."

Mind you, as Grandarse remarked, we'd have to get out of the bloody place first.

* "Gan yam" is Carlisle dialect for "Go home"; elsewhere in Cumberland it is "Ga yem".

"Aye-aye, Jock lad, w'at fettle?"

"Not bad, sergeant, thank you."

"Champion! They tell us yer a good cross-coontry rooner?"

"Oh . . . well, I've done a bit . . ."

"Girraway! Ah seen ye winnin' at Ranchi – travellin' like a bloody trail 'oond w'en the whistles gan on. 'Ere, 'ev a fag."

"Ta very much, sarn't. M-mm, Senior Service . . ."

"Sarn't's mess issue, lad. Tek anoother fer after. Aye, ye can roon . . . woon a few prizes in Blighty, did ye?"

"Well, now and then . . . seven and six in savings certificates, that sort of thing . . ."

"Ah'll bet yer the fastest man in't battalion, ower a mile or two. Aye, in the brigade, likely – mebbe the division –"

"Oh, I dunno about that. There must be some good runners –"

"Give ower, Jock! A fit yoong feller like you? Honnist, noo – wadn't ye back yersel agin anybuddy in 17th Indian? Well aye, ye wad! Ootroon the bloody lot on them, eh?"

"Well, I'd be ready to have a go . . ."

"Good for you, son. An' yer a furst-class shot an' a', aren't ye? Good . . . yer joost the man tae be sniper-scout for the section."

"Eh? Sniper-scout? What's that?"

"Weel, ye knaw w'at a scout does. W'en the section cooms till a village, the scout ga's in foorst, t'see if Jap's theer."

"To . . . er, draw their fire?"

"Use yer loaf, man, Jap's nut that bloody stupid! Usually, 'e let's the scout ga through, or waits till 'e's reet inside the position an' then lays 'im oot, quiet-like. So the scout 'es tae keep 'is wits aboot 'im, sista, an' as soon as 'e spots Jap, 'e fires a warnin' shot . . . an' boogers off. So 'e'd better be a good rooner, 'edn't 'e?"

"Does it matter? I mean, if he's surrounded by bleeding Japs, he might as well be on crutches –"

29

"Doan't talk daft! If 'e's nippy on 'is feet 'e can git oot, easy! Didn't ye play Roogby at that posh school o' yours?"

"Yes, but the opposition wasn't armed. Oh, well. Here – you said sniper-scout. Where does the sniping come in?"

"Aye, weel, that's w'en we're pullin' oot of a position, nut ga'in' in. Sniper-scout stays be'ind, 'idden in a tree or booshes or summat, an' waits till Jap cooms up . . ."

"And then snipes one of them?"

"Aye, but nut joost anybuddy. 'E waits for a good target – an officer, or mebbe one o' the top brass, if 'e's loocky – "

"Bloody lucky, yes."

". . . an' then 'e nails 'im – "

" – and boogers . . . I beg your pardon . . . buggers off."

"That's reet, son! 'E gits oot an' ga's like the clappers – "

"Being a good long-distance runner. I see. Flawless logic. Well, it must be a great life, as long as it lasts – "

"Well, it's a job for a slippy yoong feller, nut owd fat boogers like Grandarse, or 'alf-fit sods like Nick an' Forster. Ah'm glad ye volunteered, Jock. 'Ere, 'ev anoother fag."

"Thanks, sarn't, but I wouldn't want to spoil my wind. By the way, does a sniper-scout get extra pay? You know, danger money?"

"Extra peh! Danger mooney! Ye've been pickin' oop sivven an' six at ivvery cross-coontry in Blighty, an' ye're wantin' mair? Ye greedy lal git! It's reet enoof w'at they say aboot you Scotchies, ye're a'ways on the scroonge . . ."

The battle of Meiktila was a hard and bloody one, the
enemy garrison having to be killed almost to a man.
Even at Meiktila the prisoners taken were wounded . . .
never out here have hundreds of thousands surrendered
. . . as the Germans have done in the European
campaign.

Regimental history

Slim was the finest general the Second World War
produced.

LORD LOUIS MOUNTBATTEN,
Supreme Commander, South-east Asia

Slim was the chap . . . he made do with the scrapings
of the barrel.

EARL ATTLEE

THE INCIDENT OF the three bunkers and my tin of fruit/carrots
is engraved on my memory because it was my baptism of fire and,
incidentally, the closest I came to participating in our capture of
Meiktila. I say "our" inasmuch as the battalion was in the thick
of the fighting for this vital strongpoint, which was vicious even
by the standards of the Burma war, and won two decorations and
a battle honour, but of this Nine Section saw nothing, and suffered
no more than tired feet and ennui from marching around in the
sun. They did not make philosophy about this, knowing that these
things average out. That may seem obvious, but I had yet to learn
it, and I'm not sure that I ever did altogether: it always seemed
rather unjust that while one company might be eating mangoes
and bathing its feet, another should be getting all hell shot out of
it, or that two sections could go in together and one wouldn't even

see a Jap all day, while the other lost half its strength in clearing bunkers not far away.

Another discovery was that the size and importance of an action is no yardstick of its personal unpleasantness. A big operation which commands headlines may be a dawdle for some of those involved, while the little forgotten patrol is a real horror. The capture of Meiktila means that gallon tin to me, while other epi-sodes which can still enliven my nightmares receive only a passing mention in regimental accounts, if that. Mention Meiktila to any surviving pensioner of my old section and he will sip his pint, nod reflectively, and say "Aye"; but drop the name of a little unheard-of pagoda that doesn't even get into the index of the big official history and he will let out an oath, sink the pint in one gulp, and start talking.

(It's an illustration of the fortunes of war, a phrase that always reminds me of a night later on, when I shared a cigarette with three men from another platoon, and we talked vaguely of having a pint in the Apple Tree on Lowther Street when we got home. Before dawn one of them was dead, another had killed a Jap and been wounded, and the third had slept through it – and he hadn't just been keeping his head down, either; he wasn't like that. My own contribution to the night's activities had been to come within an ace of killing a comrade, a recollection that still makes me sweat.)

But we knew that Jap had died hard in and around Meiktila; the rumour ran that in one hospital more than a hundred wounded had committed suicide rather than be taken; this proved to be true. It seemed incredible, after the hammering he'd had at Imphal; from listening to the older heads I gathered that they'd been hoping to hear of cases of surrender at this stage in the war, but apparently there had been none.

From the official map I see that we came into Meiktila on foot from the west, but all I recall is volumes of smoke rising from the cluster of low white buildings between the lakes, and the distant sound of firing and explosions. It isn't much of a place; in the six weeks we were there I never visited what was left of the town proper, but I spent three days at the airstrip on the way out after VJ Day, living on tinned salmon sandwiches and attending a camp

concert which featured a bald, bespectacled, desperately dirty com-
edian who told the story of Flossie the Frog. (I'm sorry, I can't
help my eccentric memory.) When we marched in we knew only
that it was a vital link in Jap's communications, and that he would
want it back.

Our platoon position was on the perimeter, on the crest of a
gentle slope running up from one of the lakes and looking out
across a hundred yards of flat ground to undergrowth which you
wouldn't dignify with the name of jungle, with a fairly thick wood
to our right front. The perimeter was a deep sloping horizontal
apron of barbed wire (a better protection against infantry than
any upright fence or coils of Dannet), and a few yards inside this
we dug our two-man rifle pits with the usual dog-leg pit for the
Bren. Behind us was platoon headquarters, consisting of the pits of
Lieutenant Gale, Sergeant Hutton, and Gale's batman and runner;
behind that was company H.Q., which in my memory consists of
the camp stool belonging to the company commander, Long John.
There were two brigades of us inside the wire* which enclosed the
two lakes in a box perhaps four miles by three, and when the third
brigade came in by air that was the whole of the Black Cat Division
within the "anvil", eighty miles inside Jap territory, "surrounded",
says the history, "by numerically superior forces", and waiting for
the "hammer" of 5th Div – and, in the meantime, Jap.

" 'E'll be at us like a rat up a fookin' drainpipe," said Sergeant
Hutton, and the section gave pessimistic growls, and spoke with
deep feeling of our prospects. Fortunately I'd been brought up in
Cumberland, and knew that the natives would rather moan than
eat; the British soldier is famous for complaint, but for sheer sour
prolonged bitching in adversity commend me to the English West
March. It comes out in a disgusted guttural growl rising to a
full-tongued roar of discontent, and subsides into normal conversation:

"In the shit again! Ah've 'ad it, me."

* The defence of Meiktila necessitated a proper barbed-wire apron, but later,
farther south, I don't recall wire often being used, probably because we were
seldom in one position for long. A battalion or company "box", held for a night
or two, might have a single trip-wire, but usually the perimeter consisted of our
slit-trenches.

"We'll all git killed."

"Fook this!"

"Whee's smeukin', then?"

"Booger off, Forster, scrounge soomw'eers else."

"Ahh, ye miserable, mingy Egremont twat!"

"Whee's gonna brew up, then? Eh, Wattie, you've got the tin."

"Brew up yer bloody sel'. Ah've carried the bloody thing a' day!"

"Aw, wrap up, ye miserable sods! Eh, Jock, git the fire lit, there's a lad."

"All right, you get the bloody sticks." (Evil associations corrupt good manners, you see.)

"Idle Scotch git! Ye want us to strike the fookin' matches, an a'?"

An outsider wouldn't have realised it, but they were in good spirits, and I should remark here that they were not foul-mouthed, as soldiers go. Many never swore at all, and those who did swore as birds sing, so naturally that you hardly noticed. You must imagine the above conversation punctuated by the Cumbrian's dirty, snarling chuckle; they are the only people I know who can moan and laugh together; they took pleasure in reviling each other, and I remember those section brew-ups as some of the friendliest gatherings of my life. Little, the corporal, listening, not saying much; Nixon with his pipe under the drooping moustache, spitting into the fire; Steele noisy and assertive, the lean young face eager in the firelight; Wedge working methodically at his rifle, one moment laughing, the next worrying about whether 5th Div could get through before . . . ; Grandarse sprawled contented like a captain at an inn, his *pialla* in an enormous paw, red face beaming; Parker with his sharp Max Miller banter, never stuck for an answer; the Duke yawning and making occasional remarks which invariably attracted mimicry, at which he would smile tolerantly; Stanley off in a reverie of his own, replying quietly when spoken to, then lapsing into contemplation again; Forster's twisted grin as he needled and sneered – "Ah could piss better chah than thoo brews, Jock" . . . "Reet, noo . . . whee's got the fags?"

If the knowledge that they were surrounded and outnumbered by the most cruel and valiant foe on earth worried them, it didn't show, ever. Times have changed now, and it is common to hear front-line troops, subjected to the disgusting inquisition of war reporters, confess to being scared. Of course they're scared; everybody's scared. But it was not customary to confess it, then, or even hint at it. It was simply not done, partly out of pride, but far more from the certainty that nothing could be better calculated to sap confidence, in one's self, in one's comrades, and among those at home. If I'd heard Corporal Little voice the kind of anxiety that television so loves to ferret out and harp on nowadays, I'd have wondered if he was the man for the job – and felt even more nervous myself. I was a worried man in Burma, but I hope it didn't show. Nothing put more heart into me, young and unsure as I was – most of all, fearful of being seen to be fearful – than the fact that, being a Scot, it was half expected of me that I would be a wild man, a head case. This age-old belief among the English, that their northern neighbours are desperate fellows, hangs on, and whether it's true or not it's one hell of an encouragement when you're nineteen and wondering how you'll be when the whistle blows and you take a deep breath and push your safety catch forward.

Talk about morale: Nine Section *was* morale, they and the barking Sergeant Hutton, and tall Long John, the courteous, softspoken company commander whose modest demeanour concealed a Berserker, and the tough, black-browed colonel to whom I never spoke until he warned me for a late tackle in a bloodbath of a Cumberland Rugby Cup match (Carlisle v. Aspatria) after the war, and all the rest of that lean and hungry battalion. To say nothing of the Gurkhas along the wire, grinning and chirruping, and the fearsome Baluchi hillmen looking like the Forty Thieves. And the green and gold dragon flag of the regiment planted down by the lake, and the black cat insignia of the oldest division in the Army. You felt you were in good company; Jap wasn't going to stop this lot. (The only remaining question was: was he going to stop *me*? Well, we'd just have to see; there was no sense worrying about it.)

But the biggest boost to morale was the burly man who came to talk to the assembled battalion by the lake shore – I'm not sure when, but it was unforgettable. Slim was like that: the only man

35

I've ever seen who had a force that came out of him, a strength of personality that I have puzzled over since, for there was no apparent reason for it, unless it was the time and the place and my own state of mind. Yet others felt it too, and they were not impressionable men.

His appearance was plain enough: large, heavily built, grim-faced with that hard mouth and bulldog chin; the rakish Gurkha hat was at odds with the slung carbine and untidy trouser bottoms; he might have been a yard foreman who had become managing director, or a prosperous farmer who'd boxed in his youth. Nor was he an orator. There have been four brilliant speakers in my time: Churchill, Hitler, Martin Luther King, and Scargill; Slim was not in their street. His delivery was blunt, matter-of-fact, without gestures or mannerisms, only a lack of them.

He knew how to make an entrance – or rather, he probably didn't, and it came naturally. Frank Sinatra has the same technique, but in his case it may well be studied: no fanfare, no announcement, simply walking onstage while the orchestra are still settling down, and starting to sing. Slim emerged from under the trees by the lake shore, there was no nonsense of "gather round" or jumping on boxes; he just stood with his thumb hooked in his carbine sling and talked about how we had caught Jap off-balance and were going to annihilate him in the open; there was no exhortation or ringing clichés, no jokes or self-conscious use of barrack-room slang – when he called the Japs "bastards" it was casual and without heat. He was telling us informally what would be, in the reflective way of intimate conversation. And we believed every word – and it all came true.

I think it was that sense of being close to us, as though he were chatting offhand to an understanding nephew (not for nothing was he "Uncle Bill") that was his great gift. It was a reminder of what everyone knew: that Slim had enlisted in 1914, fought in the trenches and at Gallipoli, and risen, without advantages, on his own merits; his accent was respectable, no more, and he couldn't have talked down if he'd tried. You knew, when he talked of smashing Jap, that to him it meant not only arrows on a map but clearing bunkers and going in under shell-fire; that he had the head of a general with the heart of a private soldier. A friend of mine, in another division, thoughtlessly decorated his jeep with a skull he'd found: Slim snapped at him to remove it, and then added gently: "It might be one of our chaps, killed on the retreat." He thought, he *knew*, at our level; it was that, and the sheer certainty that was built into every line of him, that gave Fourteenth Army its overwhelming confidence; what he promised, that he would surely do. And afterwards, when it was over and he spoke of what his army had done, it was always "you", not even "we", and never "I".

Perhaps the most revealing story, not only about Slim but about what his army thought of him, tells how he was addressing a unit preparing to go into action. The magic must have worked again, for some enthusiast actually shouted: "We'll follow you, general!" And Slim, with one of his rare smiles, called back: "Don't you believe it. You'll be a long way in front of me."

Not many generals could have got away with that; one cannot imagine Monty saying it. The irony was that it wasn't true; Slim almost got himself killed in the fighting for Meiktila.

He has been called the best battlefield general since Wellington, which takes in some heavy competition, from Lee and Grant to Montgomery and Rommel. Certainly no general ever did more with less; in every way, he was one of the great captains.

British soldiers don't love their commanders, much less worship them; Fourteenth Army trusted Slim and thought of him as one of themselves, and perhaps his real secret was that the feeling was mutual. I have a picture of him at a Burma Reunion, standing awkwardly but looking so content, with his soldiers jostling and grinning round him – and that day by the lake, nodding and wishing us luck and turning away under the trees.

I know I have not done him justice. I can only say what Kenneth Roberts wrote of Robert Rogers, that the thought of him was like home and safety.

WINSTON CHURCHILL HAS SAID that there is nothing more exhilarating than being shot at and not being hit. Each to his taste; I wouldn't call it exhilarating, quite, but it does bring a reaction beyond mere relief; satisfaction, I think. The first time it happened to me I didn't even realise it, at first. We were patrolling, four of us, less than a mile out from the perimeter, scouting for any sign of impending counter-attack on Meiktila, and had just turned back; all round there was dusty plain and dry paddy stretching away into the haze, with here and there a grove of trees in the distance and patches of scrub. Corporal Little had paused to scan with his binoculars, and I was crossing the crest of a little bund* when there was a sharp pfft! in the air above me, followed a little later by a distant crack. If the others had reacted quickly, I'd have done the same, but Little simply squatted down, and the other two looked round before following suit; there was no sudden hitting of the deck or cries of alarm. Little just said: "Gidoon, Jock," and continued his scan.

"Somewheres ower theer," called Forster.

"Aye," said Little, and lowered his glasses. "Bloody miles off. Lal† bastard. Awoy, then, let's git on."

That was all. No second shot, and not a thing to be seen, but their lack of interest, let alone concern, nonplussed me until I reflected that the shot had come from a long way off, that the chance of its hitting had been negligible, and there was nothing to be done about it anyway: searching in the general direction of the sniper would have been futile and risky. Had it been at closer range, that would have been different; as it was, Little's job was to reconnoitre and report.

* embankment
† little

38

So I concluded, and I didn't bother Little with questions. Later, when I analysed my reactions to being shot at for the first time, I realised that they were – nothing. And that, I'm sure, was because the others hadn't given a tuppenny dam about it. If they had leaped around screaming, I'd have been fit to be tied, no doubt. That incident, trivial though it was, taught me a lesson, which I pass on to any young soldier who may be interested. If you want to know how scared you've a right to be, look at the men around you. (And if you happen to be a young subaltern, remember that they're looking at *you*.)

Among the soldier's fears, that of being shot at is probably one of the least, unless it's at close range, and then there is seldom time to be afraid. He would rather not be sniped at, of course, but experience breeds, if not contempt, at least a certain fatalism: they haven't got him yet, and with luck they won't. Everyone has his own different priority of panic, to be sure, and what scares one man witless may not worry another unduly, and vice versa; my own special antipathy was to sitting about in the dark in the presence, real or imminent, of the enemy, with nothing to do but wait because those were the orders. Some, on the other hand, found having to move around in darkness even more trying, and they have a point. I suppose it depends how much faith you have in your own agility – Grandarse loathed night patrolling, for example, and was given as little of it as possible, not to spare his feelings but because the last thing you need is sixteen unwieldy stone crashing about in the undergrowth and breathing loud enough to be heard in Tokyo.

I'm sure that out of my total active service I spent only an infinitesimal time operating in the Burmese night, but in retrospect it seems longer.

The defensive scheme for 17th Div entailed incessant patrolling, both by night and day. You might think that in our situation, cut off by superior numbers, the obvious thing would have been to sit tight and let Jap come at us; having seen my share of Westerns I envisaged waves of them charging the wire while we blazed away at them. Wiser heads than mine knew that it was vital to break up his attacks before they could even be launched, hence the expeditions, sometimes in battalion strength, to fall on his concentration points, the patrols, of varying size, to spy out his movements, and the observation posts, outside the perimeter, to give warning of night attacks. And on the wire itself, the night stag, two guards per section dusk to dawn, unless an alarm necessitated a 50 or 100 per cent stand-to (half or all of the section awake and in their rifle pits).

A stag was a two-hour watch of two men, armed with rifles and bandoliers, normally standing in one pit, but at Meiktila there was an old bunker half-under the wire, and it was usual to lie on the inner slope of this, looking out across the empty ground to the scrub and wood. I don't remember it ever being pitch black; there always seemed to be half-light, and sometimes the moon turning the scene to silver and casting shadows across the landscape. It was eerie, but placid enough; you got used to the night-sounds and to the odd tricks that your eyesight can play you, causing bushes to stir when they're perfectly still, or detecting movement from the corner of your eye which isn't there when you look at it directly. You learned not to concentrate your thoughts, too, for that can take you halfway to sleep – not that this was a problem at Meiktila, where we got adequate rest. Later on it was to be different; when you're weary to the point of utter exhaustion, keeping awake on stag can be a real ordeal, for you mustn't move too much or the enemy out yonder will have you marked; you find yourself swaying and realise you were half away, and snap out of it, and a few seconds later your legs buckle and you collapse in your pit – how my knee-caps held out in Southern Burma I'll never know. You must get up at once, pinch yourself hard, and stare for all you're worth, or you'll start to sway again. And so on.

The chief irritant on stag was the "up-you bird" (I give the bowdlerised form of the name) familiar to all who have soldiered in the Far East. In fact, it is a large lizard, said to have a vicious bite, which inhabits drains in the civilised areas; where it lived in the Dry Belt, God knows. It starts up at night and drives strong men mad, for its call is a harsh whirring sound culminating in a melodious "Up you! Up you! Up you!" Half an hour of this, and you become convinced that there is a human being out there, chanting obscenely at you; it is a rare night when some blanket-wrapped form doesn't come bolt upright with a raging retort of "And up you, too!"

Apart from listening for the enemy, you had to keep an eye and ear open for night patrols returning; it's a good patrol that can arrive back exactly at its starting-point, and occasionally dark forms would emerge unexpectedly from the gloom, hissing the password. There was a gap in the wire opposite the platoon on our left, manned by a picquet with a Bren, and that was where they would re-enter.

There was a formula for the password, which always consisted of a seven-letter word – "Victory", for example. In theory, the patrol, when challenged, would identify itself, the sentry would whisper "Victory", and the patrol would prove its bona fides by responding with whichever letter of "Victory" corresponded with the day of the week, using the Morse alphabet. Thus, if it was Sunday, the correct reply was the first letter of "Victory", which is "Victor", if Monday, Ink, if Tuesday, Charlie, and so on. Who thought this up I don't know, but if he could have heard Grandarse, who seldom knew what day it was at the best of times, and couldn't spell anything longer than "pint", trying to persuade Forster that he was not a Japanese White Tiger, he would have thought of something less sophisticated. You may imagine the exchange:

Grandarse (hoarsely from the dark): Is that thoo, marra? It's me!

Forster (being awkward): Victory.

Grandarse: Ye w'at? Aw, shit, aye . . . Victory. Haud on, noo. (to a fellow-patroller) 'Ey, Wattie, w'at day is't? Thoorsdeh – awreddy? Girraway! Aye, weel, let's see . . . Moondeh, Choosdeh, Wensdeh, Thoorsdeh – v . . . i . . . c . . . aye, t, that'll be reet! Tock! 'Ey, thoo on stag, Ah'm sayin' Tock! Are ye theer?

Forster (knowing it was Thursday when the patrol left, but that midnight has passed): Booger off, yer a fifth columnist!

Grandarse: Bloody 'ell! Whee th'ell's that? Thoo, Forster, ye git! W'at ye playin' at? It's me, sayin' Tock!

Forster (relenting): It's Friday, ye daft sod!

Grandarse: Ah, the hell! W'at is't, then? Orange?

Forster: Awreet, bollock-brain. Coom in if yer feet's clean.

Fortunately this happened on a night exercise at Ranchi, not in the field, where the system worked well enough, although I sometimes wondered what would happen if a Gurkha or Baluch patrol hit the wire when Grandarse was on guard.

My own stags were marred by only one alarm. It was after a two-day duffy to the south, when we had bumped Jap in numbers, and there had been enemy activity elsewhere on the perimeter for some days previously, so I was more on edge than usual. It was the cold watch, four to six, and I was shivering as I lay alone* on the bunker-side, scanning the shadowy open ground and envying the section in their blankets ten yards to my rear. Once or twice I'd thought I'd heard something apart from the usual night-sounds; there was a little wind playing across the earth, rustling the fronds in the distant wood, just the thing to mask stealthy movement. I peered across the bunker's top, wishing there was a moon; the sky hadn't begun to lighten, and ten yards away the landscape was just a blur; a Jap fighting patrol could get to within a stone's throw undetected, if they were quiet enough ... was there something out there, beyond the shadows, or was it just my imagination? The dark seemed thicker in that direction ... and then I froze at a sudden faint noise, as though a boot had been dragged across the ground, the sound cut off almost as soon as it had started.

There was a dull thumping, too – but that was me, pressed against the bunker, with my heart moving into fourth. I eased my safety-catch forward and laid a sweating finger along the trigger guard. There had been a sound ... there it was again ... a soft, irregular scrape, as though someone were moving an inch at a time. It was closer now, not more than a couple of yards away ... now it had stopped, to be replaced by something that brought the hairs upright on my skull – the sound of breathing. That put it beyond doubt: someone – and it could only be a Jap – was in the little area of dead ground which I couldn't see beyond the bunker.

* I have been reminded that the rule of two men to a night stag was inviolable; nevertheless, I am positive that on this occasion I was on my own. The explanation can only be that the section strength had been so reduced by casualties in recent actions that two-men stags were, for a night or two, impossible.

At least it wasn't hard to do the right thing – lie dead still, and with extreme care ease my rifle forward just a little, finger on the trigger, eyes fixed on the dark curve of the bunker top . . . but, dammit, that was useless! If he wanted to get inside the perimeter, and why the hell else should he have crawled so close? – he'd come round one side of the bunker . . . or the other. Which way? I must ease myself down from the bunker-side, and back until I could cover either side – but movement meant noise . . . should I shout the alarm? I hadn't *seen* anything . . . but he was there, and if I yelled, the section would be on their feet, and he'd get somebody for certain . . . but if I lay doggo, waiting for him to move – and without warning a hideous white face shot into view over the bunker top, glared into mine from not a yard away, and vanished!

For an instant I was paralysed, thank God, or I'd have fired from pure reflex action – and that would have been deplorable, and threepence wasted. For before I could move, let alone shout, a large pale-coloured pi-dog trotted out from beyond the bunker, snuffled at the wire apron, took a discontented look at me, and mooched off into the gloom. The false alarm can never be as bad as the real thing, but it can set the adrenalin pumping just as fast. Watching the brute disappear I reflected that to the fatal perils of enemy rifles, bayonets, artillery, grenades, mortars, punjis, malaria, dysentery, and poisoned wells, I would have to add another – heart failure.*

This was an ever-present risk on that other form of stag, the o.p., or observation post, which consisted of two men well outside the wire, lying up in any convenient concealment with a Verey pistol. The procedure was simple: you lay doggo from some time after dusk until dawn to give early warning of any enemy fighting patrol advancing to the perimeter, which was done by letting them go past and then firing the Verey. After which it was advisable to

---

* Ex-Fourteenth Army men may take issue with me for suggesting that a sentry would ever alert his comrades by shouting. The approved method was to have a log-line or creeper running from the sentry to the nearest sleeper, who could be aroused silently by tugging it, and I remember doing this in jungle country farther south. At Meiktila the ground was open, and I don't recall ever using log-lines there.

leave the o.p. at speed, since the firing of the flare was a certain giveaway of your position; what happened next depended on the circumstances, as Sergeant Hutton explained:

"Git back in the perimeter if ye can, but if Jap's at the wire keep clear, or ye'll git thassel shot be soom booger or other. If ye lie off somewheres ye might git a Jap on 'is way yam, but don't git thassel killed. Yer oot theer to watch; that's yer furst job. Dee w'at Nick does an' ye'll not be far wrang."

After which Nixon and I slipped out in the dark and made our way cautiously to a fold in the ground about a hundred yards out which Hutton had marked the previous day. The grove which lay on the section's right front was now behind us, invisible until the moon came up, and even then only a vague blur, for it was a murky night. We lay in silence, listening to the "up-you" birds giving their midnight chorus, shifting only a little now and then to avoid cramp; my chief worry, since we were lying prone, was that I would drop off to sleep, so I kept a piece of stick upright beneath my chin so that it would prick me if I nodded. I needn't have troubled; knowing what we were there for, and that there was an outside chance that Jap would turn up, was quite enough to keep me wide awake.

I have said that sitting tight in the dark was my unfavourite occupation, and that is partly because, aside from straining your eyes into blackness and listening, there is nothing to do but think. No doubt it was our exposed position and my morbid imagination that turned my mind to the possibility of being taken prisoner, on which we had been lectured by a lean and rather wild-looking Highland officer at Ranchi. He spoke with authority, having escaped from the Japs himself, and discussed his subject with an enthusiasm that prompted Forster to observe, *sotto voce,* that this 'un was jungle-happy. I doubted it; he talked too much sense, with a flippancy deliberately calculated not to create alarm and despondency. Having shown us escape kit (with which we, at least, were never issued) like tiny flexible files sewn into seams of clothing, and the magnetic fly-button which, detached and balanced on a point, indicated north ("An' Ah can joost see mesel', wid Japanni wallahs efter us, pullin' me bloody fly-buttons off an' balancin' them on me knob," muttered Grandarse), he went on to

44

remind us of survival and path-finding techniques, but what stayed in the mind was his advice on dealing with captors:

"You can expect 'em to be pretty rough. They're evil little sods, and couldn't care less about the Geneva Convention, so there's a chance they'll beat you up – not just for information, but for spite. You know the drill: give 'em rank, name, and number, nothing more. Don't lie to them. Keep your head up and look 'em in the eye. If it's an officer or someone who speaks English, tell 'em they're losing face by ill-treating a prisoner; it's been known to work. But first and foremost – escape! Don't be daft about it; wait for an even chance, and go! And keep going! You know how to look after yourselves. Don't trust the Burmese unless you must; they're mostly friendly, but they're scared stiff of Jap, so watch it." The last thing he'd said was: "Whether you escape or not, don't give up. Remember they're a shower of sub-human apes, and you're better men than they'll ever be."

He was describing, absolutely accurately, an enemy well outside civilisation, but nothing we hadn't know since the fall of Hong Kong and Singapore. Like everyone else, I suppose, I wondered how I would be if they got hold of me, which isn't a happy thought in an o.p. at four in the morning . . . and Nick stirred beside me and asked in a whisper what time it was.

I had only to glance at the luminous dial of my watch to send my thoughts off at another tangent: breakfast at home, with my parents presenting the watch on my eighteenth birthday: there was the old, stiffly-laundered tablecloth bearing in its centre the faint embossed legend "Chicago Athletic Club" – not pinched by an itinerant relative, I may say, but a flawed item bought by my thrifty grandmother from the Paisley mill – and the triangles of toast in the rack, the monthly jar of marmalade with the golliwog label, the damp strong smell of the tea-cosy when my mother lifted it from the pot, the curious wartime breakfast of scrambled pow-dered egg and "Ulster fry" (one of Spam's poor relations), my father glancing through his *Glasgow Herald* before checking his battered leather prescription book and hurrying off to his round of visits and morning surgery, the little electric fire making its occasional sparks . . . and in the darkness a few yards away a shadow was moving, and it wasn't a pi-dog this time; it was small and stunted but definitely human, standing in a slight crouch, a rifle held across the body, then moving slowly forward.

I had only to slide my hand a few cautious inches to touch Nick, and his head turned; I didn't have to point. I can see his sharp face with the heavy moustache, and the movement of his lips, pursed as though to shush me – which wasn't necessary, really. We lay holding our breaths, heads close together, willing our bodies into the ground as we watched the figure advance, a slow step at a time, the dark blur of the head turning from side to side. If he held his course he would pass about five yards to our right; in that light he would have to be a bloody lynx to make out two figures on that broken ground – unless we moved. The temptation to get my hand on the stock of my rifle was strong, but I resisted it; by good chance the muzzle was pointed almost straight at him, and if he did spot us I would have to be damned slow not to get my shot in first . . . He was level with us now, treading delicately with barely a sound; he paused to look back and gestured, and other figures, equally small and ungainly, emerged from the gloom in single file – Jesus! there were eight of them, moving like mis-shapen little ghosts. It took them an eternity to pass our position, while I let my breath out with painful slowness and inhaled again; once I felt rather than heard Nick give a tiny gasp, and as the last figure faded into the dark behind us I turned my head to look at him. To my amazement he was grinning; he gave that little patting motion of the hand that says, settle down, take it easy, and when I stirred a finger towards the Verey pistol, lying between us, he shook his head. Still grinning, he put his lips to my ear and whispered:

"Goorkas! Ey, and they nivver even smelt us!"

Sure enough, a few minutes later, came the faint sound of voices far behind us; they were at the wire, making their presence known.

Another anti-climax – and another lesson, which I learned when it grew light, and silence was no longer necessary.

"How the hell did you know they were Gurkhas? They looked bloody like Japs to me!"

"They did to me, an' a' – at foorst. They're a' short-arsed boog-ers, sitha, but there's one way ye can always tell Johnnie Goorka fra' Johnnie Jap – Ah mean, w'en it's dark-like, an' ye can't mek

oot their fesses, joost their shapes. Ah didn't spot it till they was
near on past us. Always look at their ankles, Jock! The Goorkas,
see, wear short puttees, like oors, so their troosers is baggy reet
the way doon till their ankles. Noo, Jap wears lang puttees, nigh
on up till 'is knee, so 'is legs look thin, ez if 'e 'ad stockin's
on!" Nick chuckled, well pleased. "An' they walked reet by us!
Heh-hee! The boogers!"

"Shouldn't we have let on?" I realised the answer to the damfool
question even before I'd finished asking it.

"Git hired,* Jock! Ye've bin on night patrol – if soom booger
challenges from underfoot, ye're liable to do 'im! Ah want to die
me own fookin' way, not wid a kukri up me gunga!" This seemed
to prompt another thought. "Ayup, tho'. Look, we'll 'ev to tell
Tut Hutton that we saw 'em, but we'll not let on till anybuddy
bar 'im. Mind, noo, Jock – doan't tell nobuddy else."

"If you say so – but why not?"

"Ah, they're grand lal lads, the Goorkas – but, man, they're
proud! An' they tek their sojerin' seriously, an' a'." He wagged a
finger. "Ah tell ye, if they foond oot they'd coom near treadin' on
us in't dark, an' 'edn't spotted us, they'd ga fookin' crackers!
They wad, tho'! The *naik*† leadin' that patrol wadn't 'ev to git
busted – 'e'd bust 'is bloody sel', man, oot o' shame! An' Ah'm
nut kiddin'." He shook his head in admiration. "So we'll say nowt
aboot it – bar to Hutton. Awreet, Jock? Good lad." He had
another chuckle to himself. "Walked reet by us, an' a'! Nut bad,
eh?"

I sympathised with the Gurkhas, having no doubt that in similar
circumstances I could have walked through the whole Japanese
Imperial Guards Division without knowing it. "All we had to do
was lie still," I suggested.

"Aw, aye? Is that reet, Jock? Girraway! Ah'm glad ye told us."
Cumbrian sarcasm is never applied lightly. "Lissen – the Goorkas
is the best night scoots in the bloody wurrld! By God, there isn't

* Get hired = get a job. One of the Cumbrian's many expressions of derision,
referring to the custom whereby an unemployed farm worker would stand with
a straw in his mouth at Carlisle Cross during the hiring fair, waiting to be
approached with an offer of work.
† Corporal

many can say the Goorkas nivver spotted their o.p.! Noo, an' Ah'm tellin' ye!"

"Right pair of Mohicans we must be."

"Aye, laff, ye girt* Scotch git! Looksta, if they'd bin Japs, an' we'd fired oor Verey, they'd ha' bin nailed, ivvery bloody one, on the wire wid their arses oot the winder! Wadn't they?" He was quite belligerent about it. "Awreet, then! We did oor job, an' the Goorkas missed us! An' that's nut bad! That's a' Ah'm saying'!"

Well, he was infinitely better qualified to judge these things than I, and his words prompted a disturbing thought: if I'd been alone in the o.p. I'd certainly have fired the Verey, the Gurkhas would have been caught in the glare, and might well have been wiped out by a nervous Bren gunner making the same mistake as I had done. Nick had identified them by the shape of their legs – and that is something you won't find in any infantry training manual. But then, he was what the Constable of France would have called a very valiant, expert gentleman. The irony was that it almost cost him his life a few nights later.

---

* Great, big, but like "lal" or "lyle" (little) it doesn't necessarily have anything to do with physical size, being just a familiar adjective.

"'Ey, Jock, are ye any good at 'rithmetic?"

"Not much, sarn't, I'm afraid."

"Well, mek's nae matter. Ah'll keep thee reet. Noo then – 'oo many fellers is there in't British Army?"

"Gosh, I dunno. Five million?"

"An' 'oo many o' them's in Boorma?"

"Half a million, maybe?"

"An' 'oo many o' them's in this battalion?"

"About a thousand."

"An' 'oo many o' them's in Nine Section?"

"Ten, sarn't."

"So if ye're in't Army, w'at's the odds against bein' in Nine Section? Tek time, noo."

"I haven't the least idea."

"Iggerant booger. Ah'll tell thee. It's 'alf a million to one."

"If you say so. I'm fascinated."

"Ye will be. Ye're the section scout, aren't ye?"

"I am, and I think I begin to see where your elaborate calculation is leading, sarn't –"

"Shurroop an' charge yer magazine. Noo, 17th Div's ahead o' Fourteenth Army, an' this battalion's leadin' 17th Div, an' Nine Section's oot in froont, foorther sooth than any oother boogers in Sooth-east Asia Command – are ye follerin' this, Jock?"

"With interest. Sarn't Hutton, do you know what a sadist is?"

"By, Jock, yer a loocky yoong feller! The odds against bein' the leadin' man in the whole fookin' war effort against Japan is five million to one –"

"And I'm the one. Thank you very bloody much."

"So git thasel oot on point, keep yer eyes oppen, an' think on – me an' Choorchill's watchin' ye!"

The fight to retain Meiktila was to be long and bitter since the Japanese concentrated every unit and formation they could to break Fourteenth Army's stranglehold ... It is a tribute to the Japanese that nobody had any doubt that, rather than break off the fight and withdraw, they would launch a counter-offensive with every unit they could assemble ...

Although 17th Division was surrounded ... by numerically superior forces, Cowan's policy was to retain the initiative by using a very small number of troops for static defence and sending out columns in all directions to strike at Japanese communications and enemy forces which had cut his own land communication ...

Official history

WHAT I HAVE DESCRIBED SO FAR was the "static defence" of Meiktila, and so far as that was concerned Nine Section had it cushy—doing stag, mounting the occasional o.p., keeping our weapons clean, and waiting to be sent out Jap-hunting in force with the Sherman tanks of Probyn's Horse. Jap attacked the wire elsewhere, I believe, but never in our sector, and while we were inside the perimeter life was tranquil. Snapshots of memory:

Playing in one game of football on the bare space behind our rifle pits, and being impressed by the brilliance of a young centre-half from Workington who came close to an England cap a few years later, and the speedy reflexes of an officer from another platoon; he was a Cameron Highlander, and I had occasion to note his speed later on. Also the bone-shattering violence of the man marking me, the Regimental Sergeant-Major, no less, who was completely bald (what Parker called "a lovely head o' skin") and who gave me the only wound I received in the war, a neat little scar on my left knee.

Watching someone do Number Two Field Punishment. Number One, which consisted of being tied to a gun-wheel, had gone out by that time, but Number Two looked decidedly unpleasant: having to run in circles, wearing full equipment, which included the big pack, pouches, rifle, etc., in the boiling sun under the supervision of a blue-chinned member of the Provost staff. I don't know what the accused had done, but he came off in a state of near-collapse. It did him no permanent damage, for only last year, as a sprightly pensioner, he was singing his head off at our reunion in Carlisle Cathedral. (If that kind of punishment seems barbaric, it should be noted that in the Chindits there was at least one case of *flogging*, with parachute cord. I think it was for sleeping on stag. The officer who ordered it was a charming man and a splendid soldier, with whom I had a friendly correspondence after the war. On the whole, though, much as I admired him, I think that if he'd tried it with me I'd have shot him.)

Being mocked for using a knife and fork. We had three meals a day, ideally: breakfast, tiffin, and supper, punctuated by brew-ups of tea whenever we got the chance. As I remember, breakfast was bacon, beans, burgoo,* and bread; tiffin was liable to be bully beef and biscuits and tinned fruit; supper would be either bully stew (a waste of good bully beef, in my opinion), or Maconochie's superb stewed steak, which came in dark green cans as part of the compo ration, a large tin container holding a day's food for the section, including potatoes and vegetables. These, with eggs boiled to bullet hardness, tinned fish (which we never ate, but used for barter), rice pudding, and occasional duff, were the basic foods, and very good they were. In Meiktila, and for most of the campaign, all food was dropped from the air, and later in the campaign, when the monsoon made flying impossible, we were on half rations for a month. This was no great hardship, since by then we were down south and could get mangoes, bananas, and occasional livestock from the villagers, usually by barter.

When we were away from the company cookhouse we made

* porridge

our own meals over the section fire, and it was on such an occasion that I remember being jeered at because, unlike the others, who scooped their stew from their mess-tins with their spoons, I insisted on using my knife and fork. ("'Ey, Nick, git a napkin for fookin' Lord Fauntleroy!") This, I maintain, wasn't affectation; I just wasn't at ease eating meat and potatoes with a spoon; it didn't feel right, and no doubt stamped me as hopelessly bourgeois and Christopher Robin. I noticed that the Duke, the section's aristo, shovelled his Maconochie's down with a spoon in the best Grandarse style.

Occasionally we had K-ration, that American abomination designed, I believe, by Wingate. It contained, among other things, a tiny tin of hideous eggy gunge, a nutty candy bar, three Camel cigarettes, and three sheets of toilet paper, which drew Rabelaisian comments from the section, who wondered if them Yank boogers ed nivver 'eerd o' grass.

I cannot leave our rations without mentioning that splendid item on which, in its various forms, British servicemen have thriven for centuries: the small, square rough half-biscuit half-oatcake known as hard tack. I, at least, never got tired of them; topped with little cubes of bully and accompanied by floods of tea, they make one of the great meals, and were in every way superior to the bread issue which, like all Indian loaves, was shiny, musty, and slightly stale.

The discovery that I had a genius for brewing tea. I am not modest about this: I am probably the greatest tea-brewer in the history of mankind. It is an art, and I have the unanimous word of Nine Section (even Forster, eventually) that I brought it to the pitch of perfection. They were connoisseurs, too, or at least I like to think that I imposed connoisseurship on them, once I had weaned them away from "Gurkha tea", which consisted largely of condensed milk, to which the Gurkhas were addicted. Show me the Indian soldier who isn't.

Brewing up is not merely a matter of infusing tea; making the fire comes into it, and when you have lit and maintained fires in the monsoon, you have nothing more to learn. That came later; at Meiktila it was a simple business of assembling bamboo slivers, igniting them (no small thing, with Indian "Lion" matches which

invariably broke and sprayed the striker with flaming phosphorus),
and bringing about a gallon of water to the boil in the section
brew-tin. This was a jealously-guarded article, about a foot cubed,
made by cutting a compo ration tin in two and piercing the rim
for a handle of signal wire. The casting in of the tea leaves from
the section box was the crucial thing, followed by the ceremonial
dropping in of two broken matchsticks to attract stray leaves;
remove the tin from the heat, invite the guests to scoop out the
brew with their piallas, and tea was served, each man adding
sugar and condensed milk to taste. The ritual was complete when
Grandarse had sipped, appraised, and exclaimed, "Eh, Christ,
thoo brews a canny cup, Jock!" If he hadn't said it, or had even
varied the phrase, it would have been like someone passing the
port to the right.

"W'en we git back," said Steele, "ye'll ev to oppen a shop,
doon Botchergate, near th'auction mart. Brewin' chah; ye'll mek a
bloody fortune."

"Jock's Brewshop," said Grandarse. "Ey, wid a sign – a Black
Cat, wid its arsehole wreathed in smiles."

"Hire a bloody big Sikh durwan,* an' a', wid a lathi.† Keep the
coostomers in order."

"Tanner a cup – naw, mek ivverybuddy bring 'is own pialla. Ye
knaw, giv it atmosphere. Or ev a stack o' piallas an' mess-tins at
the door."

"Wot 'e wants," said Parker, "is to make it real authentic. First
off, it ain't a shop – it's a backyard, knee-deep in shit. An' naow-
body gets any chah till 'e's dug a slit-trench, see? 'Ere, an' it all
'as to 'appen in the pissin' rain! Issue picks, shovels, an' piallas at
the door, then get soaked – you'll mebbe need a shower, Jock –
then aht they goes, digs their pit, an' you give 'em a brew-up. Two
chips a time, 'ow abaht that?"

"It sounds attractive," I said. "Think anyone would come?"

"Bleedin' millions – Yank tourists, an' that. 'Re-live the joys of
active service wiv ahr gallant lads. 'Ave an authentic Fourteenth
Army cuppa from Jock, brew-artist supreme!' I tell you, they'd

* porter
† long staff, the truncheon of Indian police

come flockin'! You could import them big ants, an' put 'em in the sugar – ahr bleedin' tin's got thahsands of the bastards!"

"You wouldn't want to hire a Jap sniper, too?"

"Nah, that be overdoin' it . . . I dunno, though, you might give 'im blanks an' let the customers kill the little sod."

They elaborated, with unmentionable details; I took it as a great tribute.

"Aye, but, think on," said Forster. "Ye'll ev t'mek it pay. Rob the boogers blin', eh, Jock?" And he rubbed finger and thumb together, Shylock-like, and quoted: *"Tora cheeny, tora dood"*.

Which means, in Urdu, "a little sugar, a little milk", and set him off singing "Deolali Sahib", one of the forgotten soldier songs of India, to the tune of "There is a happy land".

> *Tora cheeny, tora chah,*
> *Bombay bibi, bahut achha!*
> Sixteen annas, *ek* rupee,
> Seventeen annas, *ek* buckshee.
> Oh, Deolali Sahib! Oh, Deolali Sahib!
> May the boat that you go home on
> *Niche rakko pani,* sahib!

I give only the printable lines, noting that "bibi" is a girl, "bahut achha" means very good, and the last line translates literally as "under rest water", which was the nearest soldier's Urdu could come to "sink to the bottom of the sea". It is an odd reflection on our present standards that if "Deolali Sahib" were sung on television today its obscenities would pass unremarked, since they are all in regular use in the media – but there would certainly be a prosecution under the Race Relations Act.

Like most of our songs, it was sung either on the march or when travelling by truck. Camp-fire vocalising was almost unknown, and Forster's was the only case I remember, not so much for itself but because it was followed by Parker's rendering of a ditty picked up in the China wars, to the tune of "Bye-bye, blackbird".

Wrap up all my care and woe,
Here I go, swinging low,
Bye-bye, Shanghai!
Won't somebody wait for me,
Please get in a state for me,
Bye-bye, Shanghai!
Up before the colonel in the morning,
He gave me a rocket and a warning:
'You've been out with Sun-yat-sen,
You won't go out with him again',
Shanghai, bye-bye!*

It was a section favourite, and perhaps I remember so vividly hearing it for the first time, sung softly in the firelight with Parker moving his pialla to the music, because that was almost

---

* While Parker's song has an obvious origin among the mercenaries of the pre-war era, "Deolali Sahib" is considerably older, probably from the last century. Many of our marching songs were of even greater antiquity; I cannot guess where the famous "One-eyed Riley" originated, but "Samuel Hall" dates at least from the time of Captain Kidd, and "Three German Officers Crossed the Rhine" is an echo from the Middle Ages – the Three Captains, or the Three Knights, have been in folk-song for many centuries. Unfortunately most of them are obscene in the extreme, and I am too old-fashioned to quote them. In my time they were sung with vim, especially the scatological bits; maybe they still are.

One which was entirely clean was "South of Meiktila", a parody of "South of the Border", which is now to be found in anthologies. I mention it because I was present at its composition, in the back of a truck jolting down the Rangoon road after we had cleared Pyawbwe. It is, with respect, a pretty execrable piece of work, but it is exclusively about my old battalion, like that other jolly little parody of "Argentina", which begins:

Oh, you can climb a big hill
On a mepacrin pill

A favourite pastime was to sing popular songs partly in Urdu, with no regard for the niceties of that language. Thus:

I'd rather have a paper doll	became	*Ham* rather have a *coggage bint*
To call my own,		Of *mera* own,
A doll that other fellows		A *bint* that *duser admis*
Cannot steal . . .		*Klifty nay* . . .

What the British soldier was capable of in mistreating Urdu may be judged from his translation of "You would, would you?" as *"Tum lakri, lakri tum?"*. *Tum* is "you," *lakri* is "wood".

the last time I brewed up for the whole of Nine Section as it was at the start of the campaign. Next day our part in the "static defence" of Meiktila ended, and we went out in strength to look for Jap.

The method was simplicity itself. A company, or perhaps two (more than 200 riflemen) would climb on the battered Sherman tanks and rumble out of the perimeter; if authority had marked down a Japanese concentration, the tanks would often take us all the way; if it was a probe, we dismounted and marched, sweeping the countryside until the enemy was encountered. Riding the Shermans spared the feet, but it had its disadvantages: after an hour or so the metal became so hot that you had constantly to change position to avoid being roasted, and the water chaggles took considerable punishment; by then we were coated so thick with dust that our faces looked as though we were wearing Number Nine make-up, and it was almost a relief to slide down and walk.

There are two great descriptions of marching: Kipling's poem, "Boots" (a remarkable work of art since he can have endured the pain of foot-slogging in the sun only at second-hand) and P. C. Wren's passage in *The Wages of Virtue*. I marched far farther in training in England, and in India, than ever I did in Burma; twenty-two miles in a day is my record, and that was in North Africa after the war. It is painful, too, not so much on the feet as on the back and shoulders, where the equipment chafes – the official wisdom is that you should wear the small pack high up towards the neck, but I noticed that Nine Section let them hang slack. Your feet are either fine or useless; my soles, by the end of the campaign, were white, spongy, and entirely devoid of feeling, but that was the monsoon; not until fifteen years later did they return to normal. At first they just became raw, and by Pyawbwe they were hurting like sin, but not to incapacitate: it is a tribute to my small part of Fourteenth Army, at least, that I never knew a man fall out with his feet; some of them were in horrible condition, but they bathed them and patched them and anointed them with strange things from the M.O., and kept going.

I have read, whether it is true or not, that in the Falklands War there were twenty per cent casualties from feet. I find it hard to credit, but if it is true, it was no fault of the soldiers, but of the boots.

Our Burma marches were modest – certainly by the standard of the Retreat or the Imphal Campaign – but even they could be rough if you were fighting along the way, or getting wearier by the day from night actions or stand-to's. My lasting impression is of thirst, and the yearning to reach for the water-bottle bumping on my stern, warm-to-hot though the contents were and highly flavoured of chlorine and rust. You didn't touch your water-bottle until you had to, so I ploughed moodily on, parched and sore, hating Preston Sturges, the film director, because in a copy of a magazine (*Yank*, probably) there was an article about him, describing how in his Hollywood office there was a soft-drink tank, awash with clinking ice-cubes and frosted bottles; it was enough to start you baying at the sun. And it was at such a time that Grandarse, who must have been more educated than he looked, would start to recite:

> You may talk o' gin an' beer
> When you're quartered safe out here

with coarse modifications to the verse which Kipling never thought of, but which I'm sure he would have approved. I don't recall even the North Sahara being hotter or drier than the Dry Belt of Burma; it may be significant that Grandarse, having finished his recitation and stretched himself on the rocky earth with his hat over his lobster-coloured face, should exclaim:

"Wahm? Ah's aboot boogered! By hell, Ah could do wi' some fookin' joongle, Ah tell tha!" And the Duke, sighing and sweating, said thoughtfully that, on the whole, he thought Grandarse was right.

From what I saw farther south, and the jungle I encountered twenty years later in Borneo, I'm not sure I would agree. The Dry Belt might be hard and hot, but at least you could see where you were, and, with luck, the opposition.

I had my first long look at them in numbers when we made our initial probe a few miles down the Rangoon road, two companies of us with tanks of the Deccan Horse. Our own company sweep encountered little, but the other company hit a village where Jap was dug in; the attack went in, 70 Japs were killed, and two guns captured, but by dusk we were outnumbered and cut off from Meiktila, 200 men and a troop of tanks, and had to fade into the dark and make a box. This was the night a tank* brewed up on the road and we lay off in the dark, sweating in the night cold and keeping quiet while we watched the Japs swarming around the burning wreckage in a way which would have recalled Osbert Sitwell's remark about "those clever, patriotic apes of Japanese hurling themselves about", if I'd known it at the time. They looked like energetic khaki goblins, and when I whispered this to the Duke, lying alongside, we discovered that we had both suffered infant nightmares from George MacDonald's goblin stories; his imps had had tender feet, without toes, and could be laid out by stamping on them; at this point Sergeant Hutton told us to fookin' shut up, and a moment later the altercation broke out in the dark behind us, between Forster and a Sikh over the possession of a chaggle – it lasted all of three seconds before being snarled to silence.

"Stupid sods!" muttered the Duke. "Can you beat it? Forster's thirsty, so 200 men risk getting killed!"

The only other memory I have of that night is of the anxious, sweating face of a tank officer thrust close to mine, asking if everything was okay. He was crawling round the perimeter – which consisted of men lying on their weapons, since there had been no time to dig in – and when I said we were fine he exclaimed: "Thank God for that! Well done, well done!" and scuttled off on all fours. It seemed an odd inquiry – obviously everything was okay, inasmuch as Jap hadn't found us; if he did, it wouldn't be. Another lesson noted: if you're jittery, keep it to yourself; my nerves were fine until he arrived; afterwards I was decidedly restless.

There wasn't a Jap to be seen at dawn, but since they were in large numbers between us and Meiktila it was necessary to get

* My impression was that it was a truck, but the official history says it was a tank.

into cover without delay: when a small force is cut off, as we were, the best it can do is hole up, wait for a chance to slip out, and in the meantime annoy the enemy in any way it can. It was something new to me, this Fourteenth Army attitude of regarding a defensive position not as a place where you waited to be attacked, but as a base from which you sallied out to observe or clobber the foe. It was done on a big scale at Meiktila, and on a small one in the little village where we joined up with the rest of the battalion later that day, after a quick march through the dry paddy on which Grandarse trod on a krait, which is among the most venomous snakes on earth. It was a nasty shock to both of them; he cried "Ya booger!" and went up three feet, and the krait shot out from under and disappeared into a crack in the sunbaked earth.

The village was a neat little stronghold, surrounded by a high embankment with openings north and south where the road ran through. This bank, which was plainly pre-war, had evidently been built as a defence against the ubiquitous Burmese bandits, and once we had strung wire beyond the outer slope and dug our pits on the inner one, we were nice and snug. The section brewed up, and while the light lasted I started writing a short story about a sixteenth-century Highlander cruising through the wilds of Lochaber who suddenly becomes aware that he is being stalked by a beautiful young woman who is even more expert a woodsman than he is. Considering our position, Freud, had he been there, would probably have said something trenchant, but all I got was Sergeant Hutton snapping:

"Stop bloody scribblin', git off yer arse, an' git fell in wid your rifle an' kukri. Yer gan on tiger patrol. Put yer p.t. shoes on, leave yer 'at, an' report to Mr Gale."

"Are you going?"

"Nah, joost 'im and you and two oothers. Ye evn't done a tiger patrol* afore, ev ye? Nah, neether 'as Gale." He considered. "Aye . . . 'e's joost a lad – but 'e's a good lad. Reet, git crackin'."

Gale was perhaps a year or two older than I was, about twenty-two; he'd joined the battalion when I had, so he was not experienced. But he was, as Hutton said, a good lad, brisk, active, and

---

* In effect, a fighting patrol as distinct from a purely reconnaissance patrol

with a gift of easy command, neither too stiff nor too affable, the kind of subaltern that the British Army has turned out by the thousand for centuries, and who, with the tough, worldly-wise Huttons, has been its sheet anchor.

Nixon and Parker were the other two; they and Gale were lightly shod and armed as I was. We assembled in a little basha in the gathering dusk; other patrols were forming up, and Long John was issuing orders to Stanley and a man from another platoon who were going out to an o.p. in front of our position. It was all very business-like and unhurried, quiet voices and shadowy figures, an occasional soft laugh among the mutter of orders, magazines being charged and safety catches going on, feet shuffling, the light of the storm lantern reflected on faces. Gale drew us aside and briefed us: there had been a lot of Jap movement in the country around, and a big force was believed to be moving up towards Meiktila. It would probably pass some way to the east of our village, but flanking units or patrols were sure to bump us shortly; in the meantime the battalion would be scouting every village within a ten-mile radius, watching for any concentration and doing whatever mischief we could.

"Tonight we're recce-ing a couple of villages, see if Jap's in residence, pick up news." He looked at me. "You're the cross-country expert – right, if we run into trouble, and I shout "Runner!" you get out, fast. Understand? Don't wait for anything, get back to the battalion, tell 'em whatever we've found. Okay?" We all nodded. "Let's go."

His voice was level, but I could hear the suppressed excitement in it, and wondered if he felt the same rising shiver at the back of the throat that I did. The villages might be stiff with Japs, likewise the countryside; suppose we got in among them, just four of us, and it came to a dirty mêlée in the dark? Well, I would just have to wait for the shout of "Runner!", doing whatever seemed best in the meantime. For the life of me I couldn't decide whether being the best long-distance runner in the platoon was a good thing or not; it really wasn't worth considering.

We slipped out of the perimeter and stopped about a hundred yards out, kneeling in a rough diamond formation to look and listen. Behind was the dark loom of the village, with a light here and there; the paddy itself was half-dark, and I could easily make out the three dim forms; when we went on Gale led, with Parker and Nixon on either flank and a little behind him; I was the back point of the diamond. They went very quietly, pausing only when Gale stopped or sank to one knee; from the gloom around us there was hardly a sound; if Jap was out there he was being just as silent as we were.

Now, I know I must have been scared, but I don't remember it – not to compare with other occasions, where the memory of fear remains as strong as when I felt it. Looking back, I can say that night patrolling in enemy country, while not the ideal form of relaxation, was less hair-raising than I'd expected; put it another way, it was preferable to lurking in an o.p., for my money. Every normal person fears the dark, but if you have to face it there is great reassurance to moving quietly in good company, travelling light and knowing that you have been well trained in the basics – take your time, don't lose contact, when in doubt sink down and listen, and try to remember that darkness is a friend. The know-ledge, which came later, that Jap was certainly no better in the dark than we were, was absent on that first tiger patrol; even so, the confidence with which Gale moved ahead, and the sureness and silence of the other two, gradually induced a feeling that had at least as much excitement as fear about it.

Reading that last paragraph again, I wonder if I've gone mad at long last. It is one thing to sit quietly typing in one's study, recalling in safety the perils of fifty years ago and knowing perfectly well that the neighbourhood is not full of malevolent Tojos waiting to kill me (if it were, and I, an overweight pensioner, were fool enough to go out looking for them, I'd blunder about in the dark, falling over everything, and probably die of apoplexy), and quite another to have to do the real thing. No, what I mean to convey is that there are worse things than night patrolling, as we shall see. It is a matter of taste: offered the choice, which at this stage I am comfortably certain I shan't be, between roaming the Burmese night on the off-chance of meeting Jap, and clearing an occupied bunker, I'd take the former, as offering a better chance of a happy return. But on the whole I'd much prefer a pint black-and-tan.

There were no Japs in the first village, but there had been a few hours earlier. We skirted the place before going in, Gale conferring with the headman through the good offices of a smooth young villager who announced himself as a B.A., Rangoon University. About fifty Japanese had passed through during the morning, heading north; they had assured the headman that the British were about to be driven out of Meiktila and across the river; already many had been ambushed and killed in unsuccessful attempts to break out, and the village was to keep an eye open for stragglers. This, said the young man, beaming ingratiatingly, the headman had pretended to believe, but he knew it was untrue. It occurred to me that the Japanese had been treated to the same wide grin that morning.

We three kept in the shadows while Gale was talking; there could be no question of searching the place. If there had been Japs concealed they'd have been shooting us up by now, and the villagers seemed easy and friendly enough, the old women sitting smoking in the shadows before the bashas, the children staring and grinning openly.

We left from the north end of the village, circled it at a distance and made south-east, so far as I could judge. The second village was about a mile farther on, and was fast asleep. We came in quietly, among the silent bashas, freezing when somebody sneezed. A light appeared in one of the bashas, and presently a very old man shuffled out, demanding our business. He was fairly truculent, unlike most Burmese villagers, especially when there are warring armies in their neighbourhood. No, he'd seen no Japs for days, but they were coming soon, everyone in the village was very frightened and would we please go away. I guessed Gale was wondering what to do next, when the sound of firing was heard, off to the south. At this female hysterics broke out in the bashas, the old man shouted and ran for cover, and we left. The firing died away, but it was far outside our little theatre of operations, and we made for home.

"Somebody's 'avin' a duffy" was Parker's only comment. I supposed it was one of our patrols clashing with a party of Japs, but I never found out. We hit the road south of our little base, and came in through the wire without trouble, one member of the patrol at least effervescent with relief and not a little pleased with himself. Very well, nothing had happened, but at least I'd been out there and back again, like the Wolf of Kabul and Hawkeye, and hadn't come to grief or made an ass of myself. Gale thanked us and told us to get our heads down, while he went off to report. Men from other returned patrols were dispersing, and I talked to a couple of them, concealing my elation and acting nonchalant.

"W'ee wuz doin' the shuttin',* then?"

"Don't know. We heard it, about a mile off."

"Aye? There's summat up, doon theer. Feller in H.Q. Company was sayin' Jap's mekkin' a big push – aye-aye, Nick, hoo'sta gan on?"

"Nut sae bad. Any news?"

"Ye w'at? Ah'll tell thee the fookin' news – we're oot 'ere, git oorsel's coot off! W'at a bloody balls-up, eh? Couldn't roon a bloody raffle! Isn't that reet, lad?"

I made a non-committal noise, like John Wayne at Fort Apache.

"Aye! Ah, weel, Ah's gan git mesel' some Egyptian p.t., afore Jap distoorbs me beauty sleep. Neet, lads . . . 'ey, 'aud on a minnit, son! Ah knaw yoo . . . is thoo f'ae Carel?"

I admitted I was from Carlisle.

"Ah thowt sae! Girraway! You're Doctor Willie's daft son, up Currock!"

I couldn't deny it, and he grinned and shook hands.

"Your dad wuz oor doctor, afore we mooved oot t'Ivegill. Weel, noo, w'at aboot that? An' yer in Nine Section – alang wid that owd booger? Bad loock, son . . . 'e belangs in the Charpoy Chindits, 'e does! Don't ye, Nick? Well-away . . . Doctor Willie's lad!"

I knew his family's name, but not him personally; we talked for a few minutes more, joked about having a pint back home some day, and parted. All of a sudden I was ready to sleep on my feet; there was a fifty per cent stand-to, and half the section were in their pits, but Parker was already in his blanket, and I flopped down beside him, excited and drowsy all at once. It had been a big night for a young soldier, but here I was, back. It crossed my mind that I hadn't said my prayers for longer than I cared to remember, and I was in that thankful state when it seemed like a

* shooting

good idea. Long ago, when I was little, my father had used to kneel beside my bed, holding my hand and saying them with me; I could still feel the prickle of his moustache on my forehead when he kissed me good-night, and then the landing light would go off, the door far off downstairs would close, and I would stare up at the odd pattern on the ceiling where the distant street light shone in above the curtains. It would be shining* just the same now . . . and I'd been on night patrol in Burma, and an idea had come to me out there for the short story I'd started . . . suppose the Highlander came to a village at nightfall and there were a party of armed Camerons hunting the beautiful girl who'd been stalking him . . .

I came awake to the crash of explosions and the hard ground vibrating under me. All round men were starting up, there were yells of command in the darkness, the stutter of a Bren, the thump of grenades, flashes in the black, random shouts. I rolled into my pit, blanket and all, scrambling for rifle and pouches. Parker tumbled in beside me, and we ducked instinctively as tracer streaked across our front beyond the wire. There were exclamations and blasphemous inquiries from the pits on either side, and then the word was passing along: "Jap's inside the wire!"

"Ah, sod it!" said Parker, fumbling in the dark, and light flashed on his kukri as he laid it on the lip of the pit. "Wot the 'ell! Those are mortars – our three-inch mortars!"

They were thumping away at the southern end of the village, away from us. That was where most of the firing was; beyond our wire there seemed to be nothing doing, but men were hurrying past close behind us, someone was yelling: "Reiver platoon!", and I thought I heard Long John's voice, and then Hutton's bawling: "Eight section, close on me! Coom on!" The firing was sporadic, a few shots, a burst of automatic, then a scream that froze the blood, and from the left end of our position a shocking worrying sound, as though a dog were tearing at something.

"Jesus wept! Come on, Jocky!" Parker was out of the pit, and I was following when a burst of fire came from beyond the wire, right to our front. Parker dropped, and I stopped dead, staring at

---

* But only in my imagination, not in blacked-out Britain.

the darkness outside the wire – there were figures there, running, and they couldn't be any of ours. Parker was on one knee, firing towards them; I emptied my magazine, rapid fire, working the bolt for dear life until it clicked on an empty chamber. I heaved out of the pit, scrabbling for my bandolier; Parker had vanished, but another figure, rifle in hand, was on the top of the embankment before my pit, not a yard away, and even as my hand, rummaging in the dark for that damned bandolier, fell on the hilt of the dirk in my small pack, I froze in genuine horror.

It happened in split seconds, as such things do, but in retrospect it seems to have lasted forever. The figure was plainly silhouetted against the half-dark night sky, it was short and crouched and furtive, but what shocked me into momentary numbness was that it seemed to be wearing knickerbockers, loose above the knee, tight beneath. All in an instant I remembered how Nick had identified the Gurkhas a few nights earlier, realised that this was a Jap inside the wire, that my rifle was empty, that my hand was on my knife-hilt . . . the figure took a quick step, his foot slipped over the edge of my pit, as he stumbled I grabbed him with my left hand and heaved him bodily across the pit, my right hand whipped the knife out, down and up in a frantic lunge, and the fallen figure exclaimed: "Fookin' 'ell!"

God bless the electric impulses of the brain. I couldn't stop the thrust, but I did open my fingers, the knife dropped, and my open hand hit him one hell of a clout in the kidneys. He yelped, echoing me, I should think, and then he fell into the pit, swearing, and I dragged him upright with my left hand still clutching his shirt.

"Nick! What the hell are you on!"

I probably sounded hysterical for he said:

"Bloody 'ell, Jock! Ye've bloody ruined me!"

"You dumb sod!" I remember shouting, and then the section Bren interrupted me, and I let him go and found my bandolier, my hands shaking as I jammed in fresh clips. The air was thick with cordite smell, the shooting farther along the wire redoubled, the mortars were thumping away, and down at the south end a star-shell burst high up – at least, I think it must have done, for suddenly it was light for a moment, and Corporal Little was running past the pit shouting: "Come on, Nine Section!"

I scrambled out, Nick swearing in my wake, and ran after Little, who was heading down into the village. That was the moment when I caught a fleeting glimpse of Long John; he was issuing an order to someone, I think, but you couldn't hear above the firing; he had a rifle in one hand, the bayonet bent almost at right angles – I learned later that he'd bayonetted a Jap, and couldn't get it out until his batman reminded him that the way to free a bayonet is to fire a shot into the body. The theory is that it lets in air, or releases pressure on the blade, or something; how it worked with *that* bayonet, God knows, but it did. Hutton was striding towards us out of the dark.

"W'eer the 'ell ye gan, Tich?"

"W'eer d'ye want us?" shouted Little.

Hutton swore, jerked his head round towards the firing, and made up his mind.

"Nivver mind that! They're in doon yonder! Git in yer pits an' watch the wire! They're all ower the bloody place!"

Stanley was beside him, trying to attract his attention – he had been on o.p. beyond the wire. Hutton spoke to him, and as we ran back to our pits Stanley followed us, throwing himself down beside my pit. Rifle fire seemed to be rattling everywhere, the flashes of the mortar explosions were visible over the bashas, and from the road within the village came the sharp crash of grenades.

"Where's Wells?" shouted Stanley, grabbing my shoulder.

I didn't know who Wells was, even. Stanley cursed, stood up, looked about him, let out a stream of oaths – which wasn't like him at all – and suddenly ran off, down into the village. Someone shouted after him, but he was lost in the darkness, and here was Hutton again, running in a crouch.

"Fook me! Gidoon!" He was kneeling by my pit. "W'ees got grenades? Coom on, man – gi' them 'ere!"

I was half into my webbing by now, so I tore open a pouch, Hutton grabbed my grenades, and then he was off towards the road. He disappeared behind a basha, and a moment later we heard one of the grenades going off on the road. Little came crouched out of the dark, dropping beside my pit.

"W'ee's that? Jock? W'ee's wid thee?"

"Nobody! I don't know where Parker is."

"Back theer! 'Ev ye seen Stanley?"

"He went off, that way!"

He swore. "All 'ere, bar him, anyway. Watch yer froont!"

There was nothing outside the wire now but empty dark; behind us, in the village and down towards the south entrance, it sounded like Dunkirk, and then gradually the firing died away. There were a few more mortar explosions, but the voices that sounded in the dark were less urgent now, and I had time to get my breath back, wondering what the hell had happened.

The attack had been one of those mad accidents. A column of Japanese had come up the road from the south in trucks, driven right up to the wire, climbed out, and then realised that we were in the village. They'd attacked the wire, with our mortars hammering their trucks and their drivers trying to reverse or turn round and ruining their gears while the bombs rained down on them; it must have been chaos out yonder, but about a dozen Japs had got inside the wire, and a hand-to-hand battle had broken out. Most of them had been killed on the road within the village, by grenades. As many more were killed by patrols which went out at dawn to look for stragglers, and others had died outside the wire during the night's fighting; whether Parker and I had done any damage with our expenditure of about five shillings' worth of ammunition we never knew. The word passed that more than fifty Japs had bought it, for the loss of three of us, including one of the men I'd talked to just before turning in.

My knife was still lying at the bottom of my pit when dawn broke, and I was considering its eight-inch blade and feeling slightly sick at the thought of what I'd nearly done with it, when Nick loafed over, mess-tins in hand, rubbing his back-ribs.

"By, yer a stark booger, you! Sic a bloody belt – man, ye joost aboot kilt us!"

How little you know, I thought – and decided then and there not to tell him how close he'd come to dying not Tojo's way, or his own way, but my way – or that only his penchant for four-letter exclamations had saved him at the last instant. After all, you don't want your comrades-in-arms thinking that they can't even go to the latrine at night without the risk of being knifed by the maniac in the next pit. But one thing I must tell him, for his own safety in the future – for he still had on the p.t. shoes he'd worn on patrol, and his trousers were still tucked inside the socks, grey, long, soldiers for the use of, giving him that fashionable stream-lined look almost up to the knee.

I waited till we had been to the cookhouse, and had returned with our bread, tea, and burgoo, keeping a wary eye open for the kites which could swoop down like Spitfires and whip half your breakfast with surgical skill. When we were settled and munching contentedly, talking of other things, I asked casually:

"Why d'you wear your socks like that, Nick?"

"W'at for not? Me legs was cold."

"You want to watch it, marra. One of these nights somebody's liable to take you for a Jap – remember what you told me in the o.p.?"

He surveyed his legs. "Girraway, man! Do Ah look like a fookin' Jap, me?"

"From the knees down – yes."

No penny dropped. "Aw, git 'ired, man! Ye knaw, Jock, for an eddicated feller you doan't 'alf talk soom crap!"

Well, there was no denying that, so I said no more about it; no one ever did take him for a Jap by night after that, and my near-murder has remained a secret until now.

I was not the only one in the section guilty of *suppressio veri* over the night's work, but Stanley had a much more creditable reason for his reticence.

He had been in the o.p. with Wells, and when Jap arrived they had cut out for the wire. Stanley had made it into the perimeter, only to find that there was no sign of Wells. So he had slipped out again, without a word to anyone, when the fighting was at its height, into the Jap-infested dark, to look for him. By sheer luck he found him, near the o.p., dying of bayonet wounds; there was no way of helping him, but Stanley had stayed with him; he could have sought cover for himself, but he didn't. I suppose he brought the dead man in at dawn, but my informant – who was not Stanley himself – wasn't sure of all the details: he had only learned the bare facts months later.

I lost touch with Stanley after the war. We served together for most of the rest of the campaign, and he is one of the few men of whom I can say that we literally fought side by side (that came later), but I never knew him well; the picture of the tall, quiet, fair youth is not as sharp in my mind as that of Grandarse or Nick or most of the others. But whenever I heard the word "hero" loosely used, as it so often is of professional athletes and media celebrities and people who may have done no more than wear uniform for a while, I think of Stanley going back into the dark.

A FEW MILES SOUTH of Meiktila there was, and probably still is, a wood containing a little temple. The trees were very tall and close together on its outskirts, forming a thick protective screen, but within the wood they were more widely spaced, with dim clearings under the high spreading branches. How wide the wood was I never discovered, but it can't have been more than fifty or sixty yards in depth, and beyond there was open ground stretching to another belt of trees. It must have been quite a pretty place, with those shaded clearings and the tall trunks reaching up to the high foliage through which the light filtered. I sometimes wonder what it looks like now.

That wood and a nearby village were among the places used by the Japanese as concentration points for their counter-attack on Meiktila, and I believe our intelligence pin-pointed it as a result of a chance discovery made following the night action I've just described. Among the Japanese killed by our dawn patrols outside the wire was an officer – I heard he had taken cover in a culvert – and on his body were found plans listing the Jap concentration points: one of them was the temple wood, and our div command marked it for urgent attention.

Nine Section, of course, was not aware of this. Following the night action the whole battalion withdrew to Meiktila, after an excursion which had lasted several days, accounted for more than a hundred Japanese, and more importantly had helped to embarrass his build-up. Similar actions had been fought all round Meiktila at this time – the official history likens Cowan to a boxer using straight lefts to prevent his opponent getting close in, and it's a good simile: Jap was never given time to settle for a major assault.

Nine Section's impression – and it is still mine – is that Jap had taken far worse than he gave, and I am surprised by the official history's statement that our battalion took 141 casualties in two days during our foray from Meiktila. The regimental histories don't confirm the figure, and I wonder if the official version isn't referring to a longer period. But not for me to argue; I can only say that if the battalion did take that kind of punishment, we weren't aware of it.

We came back to Meiktila and spent the next week or so in our pits, watching the wire, brewing up, and waiting, and in that time other units of 17th Div threw two of Cowan's straight lefts at the little temple wood and its adjacent village. According to the official history the first attack ended in failure, with three tanks brewed up, and Jap following our withdrawal uncomfortably closely; the second attempt was also repulsed, and two more tanks were lost. Then it was our turn.

We rode out on the Shermans of Probyn's Horse on a fine sunny morning, knowing that something was in the wind, for three men had been added to the section. One was a lance-corporal (for some reason we had been short of a section second-in-command until now), another a rotund South Cumbrian, a sort of miniature Grandarse, called Wattie, and the third was reputed to be a recaptured deserter, and looked it. So Corporal Little had been told, anyway; he and I were riding on the front of the tank, either side of the gun with our backs to the turret, flanked by Forster and the Duke, and with Grandarse, who needed room, reclining on the sloping front at our feet and delivering judgement:

"Ah doan't see the point o' desertion, mesel'. Not oot 'ere, anyways. Ah mean, in Blighty a feller can stay on the roon, livin' in the railway Naafis an' Toc H canteens, but w'eer the 'ell ye gan to ga in India – unless yer Jock theer, an' look like a bloody wog –"

"Much obliged."

"No offence, lad, but ye doan't 'alf ga broon. Admit it, noo. Put a *dhoti* on ye, an' ye could git a job dishin' oot egg banjoes at Wazir Ali's.* Any roads, w'at Ah'm sayin' is that if ye desert oot 'ere – Ah mean, in India; ye'd 'ev to be doolally† to booger off in

---

* The military canteens run by the contractor Wazir Ali were famous throughout India; probably the best-remembered was at Deolali. An egg banjo is a fried egg between two slices of bread.

† mad

Boorma – the ridcaps is bound to cotch thee, an' court-martial gi'es thee the choice o' five years in Trimulghari or Paint Joongle, or coomin' oop t'road to get tha bollicks shot off. It's a moog's game."

"You don't have to be a deserter to be sent up the road and have your bollocks shot off," said the Duke. "Or hadn't you noticed?"

"Mind you," continued Grandarse, "there's this to be said for bein' a deserter – they say that if ye ask t'ga oop the road, an' ye gits kilt or wounded, the Army reckons ye've made amends, like, an' scroobs yer record. Ah doan't think that's bloody fair – they gid me sivven days in close tack for ga'in' absent in Blighty once, an' if Ah git kilt, it'll still be on me crime-sheet."

"That's 'cos ye didn't try 'ard enoof," said Little. "Ye've got to commit a big crime to git a big remission."

"Why did you go absent, Grandarse?" I asked.

"Aw, there was this tart in Silloth. An' Ah was yoong an' daft." He sighed. "She wasn't woorth it. Ah was grossly deceived. Aye, things 'as coom tae siccan a pass, thoo can't tell mistress f'ae servant lass. She wore troosers, an' a'. Bloody foony. Ah fancied 'er in troosers."

"Yer a bloody pervert, you are," said Forster.

"Oh, aye, lissen to Dr Freud!"

"Oo's Doctor Freud?"

"A fookin' professor."

"I don't suppose that's what they called him in Vienna," said the Duke, "but it's a not inaccurate description."

"Anyways," said Grandarse with finality, "if Ah was ivver daft enoof to desert, an' got done for it, Ah'd sooner tek the chance of a bullet in me bum than spend five year fillin' an' emptyin' wells in't glass'oose! So theer!"

Someone said unkindly that anybody shooting Grandarse could hardly fail to hit him in the bum, and Grandarse retorted that at least he wadn't git 'is brains blew oot if they did, not like soom clivver boogers; they were having to shout to make themselves heard above the rattle of the tracks as the Shermans rumbled over the sunlit paddy, and the swirling dust was becoming a nuisance, so I withdrew from the conversation to read for the third or fourth time the letter that had arrived from home last night.

My parents knew I was in Burma, and that (with the possible exception of air crew) it was generally believed to be the worst ticket you could draw in the lottery of active service. Those months must have been the longest of their lives; whatever anxieties the soldier may experience in the field can be nothing to the torment of those at home. I don't know how parents and wives stand it. Perhaps family experience is a help: every generation of my people, as far back as we knew, had sent somebody to war, and my grandmother's comment on Chamberlain's speech on September 3, 1939, had been simply: "Well, the men will be going away again." Her uncle had served in the Crimea, her brother had died in the Second Afghan, two of my aunts had lost sweethearts in the Great War, my father had been wounded in East Africa, and two uncles had been in the trenches; probably it was a not untypical record for a British family over a century, but whether it made my absence easier or harder to bear, who knows?

One thing was certain: they were not going to distress me by letting a hint of worry show in their letters, which were full of news and trivia and comedy. (I hope mine were, too; I was guiltily aware of being a poor correspondent who wrote briefly and usually when I wanted something; my last had contained a request for cigarettes.) My father wrote that they were on their way, and described how my aunts, those genteel maiden ladies, had exclaimed in dismay on learning that I had started *smoking,* at which my grandmother, a lively nonagenarian, had demanded to know if they would deny the solace of tobacco to a man who was standing at Armageddon; she had added mischievously that there were worse temptations than cigarettes for a young soldier in the Orient, and she didn't mean drink, either. This had opened up such visions of their nephew's possible depravity that they couldn't sleep, and in the waking small hours my elder aunt had been sure she'd heard the rattles which meant that the German bombers were dropping poison gas; she had ventured out, in dressing-gown, slippers, and gas-mask, with her handkerchief steeped in eau-de-cologne, and the A.R.P. wardens had found her shining her torch on the local pillar-box to see if it had changed colour.* And so on

* The tops of pillar-boxes were treated with a special paint which reacted in the presence of poison gas.

... my grandmother had taken to referring to two of the Nazi leaders as "Ribbonstrip" and "Gorbals"; my father had been to see *A Night at the Opera* and wished that *he* could swing on trapezes like the Marx Brothers; there had been unpleasant scenes, with allegations of fixing and corruption, at the church jumble sale, because the minister's daughter had won the prize doll by correctly guessing its name ("Wellwoodina"!); my father and mother, respectively Liberal and Conservative, were thinking of voting Labour at the forthcoming election because the candidate was one of my father's patients and an old friend – it was a picture of that happy, funny, eccentric family of mine and their little world, so far and yet so near.

Corporal Little asked me what I was grinning about, and Forster opined that it was a loov-letter frae soom bint, an' yer wastin' yer time, Jock, she'll be gittin' shagged by soom Yank pilot, and Grandarse said, leave the lad alone, he'll larn for hissel'. Oh, yes, you got the cream of intellectual discourse in Nine Section.

The tanks rumbled to a halt not far from a low bund, and about fifty yards beyond it lay the temple wood, dense and silent in the sunlight. We debussed, and Long John and Gale and Sergeant Hutton passed among us, checking that all was as it should be. There were three companies of the battalion spread across the paddy facing the wood, with the Shermans at intervals, but we were aware only of the sections immediately on either side. And there we waited, the section in a rough line, settling our equipment, taking a last swig from the chaggles, charging our magazines, and finally, at a word from Little, fixing bayonets.

So it was going to be a pukka attack – until that moment I, for one, had not been sure what the object of the operation was; the strength of our force, the presence of the tanks, had suggested something big, and now it was confirmed. The screen of trees beyond the little bund looked peaceful enough, but Jap would be there, well dug in; he would be watching us at this moment.

There are few sounds as menacing as a bayonet being fixed. Mine was the old sword type with the locking ring clicking into place with the smoothness of good Edwardian machinery; Grandarse, on my immediate right, was nipping his fingers with one of the new pig-stickers, and cursing, his face crimson in the heat; on my left Parker was drawing his kukri and re-sheathing it, and automatically I reached back to make sure mine was loose in its sheath, and that my knife-hilt was handy in my small pack. Suddenly it seemed very hot indeed, with hardly a breath of wind; just behind us the Sherman's engine coughed and roared; a bearded and turbanned head peered out of the turret and shouted in Hindustani to someone inside and the roaring died to a murmur.

Little came towards me, two grenades in his hands. "Gi'es yer Bren magazines, Jock, an' tek these; they're Stan's." Stanley was number two to Steele, the Bren gunner, and Little was seeing to it that he had plenty of spares.

"Are we going in, corp?"

"Aye, in a bit. When the Yanks 'ev doon their stoof."

He nodded past me, and as I tested the grenade pins and put them in my pouch I turned to look; I had been aware of a far-off murmur, growing louder; from behind us three distant dots in the sky were coming closer – Tomahawk fighters in camouflage paint which covered the famous shark's jaws with which the Flying Tigers decorated their engine cowlings. They came roaring in at tree-top level over us and zoomed up in a climb as they passed above the wood, banking as they soared up into the blue.

"Advance to the bund!" shouted Hutton. "Take cover – an' keep yer 'eids doon!"

We moved forward and lay against the low bank, and from overhead came the thundering whine as the first Tomahawk hurtled down in a steep dive; while it was still behind us two small dark objects detached from it, falling at a steep angle to land on the edge of the wood with a crashing double explosion and sheets of orange flame. Smoke and dust billowed up, obscuring the trees, and then the second Tomahawk came, repeating the performance, with the third on its heels. The ground shook as they pounded the wood, which was now entirely hidden by a great cloud; in came the Tomahawks again, unloading their bombs, and this time three of them failed to explode. The aircraft banked away in a great arc, and soon the whine of their engines died away; that was the air strike over, and now it was the Shermans' turn.

As the engines roared, Grandarse, lying on the bank two yards away, looked along at me.

"Loocky boogers, them Yank pilots. They'll be sittin' in the Casanova in Cal the neet, suppin' cocktails. Warra life, eh?"

Parker must have heard him, for he laughed on my other side and turned on his back, looking up at the sky, and hummed:

> I'd like to be a wop a.g.
> I'd fly all over Germanee
> And blow the Huns to buggeree
> It's foolish but it's fun!

"Aw reet, pipe doon!" said Hutton, but he was grinning; it must have been a new one to him. But now the Sherman was clanking forward, through a gap in the bund; the great mass of dust-coloured steel rolled on a few yards, and stopped. Its hatch was closed, but the big gun was traversing from side to side, and lowering to the point-blank position. Suddenly it crashed, the tank shook, and the shell burst with an almighty roar in the depths of the wood. Up and down the line the other tanks began blazing away, and then the machine-guns started chattering, and the whole screen of trees was shaking as though in a gale; through the slowly-dispersing haze left by the Tomahawks' bombs we could see the foliage being ripped to shreds. All along the bank men were craning as they watched; I stole a glance behind and saw Hutton was on his feet; farther along Long John was checking his watch; Gale, rifle in hand, his bush-hat at a rakish angle, was talking to his runner. Abruptly the firing stopped.

"On yer feet!" roared Hutton, and as we stood up: "Wait for it!"

This was it, then, the moment you read about in books and see in films – and by God it was happening to me. Ahead the wood still seemed to be sending back the echo of the cannonade, but now the foliage was steady again, and the dust had settled. There was a long moment's stillness, broken only by the growl of the Sherman, holding its ground twenty yards ahead, not more than thirty from the edge of the wood. A branch, hanging by a thread after the bullet-hail, suddenly fell, sending up a little swirl of dust. I glanced right: Grandarse had one foot on the bank, leaning forward; beyond him were two of the new men, the lance-jack and the reputed deserter. Parker, on my left, had his rifle at the port, and beyond him Steele was adjusting his Bren sling, the big l.m.g. resting on his hip; Stanley was removing his hat and replacing it firmly. I found I was hissing through my teeth, and recognised it as "Bonnie Dundee", but I hadn't time to digest this peculiar reaction when Little was walking forward between Parker and Steele, crossing the bank, and Hutton was shouting again:

"Ad-vance! Keep yer distance, noo! Advance!"

Up the bank and over, the shuffle of boots in the morning quiet, the slight creak and rustle of equipment, the dark green figures on either side moving in a slow, steady advance; the stationary tank, its tracks clogged with earth and coarse grass, ten yards to my right front, the slight figure of Little, rifle at the trail, his head obscured by the tilted bush-hat, to my left and out in front – and there was a faint crack, like a cap-pistol, from the wood, and Little gave a sharp cough, spun half-round, and went down like an empty sack.

Hitting the deck, face down on the scrubby earth, automatically whipping rifle to shoulder in the lying position, puffs of dust leaping from the ground to my left, Parker rolling over, yelling, the left breast of his bush-shirt blood-stained; a scream from the right, a blinding cloud of dust and gravel striking me in the face, the rattle of machine-gun fire from the wood and the irregular cracks of rifle-fire. Someone was bawling "Covering fire!", and I was shooting obediently into the wood at ground level, aware that on my right Grandarse was doing the same, and that Parker was crawling rapidly back to the bank – one glance I took, and he was dripping blood as he scrambled to the bank and over. Caught in the bloody open, flat-footed – Jesus! beyond Grandarse the lance-jack was trying to pull himself clear, with his leg trailing, and the deserter was absolutely sitting up! (I still don't know why.) I pumped off another couple of shots, realised the futility of it, looked left, and Steele had the Bren at his shoulder, left hand on the stock, right hand reaching forward for the magazine. There was a sharp clang, a silver streak appeared on the side of the magazine, and Steele reared back, his face contorted, scrambling up on to his knees. Blood was streaming down his arm – the bullet had gone through hand and shoulder. He yelled something and –

77

this I shall never forget – actually shook his uninjured fist at the wood before turning to run for the shelter of the bund.

And there was the Bren gun, the section's most precious possession, lying unattended.

I've asked myself a thousand times: did I hesitate? God only knows, and perhaps some day He'll tell me, for I genuinely am not sure. Probably I wanted to, and this is what has made me wonder; that, and the knowledge that with four men hit all around me in as many seconds, and the shots kicking up the dirt in what seemed to be your proverbial hail of lead, that Bren was about as untempting an article as I've ever seen. And then I was starting to crawl towards it, and Hutton, flat on the ground behind me, was yelling and signalling to Stanley, the Bren's number two, and Stanley, who had been face down just beyond it all the time, was grabbing its handle and hauling it away.

"Jock!" It was Hutton. "Coover 'im!"

For what it was worth I started to fire into the wood, and Stanley and Bren rolled over the bank and out of sight. Behind me Hutton spoke, more quietly now.

"Awreet, haud tha fire! Heid doon!"

I put my head flat on the butt, reaching behind me for another clip from my bandolier, moving cautiously in the belief that any obvious movement was liable to attract those goddamned Jap snipers. To my right Grandarse was lying as close to Mother Earth as his great belly would let him; he looked towards me and blew out his cheeks. There was no one on my left, just two patches of blood where Steele and Parker had been hit. Christ, I thought, are Grandarse and I the only ones left? Intermittent cracks were sounding in the wood, but they didn't seem to be coming this way; the Sherman's l.m.g. was rattling away, and in behind it an Indian soldier (don't ask me where he had come from) was leaning against the metal, clutching his thigh; his trouser leg was sodden with blood.

"Grandarse!" Hutton again. "When Ah say *jao*,* git oot of it! Jock – five roonds rapid, fire!"

I blasted away, and through the din heard Hutton's "*Jao!*"

* go!

and the sound of a great body taking flight. "Reet, Jock – *jao!*" Grandarse was still short of the bank when I went over it like a bird.

The first thing I saw was Steele, a yard away. He was white as paint, his eyes shut, but his jaw was working up and down. An orderly had torn away his shirt, and his shoulder and chest were a mass of blood; the orderly was padding the shoulder wound while another wrapped a gauze dressing round his hand. Beyond him Parker was propped up against the bank, stripped to the waist, holding a field dressing to his shoulder; Gale was bending over him, then turning away to shout. A jeep came bouncing up to the bank, and Gale helped Parker to climb in; the orderlies were lifting Steele on to a stretcher, preparing to load him in also. I didn't see them, but the lance-corporal and the alleged deserter had both been hit. Farther along the bank rifles and Brens were firing, the Sherman guns were crashing again. I realised that I was sitting idle, breathing hard, and that one knee was painful where I had grazed it in hitting the deck. I would guess that perhaps three minutes had passed since we started to advance. I jerked open my bolt, ejecting a spent case, and saw that my magazine was empty. While I was charging it, a tall lance-corporal whose face, in my memory, is that of the late Lyndon Johnson, came running in a crouch to confer with Hutton. They peered over the bank, and Hutton signalled to me.

"When Kang ga's ower the top, you give 'im cooverin' fire as 'ard as ye can! Stanley, you give automatic fire! Reet, Jack – on ye go, son!"

Kang took a run at the bank and went over, dodging from side to side as he ran towards the still, green figure of Corporal Little, face-down on the earth. Kang dived down beside him, and even as I was firing I could see that he was speaking; I reloaded, and began firing again as he came ziz-zagging back towards us. Halfway he stumbled, Hutton swore, and then Kang came tumbling over the bank in a shower of dust, gasping and clutching his forearm; blood was running between his fingers. He shook his head.

"*Bus,*" was all he said, and Hutton groaned deep in his throat. Two more jeeps were pulling up, scattering the earth, and the wounded were being helped into them. The one carrying Parker and Steele was reversing with a rasp of tyres, and Parker, his dressing in place, actually grinned and waved with his sound arm. All along the bank men were lying, waiting; I think I remember Long John on one knee, talking to Gale, and pointing off to the left. The firing along our front had died away to an occasional shot or Bren burst; the tank firing had stopped, and the wood itself was silent. They had stopped us almost before we had started, and now they would be reloading in their pits and bunkers, waiting for us to try again.

I remembered the wounded Indian, and took a cautious look over the bank. He was standing up now, talking to the bearded Indian, who was presumably the tank commander, and was looking out of his hatch – something which, in his position, I'd not have done for a pension. I had the impression, from their gestures, that the wounded man wanted to get into the tank, and was being denied. Grandarse rolled up beside me.

"Tich 'as 'ed it! Fook me!" His face was purple, running sweat. "That shows ye w'at air strikes an' tanks is woorth! Fookin' 'ell!"

"Will we go in again?"

"We'll fookin' 'ev to! Not by the front fookin' door, tho'! 'Ey, w'at the 'ell's ga'n on? That booger's 'ed it, an' a'!"

He was peering over the bank at the Sherman. The hatch was down again, and the wounded sepoy was dragging himself in behind the tank, feebly, a foot at a time. He rolled over on his back, his whole trouser leg was black with blood to the thigh, and then he was dead – you could tell from the way the body seemed to subside, as though something had been let out of it.

"Awoy!" said Grandarse, and scrambled to his feet. Hutton was waving to us, and we doubled towards him, crouching to keep under cover of the bank. The rest of the section, what was left of it, was there: Stanley with the Bren, Nixon, Wedge, the Duke, and other men whom I didn't know – this presumably was Nine Section reconstituted; in less than a minute we'd lost over a third of our original number.

Then Gale was leading the way to the left, along the bank which must have curved in towards the wood, for presently we were on the edge of the trees, taking up firing positions. I have to say that

I am not sure how we got there; it is another of those hiatuses in memory when nothing much happened to compare with the minute of frenzied violence which had followed our advance over the bank, or with what was to follow when we got into the wood. That day's battle, for me, was in two distinct parts, both of them vivid in my mind, but the connecting period is hazy. No doubt my mind was too full of what had happened to notice; I don't know how long a time elapsed in making that leftward movement, or how far we came from our original position on the bank, or what units of the company were on either side, or behind. Fighting was going on elsewhere – a young corporal was winning the M.M. clearing bunkers single-handed at about this time – and the interval may have been five minutes or thirty. Battle concentrates your attention on your own immediate front, and all I was aware of, now, was the fringe of trees in which we lay, and the shadowy interior beyond. The snipers who had cut down Parker and Steele and Little and the others must be in the wood ahead and to the right.

Stanley, lying next to me, touched me on the shoulder. Beyond him Gale was on his feet, motioning the section forward and stepping ahead into the wood; someone muttered something about bunkers. Stanley and I looked at each other; what he saw, God knows, but what I saw was his sweating face with the lips drawn back from the teeth. He adjusted the Bren sling; I waited until he was ready and we rose together and moved warily through the fringe of trees. There was undergrowth to our front, so I moved to the right with Stanley at my left elbow.

It was dim after the glare of the open country, but through the trees immediately to our right front I could make out a clearing. What I couldn't see was any sign of a bunker, but they must be in there somewhere, so I took a nervous glance to see that Stanley was still there, and moved on slowly through the trees, safety catch off, finger just touching the trigger. There was no one to my right, and the section was now out of eyeshot to my left; for a moment Stanley and I might have been alone in the wood, but I knew bloody well we weren't; the one comfort was that its other inhabitants hadn't seen us yet. I nerved myself to go on walking, as softly as could be, scanning the clump of bushes ahead, the tree trunks on either side, and the clearing beyond. There wasn't a sound, or a sign of a Jap, and if firing was taking place farther off, I wasn't aware of it. A few more steps brought me to the bushes, and I knelt down, listening.

The simple truth about war is that if you are on the attack, you can't do a damned thing until you find your enemy, and the only way to do that is to push on, at whatever speed seems prudent, until you see or hear him, or he makes his presence known by letting fly at you – as witness our first advance over the bank. Now it was the same thing over again, the difference being that the left flanking movement had brought us inside his position, and it was a question of who saw whom first and shot the straighter.

Life closes in; I had no idea of what was happening elsewhere, no thought or use of the senses to spare for anything but what I saw as I knelt behind the bushes – across the clearing, maybe ten yards away, was the bunker. It was a big one, three-man at least, a mound of hard red earth about four feet high, and probably the same depth underneath. There was a wide firing-slit at ground level, but what lay behind the slit was darkness. No movement, and nothing in the trees beyond the bunker.

I looked at Stanley, a yard behind me, his Bren at the ready, and then I was going like a bat out of hell for a palm on the other side of the clearing. There was a crack from the firing-slit, but it was threepence (or three yen) wasted, and as I fetched up at the tree, its trunk between me and the bunker, Stanley ran forward, firing from the hip at the firing-slit. Dust flew from the bunker as the Bren burst hit it – and then the bloody gun jammed, Stanley yelled and tugged at the magazine, I thought I saw movement inside the firing slit, and as Stanley jumped aside I found myself running forward, firing into the slit – three shots, I think, and I believe there was a return shot, and then I was diving down beside the bunker wall, about a yard to the side of the firing-slit, fumbling for a grenade.

I was facing back the way we'd come, and there were dark bush-hatted figures running through the trees, and the wood was suddenly alive with small-arms fire, rifle and automatic. I yanked out the grenade pin, let the plunger go, forced myself to count one-thousand-two-thousand and stretched sideways, back flat on the bunker, to whip the bomb through the firing-slit. One thousand-two-thousand-three – an ear-ringing crump, and I was snatching for a second grenade when Gale came running past, gesturing, and I followed him round the bunker side. There was the bunker entrance, a low narrow doorway, and Gale had a green 77 phosphorus grenade in his hand.

He threw aside the black safety cap as he reached the doorway, and was in the act of tossing the grenade inside when he suddenly stood straight up, his bush-hat fell off, and the side of his face was covered with blood. He fell full length, landing almost at my feet, and someone grabbed him and pulled him away. I was at one side of the doorway, and a small sharp-faced sergeant whom I didn't know was at the other, with a tommy-gun. Gale's phosphorus bomb hadn't exploded – they're dicey things with a tape which unwinds in flight and a ball and spring mechanism – but I had my second 36 grenade in one hand and my rifle in the other. The little sergeant also had a 36; he nodded, we pulled our pins together, he waited *three* seconds that seemed like hours, and we tossed them in, flattening against the bunker. On the heels of the double explosion he darted in, Thompson stuttering; two quick bursts and he was out again.

"Three on 'em!" he shouted, and his jaw dropped as he stared past me. I turned to see a Jap racing across in front of the bunker, a sword flourished above his head. He was going like Jesse Owens, screaming his head off, right across my front; I just had sense enough to take a split second, traversing my aim with him before I fired; he gave a convulsive leap, and I felt that jolt of delight – I'd hit the bastard! – and as he fell on all fours the Highland officer with whom I'd played football dived on him from behind, slashing at his head with a kukri. Someone rounded the bunker, almost barging into me; it was Stanley, shouting: "Where? Where?" – in that kind of mad scramble all that matters is seeing the enemy. He had a Bren magazine in one hand, and was trying to change it for the one on the gun; I grabbed the barrel to steady it, burned myself, yelped, and seized the folded legs while he pushed the full magazine home – one of his puttees was coming loose, a yard away Gale was lying dead with two men bending over him, the whole wood was echoing with shots and explosions and yelling voices. Stanley ran past me, dropping the empty magazine – and as some Presbyterian devil made me pick it up I noticed Gale's hat lying in the bunker doorway, and the little sergeant was shouting and running towards a second bunker.

The sixty seconds I have just described, being among the most eventful of my life, I have been able to relate almost step by step; after that it was more disconnected. There were half a dozen men at the second bunker, feeding in grenades and firing through the slit, a Jap was shot and bayonetted in the entrance, and then we were past it, making for the far verge of the wood. Shots came from an earthwork to our left, a man had his bush-hat shot from his head – usually when a hat is hit it stays in place, but this one spun off like a plate, landing several feet away – and a Jap appeared between the trees and I shot him and he fell against a trunk, and the little sergeant dropped his tommy-gun and swore and picked it up again – the sequence of these things I can't be certain of because it all happened so quickly – or seemed to. I've spoken at the start of this paragraph of "sixty seconds" because I can't believe it took any longer, and probably the rush from the first bunker to the second and on to the wood's edge took about the same – but if that little sergeant were to appear and tell me it took twenty minutes, I couldn't contradict him. We were in that wood four hours, according to the regimental history, killed 136 Japanese, and lost seven dead and 43 wounded ourselves in the whole operation, but I wasn't conscious of time, only of the highlights of action. The fight at the first bunker is crystal clear, but the rest is a series of unrelated incidents.

It was a hectic murderous confusion: the whole section was in the wood, but Stanley is the only one I remember – indeed, Gale is the only other I can positively identify from the entire platoon. The little sergeant was there most of the time – when we were lying on the edge of the wood, covering the open ground beyond, I heard him asking for a field dressing – but which platoon he belonged to I never knew. When we opened fire at Japs moving on the open ground, the men on either side of me were strangers; one of them kept seeing Japs in the trees beyond the open space, and blazed away, cursing, but I believe it was wishful thinking.

Then we were withdrawing. Behind us the company were leaving the wood by the way we'd come in, and when we on the far side were ordered to fall back we went quite slowly, with the little sergeant shouting hoarsely to take our time. He knew his business, that one, for as we retreated past the cleared bunkers to the front of the wood he kept up an incessant patter of orders and encouragement (I have an idea he was a Welshman) keeping us in a rough line, well spaced out, firing as we went, for Japs were filtering into the trees we had just left. He was next to me, firing short bursts; I had a shot at one running figure among the trees, and he went down, but I think it was a dive for cover.

There was a film called *Honky Tonk*, in which Clark Gable had to back out of a saloon, covering the occupants with his gun and remarking: "This reminds me of the days when we used to do all our walking backwards." The words came back to me in the temple wood, as such things will, and at some point the man on my left dropped to his knees shouting: "Look what I've got!" I didn't identify the object, but what he did get a second later was a bullet in the leg from an unseen Jap, and he rolled over shouting: "They got me! The dirty rats, they got me!" It wasn't a bad wound, a furrow just above the knee, and he hobbled out of the wood under his own steam, blaspheming painfully.

That was the battle in the temple wood, an insignificant moment in the war; its importance is personal. It was typical of the kind of action that was going on all around Meiktila, and if figures mean anything, we won it, although I am still puzzled about its conclusion. Japs were re-entering the wood as we left it, but they cannot have reoccupied it, for the battalion history's tally of Japanese killed is exact, not an estimate, and must have been made on the ground afterwards, with ourselves in possession. So I conclude that the withdrawal in which I took part was not the end of the action, as I thought at the time.

This is the trouble with eye-witness: it sees only part of the whole, and is incomplete. If mine is patchy, I can only excuse it on the ground that I had never been in a fight to the death before, with the enemy at close quarters, which is, to say the least, confusing. I have tried to describe in plain terms what I saw, and can be sure of; what I thought at the time is less clear, but some strong impressions remain.

At the moment of fixing bayonets I had that hollow feeling which most writers locate in the stomach but in my case manifests itself in the throat; after we were fired on I didn't notice it. To say I was shocked at seeing Parker and Steele hit is correct in the sense that one is shocked by running into a brick wall; astonishment and fascination came into it, too. You read of such things, now you see the reality, and think: "So *that*'s what it looks like!" The thought of being hit myself occurred only in the moment before I started crawling towards the Bren, to be submerged in relief when Stanley took possession. Going into the wood I was scared stiff but not witless; given Aladdin's lamp I would have been in Bermuda. No, that's not true; if it were, I'd have kept out of the Army in the first place. Being there, with the choice made, you go ahead – and if anyone says you could always change your mind, and run away, he's wrong; you can't. It sounds pompous to say it's a matter of honour, but that's what it comes down to, and Falstaff knew it. He was quite right, though, that honour hath no skill in surgery – which is why you are perfectly entitled to be scared.

There is the consolation that once the shooting starts, the higher thought takes a back seat. Putting a grenade into a bunker had the satisfaction of doing grievous bodily harm to an enemy for whom I felt real hatred, and still do. Seeing Gale killed shocked me as our first casualties had done, and I think enraged me. I wanted a Jap then, mostly for my own animal pride, no doubt, but seeing Gale go down sparked something which I felt in the instant when I hung on my aim at the Jap with the sword, because I wanted to be sure. The joy of hitting him was the strongest emotion I felt that day; I notice I've mentioned it twice.*

Perhaps I'm too self-analytical, but I'm trying to be honest. It's hard to say where fear and excitement meet, or which predominates. The best way I can sum up my emotions in that wood is to say that a continuous nervous excitement was shot through with occasional flashes of rage, terror, elation, relief, and amazement.

* Strictly speaking I should probably have held my fire, since the Jap was between me and comrades who were advancing into the wood, but I have since learned that I was not alone in letting fly at him and breaching what battle school instructors call "fire discipline". I can only plead the heat of the moment and say that it seemed a good idea at the time.

So far as I have seen, most men are like that, by and large, although there are exceptions. A few really enjoy it; I've seen them (and I won't say they're deranged, because even the most balanced man has moments of satisfaction in battle which are indistinguishable from enjoyment, short-lived though they may be). Some are blessed with the quick reflexes which, combined with experience, enable them to keep cool, like the little sergeant. Others seem to be on a "high", like the man who cried "Look what I've got!"

I was glad to come out of it, but even then I felt what I feel now, and what every old soldier feels: a gratitude for having been there, and an abiding admiration amounting to awe for the sheer ability of my comrades. Nowadays the highest praise a soldier can get is the word "professional". Fourteenth Army weren't professionals. They were experts.

The aftermath was as interesting as the battle. Fiction and the cinema have led us to expect certain reactions from men in war, and the conventions of both demand displays of emotion, or a restraint which is itself highly emotional. I don't know what Nine Section felt, but whatever it was didn't show. They expressed no grief, or anger, or obvious relief, or indeed any emotion at all; they betrayed no symptoms of shock or disturbance, nor were they nervous or short-tempered. If they were quieter than usual that evening, well, they were dog-tired. Discussion of the day's events was limited to a brief reference to Gale's death, and to the prospects of the wounded: Steele had been flown out on a "flying taxi", one of the tiny fragile monoplanes to which stretchers were strapped; it was thought his wound was serious.* Parker was said to be in dock in Meiktila (and a few weeks later there were to be ironic congratulations when he returned to the section with a romantic star-shaped scar high on his chest; penicillin was a new marvel then).

Not a word was said about Tich Little, but a most remarkable thing happened (and I saw it repeated later in the campaign) which I have never heard of elsewhere, in fact or fiction, although I suspect it is as old as war.

---

* It was. I visited him after the war, when he had had to give up his job as a builder because his right arm could not be fully lifted, and he could not mount scaffolding in safety.

QUARTERED SAFE OUT HERE

Tich's military effects and equipment – not, or course, his private possessions, or any of his clothing – were placed on a groundsheet, and it was understood that anyone in the section could take what he wished. Grandarse took one of his mess-tins; Forster, his housewife, making sure it contained only Army issue and nothing personal; Nixon, after long deliberation, took his rifle, an old Lee Enfield shod in very pale wood (which surprised me, for it seemed it might make its bearer uncomfortably conspicuous); I took his pialla, which was of superior enamel, unlike the usual chipped mugs. Each article was substituted on the groundsheet with our own possessions – my old pialla, Forster's housewife, and so on – and it was bundled up for delivery to the quartermaster. I think everyone from the original section took something.

It was done without formality, and at first I was rather shocked, supposing that it was a coldly practical, almost ghoulish proceeding – people exchanging an inferior article for a better one, nothing more, and indeed that was the pretext. Nick worked the bolt, squinted along the sights, hefted the rifle, and even looked in its butt-trap before nodding approval; Grandarse tossed his old mess-tin on to the groundsheet with a mutter about the booger's 'andle being loose. But of course it had another purpose: without a word said, everyone was taking a memento of Tich.

An outsider might have thought, mistakenly, that the section was unmoved by the deaths of Gale and Little. There was no outward show of sorrow, no reminiscences or eulogies, no Hollywood heart-searchings or phony philosophy. Forster asked "W'ee's on foorst stag?"; Grandarse said "Not me, any roads; Ah's aboot knackered", and rolled up in his blanket; Nick cleaned Tich's rifle; I washed and dried his pialla; the new section commander – that young corporal who earlier in the day had earned the Military Medal – told off the stag roster; we went to sleep. And that was that. It was not callousness or indifference or lack of feeling for two comrades who had been alive that morning and were now names for the war memorial; it was just that there was nothing to be said.

It was part of war; men died, more would die, that was past, and what mattered now was the business in hand; those who lived would get on with it. Whatever sorrow was felt, there was no point in talking or brooding about it, much less in making, for form's sake, a parade of it. Better and healthier to forget it, and look to tomorrow.

The celebrated British stiff upper lip, the resolve to conceal emotion which is not only embarrassing and useless, but harmful, is just plain common sense.

But that was half a century ago. Things are different now, when the media seem to feel they have a duty to dwell on emotion, the more harrowing the better, and to encourage its indulgence. The cameras close on stricken families at funerals, interviewers probe relentlessly to uncover grief, pain, fear, and shock, know no reticence or even decency in their eagerness to make the viewers' flesh creep, and wallow in the sentimental cliché (victims are always "innocent", relatives must be "loved ones"). And the obscene intrusion is justified as "caring" and "compassionate" when it is the exact opposite.

The pity is that the public shapes its behaviour to the media's demands. The bereaved feel obliged to weep and lament for the cameras (and feel a flattering importance at their attention). Even young soldiers, on the eye of action in the Gulf, confessed, under a nauseating inquisition designed to uncover their fears, to being frightened – of course they were frightened, just as we were, but no interviewer in our time was so shameless, cruel, or unpatriotic as to badger us into admitting our human weakness for public consumption, and thereby undermining public morale, and our own. In such a climate, it is not to be wondered at that a general should agonise publicly about the fears and soul-searchings of command – Slim and Montgomery and MacArthur had them, too, but they would rather have been shot than admit it. They knew the value of the stiff upper lip.

The damage that fashionable attitudes, reflected (and created) by television, have done to the public spirit, is incalculable. It has been weakened to the point where it is taken for granted that anyone who has suffered loss and hardship must be in need of "counselling"; that soldiers will suffer from "post-battle traumatic stress" and need psychiatric help. One wonders how Londoners survived the Blitz without the interference of unqualified, jargon-mumbling "counsellors", or how an overwhelming number of 1940s servicemen returned successfully to civilian life without benefit of brain-washing. Certainly, a small minority needed help; war can leave terrible mental scars – but the numbers will increase, and the scars enlarge, in proportion to society's insistence on raising spectres which would be better left alone. Tell people they should feel something, and they'll not only feel it, they'll regard themselves as entitled and obliged to feel it.

It is a long way from the temple wood to Sheffield – and not only in miles. I knew a young Liverpudlian who, following the Hillsborough disaster, stayed away from work because, he said, of the grief he felt for those supporters of his team who had died on the terraces. He didn't know them, he hadn't been there, but he was too distressed to work. (Suppose Grandarse or the Battle of Britain pilots, with infinitely greater cause, had been too distressed to fight?) One shouldn't be too hard on the young man; he had been conditioned to believe that it was right, even proper, to indulge his emotions; he probably felt virtuous for having done so.

Fortunately for the world, my generation didn't suffer from spiritual hypochondria – but then, we couldn't afford it. By modern standards, I'm sure we, like the whole population who endured the war, were ripe for counselling, but we were lucky; there were no counsellors. I can regret, though, that there were no modern television "journalists", transported back in time, to ask Grandarse: "How did you *feel* when you saw Corporal Little shot dead?" I would have liked to hear the reply.

APART FROM BEING a first-class soldier, the new corporal, Peel, was genial and sensible; the other additions were Wattie, who had been with us at the temple wood, and a big humorous Yorkshireman, Morton; all three fitted in smoothly, and there was general satisfaction. Stanley was confirmed, to his quiet disgust, as Bren gunner, with Wedge as his number two – a billet which I had sought because Stanley and I had become muckers as a result of the recent action, but which Sergeant Hutton had refused me. I found out why the day after we returned to Meiktila, when he told me to report to company office.

"What the hell have I done?" was a natural reaction, and he gave me one of his rare, sour grins.

"Weel, w'at 'ev ye done? Nowt? Then doan't fret tha bloody sel'. Git yer belt an' titfer, do thasel' oop, and doan't keep Long John waitin' – moove!"

Company office in the field consisted of a camp stool with Long John sitting on it. I strode up and saluted, he gave me a courteous good morning, looked me up and down, and dropped his bombshell: a promotion to lance-corporal, second-in-command of the section.

Well, we needed one, but my first reaction was that the sun had got him; the very thought of being given authority over veterans like Nixon and Grandarse and the Duke – of having to direct them in action, took the breath away. Not that lance-jack is any great eminence; it is an appointment, not a rank, and is the worst dogsbody's job in the Army, as Hitler and I could tell you. But if anything happened to Peel – or even if the section got split up in a duffy, as frequently happened, I would be the man in command, and I didn't fancy it. I said so.

"Why not?"

"Well, sir, I'm the youngest in the section, and haven't much experience –"

"How old are you?"

"Nineteen, sir. Twenty next month." It didn't occur to me that Long John himself, with a major's crown on his shoulder, was probably younger than most of Nine Section.

"If you'd passed wosbie* last year you'd probably be command-ing a platoon in France by now – without any experience." So he knew I'd failed to get into OCTU, and also, no doubt, that I'd been a lance-corporal thrice before, and busted each time. I said that I'd like another shot at a commission, eventually. Which was like bowling him a very slow lob.

"You can't go to wosbie again until this is over." His gesture indicated Burma in general. "When it is, I'll see that you're sent up, and if you've been leading a section it'll be in your favour."

After that there was nothing to do but thank him, accept with inner misgivings, draw two stripes from the stores, sew one on each sleeve, and submit to the unbridled hilarity of Nine Section. They lay about, heaving – at least Grandarse did, purple with mirth and inviting anatomical impossibilities on himself; the others were kinder, merely begging to be allowed to lick my boots, clean my equipment, and fetch my connor† from the cookhouse. Having been through this three times before, I wasn't unduly disturbed; it wasn't like being a lance-jack at home, where your principal fear was of being defied and made to look foolish; up the road, life is serious, and such worries don't even exist.

And more important things were happening. My promotion coincided (I learn from the official history) with the Japanese decision to abandon the siege of Meiktila – if only I'd known I could have invited Grandarse to draw the obvious conclusion – but the big news which ran through the rifle pits was that six Japs had come out of the Fort Dufferin defences at Mandalay with their hands up. For all I know, this may have been latrine gossip; I

---

* War Office Selection Board, which tested candidates for OCTU (Officer Cadet Training Unit)

† food

imagine that there must have been earlier cases of Japanese surrender, even if they were just individual ones. But Nine Section took the rumour as a portent, and discussion was heated.

"Ah doot it," was Nick's verdict. "When Ah see a fookin' Japanni wallah crawlin' oot o' 'is fookin hole wid a white flag, Ah'll believe it then, not until."

"Aye, mebbe," said Grandarse, wanting to believe it. "Mind you, Jap's bin gittin' the shit knocked oot on 'im a' ower – 'ere and at Mandalay. 'E moost 'ev aboot 'ed it, by this."

"Bollocks," said Nick. "Them boogers 'ev 'ed it when they're deid. Look at that lot that committed 'arry-karry in the 'ospital. Jap doesn't pack in, noo an' Ah'm tellin' ye!"

"You, ye fookin' pessimist!" cried Grandarse. "Spreadin' alarm an' despondency! Christ, if gripin' wad ha' woon the war, ye'd 'ev 'ed it ower efter Doonkirk! Ye mek me tired, Nixon!"

"Weel, Ah'm not coontin' on 'im packin' in," said Forster. "We'll 'ev to chess the boogers a' the way to Tokyo."

"Ye'll a' be killed afore then," said Nixon, winking behind Grandarse.

"Booger me, 'e's still at it! Naw, man, think on! Jap's bin chessed a' the way doon from Imphal, 'e's bin beat 'ere, 'e's bin beat at Mandalay – bloody 'ell, ye've seen more deid Japs on the road 'ere than ye've got 'airs on yer arse – "

"Not on your arse, tho'."

"Nivver mind my arse! W'at Ah'm sayin' is, 'e moost be marchin' on 'is chinstrap by noo! An' look 'ere, Nick – suppose thoo wez a Jap – "

"Ah, so! Me Jap, me sit in bunker, wait for Glandarse, stick bayonet up honnelable jacksy – "

"If thoo wez a Jap," insisted Grandarse, "an' saw this lot coomin' – Goorkas, an' Pathans, an' Sikhs, an' them bloody great black boogers frae th'East African Division – fookin' Zulus, or summat – aye, an' us, an' a' – wadn't *you* pack in? Ah'm bloody sure ye wad! Weel, Jap isn't bloody stupid!"

"Course 'e's bloody stupid!" said Forster. "'E commits suicide, doesn't 'e? That's as stupid as ye can git!"

"Aye, but there's a limit!" roared Grandarse. "That's what Ah'm sayin', see? 'E's boond tae pack in soomtime! An' this lot at

Mandalay's the start on't, mebbe. Eh?" He looked round in wrathful appeal. "Wadn't ye say?"

The Duke remarked that one swallow didn't make a summer.

"'Oo's talkin' aboot fookin' swallers? Coom on, Tommo, w'at d'you say?"

The corporal, thus addressed, doubted if Jap would crack soon, if at all. From what he had heard officially, while driven out of Mandalay and abandoning his siege of Meiktila, he was preparing a big defence at a place called Pyawbwe.

"W'eer th'ell's that?"

"Next town down the road."

"An' w'ee's gonna tek that?"

"We are."

"Aw, fer fook's sake!" Grandarse stared in disbelief. "Is the fookin' Black Cat th' only div sign they knaw? W'at aboot the Cross Keys, or the Dagger div, or them wid the bloody spiders an' crossed spears?* Bloody 'ell, Calcutta's full o' them! Ye can't git a drink in Jimmy's Kitchen for bloody Raff an' Chindits! Git the boogers down 'ere, to Pawbee, or whativver ye ca' it!"

"Where's Fifth Div?" asked Wedge, voicing his obsession.

"They'll leapfrog us sooner or later," the corporal was beginning.

"Aye, bloody later!" fumed Grandarse. "Flamin' Arseholes!"

"– and Cross Keys div's at Mandalay," continued Peel. "I don't know about the others. Anyway, it doesn't matter. We'll be going down the road shortly."

"In the bloody crap again!" Grandarse apostrophised the heavens. "Sell the farm an' buy us oot! Ah've aboot 'ed it, me! Naw, it's not bloody fair! Ah thowt w'en we took Mike-tilla we'd

---

* Fourteenth Army's various divisions had rather exotic badges which were worn with considerable pride out of the line, but not in action. The oldest was the Black Cat of 17th Indian Division (and I was still stirred, quite unreasonably, to see it on the shoulders of Indian troops when they invaded Goa many years after the war), but equally well known was the Cross Keys emblem of the 2nd British Division. Of the others referred to by Grandarse, there were two Dagger divisions, the 19th Indian (downthrust) and the 20th Indian (upthrust); the spider was worn by 81st West African Division, and crossed assegais by the 82nd West African. Probably not even the legions of Rome embraced as many nationalities as Fourteenth Army.

git a bit o' rest – Ah could do wi' seven days at the Museum, me
– an' w'at'll Ah git? Japs! Fookin' Tojos!"

"Mind they doan't git thee," said Forster acidly.

"That's reet, Grandarse lad. There's a bloody girt big Imperial
Guardsman doon t'road, wid a Samurai sword, an' it's got thy
number on it. I'm tellin' ye, ye'll a' git killed."

"Aw, bollix! Pee – Pee-what-d'ye-call-it, Tommo?"

"Pyawbwe."

It's pronounced Pee-aw-bee, and Peel's information was correct:
we were to take it. I imagine that the reason 17th Div got the job
was because there wasn't a day to be lost, and we were nearest
and best organised for the work. Jap was digging in for a last
desperate stand on the Rangoon road: if he could hold us at
Pyawbwe for just a few weeks, until the monsoon broke, he might
stave off defeat indefinitely, for when the rains came they would
turn southern Burma into a huge swamp where no armour or
truck could operate, where the airfields would be impossible, and
where even infantry could not operate effectively. "You can't fight
through the monsoon" was the received wisdom, and if it proved
to be true Fourteenth Army would squelch to a halt somewhere
on the southern edge of the Dry Belt, and Jap would have months
in which to reorganise his defence of southern Burma.

"We'll be oop tae the goolies in watter, gittin' et tae bits by
leeches an' joongle sores, while the lal bastard's diggin' 'issel' in
a' the way tae Rangoon," was Nick's verdict. "Rain? It joost pisses
doon forivver. It'll be that deep in t'paddy, they'll efta tek the
Goorkas oot the line, or the poor lal boogers'll droon."

"Maybe Jap'll drown, too, Nick. He's just a chota wallah."*

"Droon? Them? The bastards are fireproof, watterproof, an'
too fookin' dumb tae droon. The only way they die is Tojo's way.
Ah, weel, we'll a' git killed."

But if Pyawbwe could be taken in time, and we could get a grip
on southern Burma before the monsoon set in in earnest, Jap might
be wrapped up by the end of the year, in Burma at least. The best
armies he had put into the field anywhere would have been broken
and scattered north of Rangoon; the strongest link in the chain

* little fellow

surrounding his homeland would have been broken, and the allies would be closing inexorably from all sides – Americans in the Pacific, Australians in New Guinea and Borneo, Chinese in China and Korea, ourselves in Malaya and Siam. That was how it looked then; the war in Europe might be all but won, but South-east Asia looked set for a long-drawn bloody struggle which would end only with an assault on the Japanese mainland – in 1946? 1947? There were those who spoke of 1950, even. No one underestimated Jap: he might be a subhuman creature who tortured and starved prisoners of war to death, raped women captives, and used civilians for bayonet practice, but there was no braver soldier in the whole history of war, and if he fought to a finish . . . In the meantime, Pyawbwe.

Before we left Meiktila I had my first taste of leading the section – or rather, having the section lead me, for the operation was a highly technical one of which I knew nothing and they knew everything, and then some. This often happens to young men on their first independent commands, and is very educational.

With Jap surrounding Meiktila all our supplies had been dropped from the air, and even when he began to withdraw from our northern front the road route remained hazardous, and the drops continued. Corporal Peel being otherwise engaged, I was ordered by Hutton to take the section out to assist in the collection of supplies being dropped that day, so I fell them in and marched them to the 15cwt truck which would take us out to the dropping zone, a mile or so beyond the perimeter. Usually the prospect of fatigues induced extreme lethargy and a tendency to melt into the background, but to my surprise they were not only all present but eager; even Grandarse, whose normal response to being roused was to turn over and go into a coma, was to the fore, armed with a water chaggle on either shoulder.

"Bloody thoorsty work, air drops," he explained. "Better git thasel a chaggle, corp – we'll sweat fookin' gallons the day."

Corp? This was unwonted respect, for stripe or no stripe I remained "Jock", just as Peel was "Tommo", and even Hutton, to the older hands at least, was "Tut". Not a little impressed, I told the section to take a chaggle apiece, and the truck set off looking like a water-skin bazaar.

"Best leave 'em in the trook, eh, corp?" suggested Grandarse, when we reached the drop zone. He raised one of the chaggles, opened a valve in his throat, sank most of the chlorinated contents at a gulp, and observed that he wad be oop a' neet, pishin' 'issel' cross-eyed. "By, Ah joost wish it was yell!* Ayup, let's be at it!"

The others also half-emptied their chaggles, hung them on the truck stanchions, and fell in belching, their radiators filled for the work ahead.

The man in charge was a grizzled Service Corps warrant officer, naked save for his service cap, shorts, sandals, and the wrist brass-ard denoting his rank. All round him were fatigue parties from the East Yorks, Probyn's, Gurkhas, Baluchis, Deccan Horse, West Yorks, Gunners, Sappers, Sikhs, Jats, and every outfit in the div-ision, and he was going hoarse assigning them to different areas of the drop zone. This was a hard-baked paddy bounded by mark-ers, a dusty expanse shimmering in the heat haze, for it was early April and the temperature was rising with a vengeance. It was going to be a gruelling day, and I congratulated Grandarse on his foresight about the water before reporting to the W.O., announc-ing the name of our regiment.

He winced, dropped his list, and gave me a hunted look.

"Did you say —?" he asked, as though hoping he hadn't heard aright. I repeated it, and he looked despairingly at the section.

"Oh, bloody hell!" he said, and sighed. "As if life wasn't hard enough!" He muttered something which I didn't quite catch, about the years of the locust. "All right, corporal, hold 'em there; I'll attend to you when I've detailed this lot." And he turned away like a man with a heavy load, shouting bad-tempered orders to the other squad commanders.

If I'd been sensitive, I'd have said we weren't welcome, and I'd have been right. For when he had dispatched the other parties he returned and addressed the section directly.

"Right!" he said grimly. "I know you lot. I was in Ceylon in '42, with your —th battalion. I know all about the Pink Elephant. And I remember you in Umballa, before the war." He drew breath,

* ale

while I wondered what he was on about, and continued in a quieter, almost appealing tone. "All I'm asking is, keep your hands off the bloody stuff – you know what I mean. Just bring it in and stack it, *bus*. Behave yourselves, and I'll get you a few buckshees afterwards, okay? That's a promise – but you'll have to play the game, see? Leave it to me, and I'll see you right."

It sounded like most offensive innuendo to me, but the section received it with polite interest; Grandarse was even nodding approval. The W.O. gave them a last weary look and led me aside.

"What are you doing with this shower? You sound Scotch. Ah, well, bad luck, son. Tell you what, I'll give you this stretch, near the trucks, where I can keep an eye on them. Right, carry on – here they come!"

There was no time to protest or question; the first of the big Dakotas was droning in, circling the drop zone just above our heads, the Sikh unloaders visible in its open doorway. Behind came the other planes, following the slow circle, banking slightly while the Sikhs thrust out the big bales. It was a spectacular sight, the aircraft glittering in the sunlight, the bales falling in a continuous shower; a few of them, containing machine parts and other delicate cargo, came waltzing down on little white parachutes, but most of the great canvas bundles fell in what was called "free drop", hitting the paddy with resounding thumps and clouds of dust, bouncing high and careering across the plain. The fatigue parties ran to them, and in a few minutes the zone was like an antheap as the covers were ripped away and the contents dragged out – crates and boxes and metal containers by the thousand, to be carried towards the parked three-tonners, where they were stacked for loading under the eye of the W.O. and his shouting, sweating assistants.

It was an uplifting sight, too – Fourteenth Army exercising its talent for improvisation on the grand scale, feeding and arming its spearhead deep inside enemy country, demonstrating that this was a siege which the Japanese, for all their superior numbers, could not hope to win; those leisurely wheeling American planes were symbolic, and the sight of them droning unhindered overhead must have been a bitter one to the withdrawing Japanese armies: not a

Zero in the sky*, and food and ammunition in massive quantities pouring down to their opponents.

You had to keep an eye on that pouring process, for it continued while we worked, the big bales booming down while we scattered out of the drop line; I saw one misdirected bale come streaking down to hit a jeep on the edge of the zone; it struck fair and square on the bonnet, flattening the vehicle in a tangled wreck and exploding a great cascade of Indian butter for fifty yards around.

"Ye'll be gittin' yer chapattis dry the neet, Johnny!" Nixon shouted to a party of Gurkhas, and the little men beamed and squealed, pigtails flapping on their shaven skulls as they wrestled with bundles as tall as themselves; they worked, as they did everything, with all their might, slashing the covers with their kukris, staggering away laden to the trucks, racing back for more, and bubbling with chatter and laughter, treating it as a great game. The rest of us worked as hard; in that heat it was as exhausting as any labour I've ever done, even stevedoring in Port Said, but it was exhilarating, too; our arms ached with swinging our kukris, and our hands were raw from the canvas, but we enjoyed it.

As Nine Section beavered away, ripping, dragging, lifting, and carrying with a fine energetic rhythm, the W.O. would stride over every now and then to peer suspiciously at our stacks, obviously comparing them with those of the other units. After a while he seemed to grow less anxious, and when we broke for tiffin he even remarked favourably on the amount we'd shifted.

"'Ard graft," panted Wattie, reclining against a wheel of our 15cwt and mopping his chest. "By God, it beats 'ay-mekkin'!"

"Ah could stand that, an' a'," said Grandarse, a rich cerise from his exertions. "Aye, w'at? A lang day i' the Lorton Valley, wid the farm lassies bringin' the bait† an' nasty big pints! Eh? Ah could fettle a coople this minnit, could Ah nut?"

"Pints or lassies?" jeered Forster. "That's a' the 'ay-mekkin' thoo ivver did, Ah'll bet. Aye, oonder the bloody stacks, wid yer arse gan like a fiddler's elbow. Shaggin' an' suppin', that's your

* I saw one Zero in the course of the campaign, farther south. It was greeted, inevitably, with the cry: "There's a Nip in the air!"
† food

99

idea o' woork." But Grandarse was too intent on his chaggle to retort.

"I'd sooner be working down here than up there," said the Duke, watching a Dakota wheel lazily away, its bearded unloader leaning out at a perilous angle to watch a falling bale. "You know they have to change those Sikh crews every few trips? Fact – after a while they get disoriented, forget that they're two hundred feet up. They think they can step out, that the ground's just a yard beneath them – and some of 'em do. Lost a few men that way, I heard."

"Aw, cobblers!" said Forster. "Ye tellin' us they can't tell 'oo 'igh up they are?"

"It's reet, tho'," said Nick. "Ah 'eerd that f'ae a feller that seen it 'appen. Big Sikh joost walked oot efter a boondle; they 'ed to scrape 'im intil a mess-tin; nowt left but 'is beard an' bangle." He raised his voice to the skies. "Doan't loup oot, Singh lad! This isn't Spiattri!* Ye'll nivver bounce!"

We worked through the afternoon, and none more zealous than Nine Section; when the other fatigue parties were calling it a day, sitting or lying in the shadow of their transport, draining chaggles or emptying them over sweat-plastered heads and dusty torsos, Nick and Wattie and Grandarse and even the egregious Forster were still scouring the littered plain, finding overlooked boxes, plodding back with their burdens, and generally heaping coals of fire, it seemed to me, on the head of the mistrustful W.O. It had its effect; I heard him saying "Good lads", as they trudged by, setting down the last loads with the sighs of men who have toiled well in the vineyard; Grandarse responded with hearty affability. "Aye, wahm woork, staff! Nowt like a good job weel dyun, eh?"

By the time the last crate was in place, and the three-tonners were rumbling away to the central depot, the W.O. was being almost amiable. He waited until the other parties had gone, and

* A piece of Cumbrian folk-usage. Workers in the town of Aspatria (pronounced 'Spiattri' in dialect) were noted for wearing clogs, and it was traditional that when the train reached the town the guard would cry "A' they wi' clogs on, loup oot!", or, simply "Spiattri, loup oot!" Consequently it became a folk-saying, and a native Cumbrian, reaching the end of a journey (such as debussing in the Army) may be heard repeating it.

Nine Section had completed a lengthy toilet in our 15cwt and emerged in shirts and hats, and told me to fall them in. As they fell in, tired but decent, behind them two of the W.O.'s minions were going over our truck with practised hands; he waited for their nod, and surveyed the section with a knowing, satisfied smirk.

"Good enough, then. They've worked well, corporal – and you've behaved yourselves, haven't you? Yerss, I know you have!" He was looking positively roguish. "Oh, yerss, because I had the eye down on you – and you knew it, didn't you? You couldn't old-soldier me, my sons – the name's Croft, not soft. Well, fair's fair; I'm a man of my word – over there, corporal, under that tarpaulin. Help yourselves, lads, and don't say I'm not good to you!"

Beneath the tarpaulin were a few bags of tea and sugar, a carton of Lucky Strike, and a couple of cans of condensed milk, and the section fell on them with cries of astonishment and gratitude that were touching to hear. The W.O. watched with a tolerant eye as they climbed into the 15cwt, exclaiming over his bounty.

"I didn't body search 'em," he told me confidentially. "Creates a bad impression. Anyway, no need – I've got eyes in my arse, and they knew better'n to try it on." He shook his head. "Desperate lot, your mob. Notorious – have been since Marlborough's day, I shouldn't wonder. Well, they don't call you the Reivers for nothing!" He chuckled indulgently. "I just showed I was fly to them, promised 'em buckshees – a bit o' stick, a bit o' carrot, works wonders. All right, corporal, fall out!"

If he hadn't been four ranks above me I might well have given him my opinion of his aspersions on my regiment. As it was, I felt I owed the section an apology on his behalf, but since I was up front with the driver I didn't get a chance to make it, although when we debussed I remarked to Nick that the W.O. was a cheeky son-of-a-bitch. He looked blank.

"Ah didn't knaw w'at 'e was talkin' aboot. Did you, Wattie?"

"Ah wasn't listenin'," said Wattie with contempt. "Service Corps, Ah've shit 'em. Pathetic."

We were at the pits. "Awreet," said Forster, "git the groond-sheet doon, an' let's git crackin'. 'Ey, Duke, bring them chaggles ower 'ere."

The Duke, bent under the weight of a dozen bulging chaggles, gave me an apologetic look. "I feel like one of Fagin's apprentices . . . oh, well, when in Rome. Here, Foshie."

Forster upended the chaggles one after another, and before my astonished eyes a mound of sugar grew on the groundsheet. Nick fingered it critically.

"Soom barmy booger didn't sup a' 'is watter. Ah, weel, it'll dry oot." He took off his hat, disclosing half a dozen packets of cigarettes, then stooped and opened his bush-shirt to release a deluge of cigarette packets. Forster contributed even more from within his shirt; he then pulled his trousers out of their puttees, and wriggled, and more packets piled up round his ankles. Further sensational revelations followed: Grandarse's capacious britches yielded, of all things, several pounds of loose tea ("Ah doan't fancy the flavour o' that bloody lot," said Forster) and from beneath his vest he brought out flat tins of fish in tomato sauce. "We'll swap 'em tae the Goorkas for chapattis, an' that. The lal sods'd sell their sowls for 'errin's."

It was the same with the rest of them – every man-jack had plundered comestibles about him, inside buttoned sleeves and trouser legs, under shirts, in hats; tea, sugar, and cigarettes, mostly, but of condensed milk, pipe tobacoo, tinned fish, bacon, spam, and sausage there was no lack, and by the time they were finished that groundsheet looked like Harrods food hall. I felt quite guilty, not contributing. Then they stood around and admired it.

"We'd best gi' soom t'Sivven an' Eight Sections," said Nick.

"W'at for?" said Forster, shocked. "We kliftied* the bloody stoof!"

"Gan, ye greedy booger! This lot'll last tae Rangoon, easy! Any roads, they knaw we were oot on the drop, an' Ah doan't want Jonty Armstrang gan through oor groob box w'en we're in kip. He's a thievin' bastard, yon. Tell ye w'at – we'll let 'em 'ave the bookshees that gormless Service Corps wallah gev us!"

So they did, with the loose tea and sugar that wouldn't cram into our chah and cheeny boxes, and the odds and ends of tins left over when the mortar box containing our delicacies had been

* stole

filled. Hearing Nick setting aside cigarettes for Hutton, I felt
absolved of all qualms of conscience; my main concern was how
the devil they'd managed it; lined up before the W.O. there hadn't
been a suspicious bulge anywhere, and I hadn't noticed any surrep-
titious work during the drop collection.

"Ask their ancestors," said the Duke, when I put it to him. "It's
a gift – and from what I've heard, a regimental tradition. If he'd
frisked them, they were dead men, but they had him weighed up,
I suppose. Mind you, I thought Grandarse was looking a bit too
dropsical for comfort, and if that clever W.O. had thought to walk
round them, he couldn't have helped noticing that half of them
had humps like Quasimodo. Silly ass, asking for it!"

"How d'you mean?"

"All that fly-man stuff about the Pink Elephant – it was like a
red rag to a bull. Oh, they came prepared to fill the chaggles with
sugar or tea, but it was his smart cracks that made 'em rob him
blind. He's lucky they left the wheels on his jeep."

"What's the Pink Elephant?"

"It was a pub or club sign, in Kandy or Colombo – somewhere
in Ceylon, when the —th Battalion were there. Sodding great
thing, I believe, about twenty feet high. Someone made a bet –
and it vanished. Turned up months later in the corporals' mess at
the depot, back home. So I'm told."

I reflected on all this, sitting round the fire that night, full of
illicit tea and condensed milk, excellent chapatti obtained from the
Gurkhas for looted tinned fish, plundered peaches, and enjoying
unlimited ill-gotten cigarettes, pondering the old West March saying that there's nothing too hot or too heavy, thinking about
regimental tradition, looking at the hard brown faces, and reaching a remarkable, paradoxical conclusion which I hold by to this
day: in word and deed, I never knew such honest men.

17th Division closed in on Pyawbwe from all directions. Since the last gap in the circle round Pyawbwe had been closed, the [Japanese] garrison had to fight its way out, die or surrender. It chose a combination of the first two, and when Pyawbwe was entered 1,110 dead and thirteen guns were found in the town. Pyawbwe was the only large action in the Battle of the Rangoon Road, and it finally shattered 33rd (Japanese) Army.

Official history

And then recall that exhilarating dash that carried you across the Irrawaddy . . . And there you met the Japanese Army in the open, and you tore it apart.

FIELD-MARSHAL VISCOUNT SLIM,
at a Burma Reunion

DUST AND SUNLIGHT and dry rocky plain dotted with mounds and low bunds and an occasional small broken ruin, all stretching away to a distant line of shattered buildings, and beyond them, dim through the heat haze, a long gradual slope ending in a ridge: that is Pyawbwe in my mind. We crossed the plain with the Japanese whizz-bangs exploding just overhead, and reached the line of buildings, and the Japanese died on the long slope, and my feet were killing me through all that scorching, thirsty day: that was the battle.

Those are the first images, at any rate, that I see when the name of Pyawbwe is mentioned. The incidents of the day come back in a rough, unconnected sequence only when I consider them at length, starting in a Burmese lavatory and ending with a long, sound sleep in a wrecked and rusty railway wagon; I shall fill them in as I come to them – the man who was sick, the row of bodies wrapped in blood-stained blankets in the lee of a little bank, the whine and crack of the Jap 75s, "Remember Arroyo!", the shell-burst right in Morton's face which never touched him, the cool scummy depths of the well, Long John smiling and adjusting his bush-hat, the sergeant who went stone deaf in the last stage of the advance, the rattle of our rapid fire as we knelt among the ancient rolling stock, the figures running and falling across our front on the slope, the long painful trudge back from the sniper's nest to the section's final position, the faint pfft! of shots fired by some distant Japanese optimist passing high overhead, and the Dubarry–Foster debate which brought proceedings to a close.

That is my corresponding summary to the official history's. Of the preliminary activity on the preceding days I have absolutely no recollection; we must have come down from Meiktila to the outskirts of Pyawbwe as part of Cowan's encircling movement whereby the town was hemmed in, taking up our position for the final assault in what was to be the last set-piece battle of the Second World War – at least I know of no later one. I suppose it was Jap's last big organised stand; what happened in the following months was the mopping-up of southern Burma. Pyawbwe broke him; we took it before the monsoon, and he had no hope of turning the tide after that.

The advance to Pyawbwe, as detailed in the official history, is complicated, but since Nine Section played no remarkable part in it I am content to pass it by; Jap was swept aside piecemeal, and took heavy casualties, and once Cowan had the town surrounded it was a question of closing in from all sides. Nine Section's starting point in the grand design was a cluster of Burmese bashas, not big enough to be called a village, where we had dug in the night before. It was just large enough to boast a communal toilet, of which I availed myself when I came off stag at dawn.

Burmese conveniences are curious structures, consisting of a flimsy and barely concealing cabin built on very high stilts and reached by a ladder. The cabin is the upper works, so to speak; there is a hole in the floor, and far beneath is what you might call the pan, except that there isn't one, just the ground. Why the Southern Burmese (for I never saw a skyscraper bog in the north) found it necessary to perform natural functions at such a dizzy height, I never discovered; Parker, who had returned to the section after his convalescence, and had shared the stag with me, supposed that it arose from sheer laziness; the higher the structure, the less frequently would it need to be moved to a new location, for obvious reasons. He may have been right. The Burmese of the south had discovered a dimension of leisure unknown to the West; they lived in their bashas, planted their rice, ate mangoes and bananas, sat on their verandahs and smoked by way of exercise, and enjoyed an existence of complete tranquility which even a full-scale war seldom disturbed. Probably no people on earth move so slowly or so infrequently.

Which could not be said of me, secluded in the cabin, when a shell burst close by. It would be hard to think of a worse place to be caught during a barrage, and I came down without recourse to the ladder and was crouching in my pit before the echo had died away. It must have been a ranging shot, for no others followed, but it was a sign of things to come, and I time the start of the battle of Pyawbwe from that moment.

Breakfast was a generous affair that day; guessing what was ahead, the cook-sergeant was lavish with the burgoo, bacon and beans; as a rule he was harassed and defensive, like all master gyppos, but that morning he was solicitous, even anxious, scanning our faces as we came by the dixies with our mess-tins. Perhaps he was wondering how many of us would be queuing for supper. "Git that doon ye, Jock – d'ye fancy a boiled egg an' a', son?" was a far cry from "Ah dae me bloody best wi' the bloody stoof – wadyas expect, sivven courses at the Croon an' bloody Mitre?"

Not everyone took advantage of his bounty. One of the section, a newcomer from another regiment, was sitting on the edge of his pit, hunched up, when his mucker called me over; he was giving little gasps, holding his stomach, and looking green.

"What is it, the shits?" Mild dysentery was common enough, and more of a nuisance than an illness; the genuine article, which was to become increasingly common as we went south in the monsoon, can be a killer. He shook his head, groaning, and when I pressed his lower right abdomen he yelped. I told him to report to the M.O. and went over to tell Peel, who was falling the section in.

"He'll have to go sick," I said.

"Aye," said Forster. "Sick wid nerves."

I said it might be appendicitis – being from a medical family you feel obliged to give idiotic diagnoses every so often – and Forster spat and said: "Ah doot it." Peel said nothing, and we moved off to the assembly point.

It wasn't appendicitis, but I'm not saying Forster was right; the man was in pain, and it would have taken an expert to determine what caused it. What was interesting was the section's indifference; whether he was sick or scared made no odds, since either would make him an unreliable quantity in action, and it was never referred to again. They were very practical about that sort of thing, and I don't pretend to know what went on deep in their minds, for it is a highly personal matter, and they didn't talk about it, much less show the least emotion. They belonged to a culture in which "windy" is the ultimate insult, and in which the synonym for brave is "mad", and that is all there is to be said about it.

It was at the assembly point, or shortly after, that I saw the bodies, three or four of them, entirely covered in blankets secured by log-lines; there were patches of dried blood staining the coarse khaki. My impression remains that they were not of our company; I don't remember shell-fire at this time, and can only suppose that they were casualties from an early skirmish. No one drew attention to the discouraging sight.

Then we were moving out from under the trees on to the edge of the dry plain. It was to be a two-company attack, with ourselves on the left, and we formed up in extended lines, a couple of hundred green-clad figures well spread out, with our platoon roughly in the middle behind the vanguard. This was not lost on Sergeant Hutton as he moved among us, making his last-minute checks.

"It'll be heids doon an' keep movin' the day," I heard him say to Peel. "An' we'll be the ones that catch the shit, an' a', stook in the middle." He sounded more irritable than usual, possibly because, since we had been given no replacement for Gale, he was de facto platoon commander, responsible for thirty-odd men, a job which no sergeant cares for. He came across to me. "Jock – keep close to the Bren, mind, when we git in." As 2i/c of the section the Bren gunner and his number two were my immediate concern. I said I would, and asked him why being in the middle of the advance was a bad thing.

"When Jap artillery oppens oop, he'll ga for the middle o' the target – an' that's us. So keep weel spread oot, all on ye, an' keep movin'. The farther ye git in, the less chance there is o' the whizz-bangs gittin' ye. Reet, Nick?" But Nick was enjoying his pessimism, as usual.

"Jap's got 'is eye on Nine Section," he announced. "Special orders f'ae Tojo – 'Git them boogers, me jolly lal Japs, an' there's a sivven-day pass for the gooner that puts a whizz-bang oop Grandarse'." He cackled and leaned forward to shout to Grandarse, in the line in front of us. "Are ye reet, owd lad? Nivver bother, we'll a' git killed!"

"Aw, fookin' shurroop!" snapped Forster, and for once I sympathised: Nick's eternal parrot-cry isn't exactly what you want to hear before going in under Jap artillery without a scrap of cover. Mind you, I'd have felt there was something wrong if he hadn't said it; I'd probably have been superstitious enough to regard it as a bad omen.

We waited in the sunlit morning, listening for our own divisional artillery whose barrage would signal the start of the battle, and I was interested to find myself less nervous than I had been before we went over the bund to the temple wood. It was a primitive thing, no doubt: then there had been no one between me and the enemy position; now there was the lead platoon ahead – I wasn't an old enough soldier to appreciate Hutton's warning about being in the second wave. I heard someone laugh, and saw to my surprise that it was Long John, the company commander, checking his watch as he talked to the sergeant-major. I couldn't recall hearing him laugh before; the quiet smile was more in his line, but today he was looking as though he hadn't a care in the world, joking with the C.S.M.

"Happy as a pig in shit," muttered Hutton, and added, with a sour grin that had a deep affection behind it: "'E's a lad, oor John."

That, incidentally, is about as high a compliment as a Cumbrian soldier can pay, and was a just reflection of the company's feeling. They didn't give their admiration lightly, but they wouldn't have swapped Long John for any officer in the Army. He was a wild cat in action and a gentle man out of it; forty years on I watched him finding seats for latecomers to a memorial service in Carlisle Cathedral, mild and unobtrusive as he handed them their hymn-sheets – and remembered him coming out of the dark with that bent bayonet on his rifle.*

The artillery opened up behind us with a thunder that made the ground shake, every gun in 17th Division throwing its high explosive at the Japanese positions far ahead; the green lines stirred and the bush-hats tilted back as everyone craned to see what was happening beyond the haze, with the ritual murmurs of "Send it doon, David!" – whoever David might be. The bursts were invisible, but the rumble of the distant explosions came back to us in a continuous wave of sound. For five minutes the barrage continued, and as it died away Nine Section expressed their appreciation.

"Is that a', fer fook's sake! Christ, Ah could 'ev farted better than yon! Aye, weel, that's a' we're gonna git – an' nae air coover, neether! Sod that for a game o' sojers! Bloody madness! Gooners, Ah've shit 'em!" etc. etc. Actually, by their standards it was practically a hymn of gratitude.

A word of command sounded from the platoon ahead. All around men were hitching their rifles to the trail, settling their hats, twitching pouch-straps and water-bottles to make sure all was secure, tapping the hilts of kukris and bayonets; the lead platoon was advancing out on to the plain, three extended lines of them, the right markers keeping distance from the company on our right – I'm told there were Shermans of Probyn's Horse somewhere, but I didn't see them. We moved off in the lead platoon's wake, extending as we came into the open until there was five or six yards between each man; Nick was on my immediate right and Stanley with the Bren to my left; a few yards ahead were Morton the Yorkshireman and Grandarse – and between Grandarse and the lead platoon the tall figure of the battalion chaplain, swinging along good style with his .38 on his hip.

* I was not the only one who noticed his demeanour at Pyawbwe, where he won the Military Cross: the battalion history records that "he seemed to be having the time of his life".

I wondered then, and I wonder now, what the Church of England's policy was about padres who put themselves in harm's way; giving comfort to the wounded and dying, fine, but ethical problems must surely arise if Jap came raging out of a bunker into his reverence's path; the purple pips on the chaplain's shoulder wouldn't mean a thing to the enemy, so . . . And if a padre shot a Jap, what would the harvest be – apart from three ringing cheers from the whole battalion? In my own Church, the highly practical Scottish one, it would doubtless be classed as a work of necessity and mercy, but I wasn't sure about the Anglicans. If this seems an unlikely field of speculation when you're going into battle, well, my mind had been running on religion lately. I'd been given the hand of fellowship by the Scots Kirk at Deolali (mainly because it would be welcome news to my father), and had accidentally strayed into a C. of E. communion service at Meiktila, receiving wafers and wine to which I obviously wasn't entitled, and escaping detection only by copying the actions of the other communicants. Also, after being an agnostic from the age of ten, I'd started saying my prayers again – there's nothing like mortal danger for putting you in the mood; as Voltaire observed, it's no time to be making enemies.

I came out of my reverie to realise that we'd gone several hundred yards, and were well out on the plain. The advance was swift but not hurried, about a regulation marching pace, and the rhythm of it, the steady tramp across the hard earth, and the companionship of those long green lines ahead and to either side produced a momentary exhilaration; someone nearby was whistling "Bye-bye, Shanghai" – it must be Parker, somewhere to my right – and I found I was hissing it through my teeth and keeping time in my head, left-right-left-right, as we strode ahead, watching Grandarse's small pack bumping to the step, the dust drifting past from the boots stepping out ahead . . .

Something exploded about ten feet above us with an ear-splitting whine-crack – the celebrated Jap whizz-bang, better known as the 75 or 73 calibre gun. Then another and another, whizz-bang, whizz-bang, and dust was flying among the marchers ahead, and invisible things were whistling past. They seemed to be crashing out every second now, and I found my head was flinching to each report even while my feet kept moving. People were shouting orders – no, they weren't orders, really, just the automatic cries of rally and encouragement common to advancing armies since time began: "Keep going! Keep moving! Don't stop! Keep spread out! Keep going!" And overhead those infernal things whined and cracked, deafening and staggering the mind if not the body; to my left Stanley was striding on, head down, face turned like a man walking into the wind. On my right Nick had his head hunched down on his shoulders, and I could see him swearing savagely to himself; something went shrieking past between us, the explosions seemed to be rising to a crescendo – out of the tail of my eye I saw a man in the platoon ahead go down, and then another, stumbling onto his knees, but he was up again in a second and someone was running to the first man, who lay horribly still.

Grandarse staggered and let out a bellow of pain, and I thought, oh, Jesus, not Grandarse, and Hutton ran past me and grabbed his elbow. "Y'areet? Y'areet, man?" Grandarse turned, clinging to Hutton to keep his balance, then letting go to wipe his face which was plastered by dirt thrown up by a splinter. He was roaring unheard obscenities, the whining and cracking overhead blotting out the words, and then he was plunging on, and Hutton was turning, marching backwards for a few steps, bellowing to make himself heard: "Keep ga'n! Keep ga'n! Keep spread oot!" As I passed him he was snarling in a justified way about how right he'd been – we were in the middle, catching the shit, just as he'd foretold. Whine-crack, whine-crack – and I saw a cloud of smoke and flame erupt right in front of Morton the Yorkshireman at head height, bursting right in his face. Goner, I thought – and he shook his head without even breaking stride; about seven thousand shell splinters must have missed him, by a miracle.

A deafening crash, apparently on top of my hat, and I staggered, momentarily stunned, but only by the force of the explosion. Nick was staring at me, but I signalled that I was all right – and there was a man reeling away from the lead platoon, collapsing on a little bank, blood running down his face. Someone ran to him, but the fallen man – he was a corporal, with black curly hair – waved him almost savagely away, and the man ran back to the ranks. As we drew level the corporal had dragged out his field dressing and

was mopping the gash on his temple; he waved it at Nick and me
and shouted:

"Ga'n git 'em, marras! Remember Arroyo!"

"Booger Arroyo!" roared Grandarse, and the corporal pulled
himself up into a sitting position, and as we swung past he was
trying to sing, in a harsh, unmusical croak.

> Aye, Ah ken John Peel an' Ruby too,
> Ranter an' Ringwood, Bellman an' True
> From a find to a check, from a check to a view
> From a view to a death in the morning!

He was a romantic, that one, but whoever he was I'm grateful
to him, for I can say I have heard the regimental march sung, and
the regimental war cry shouted,* as we went in under the Japanese
fire. I don't know how many casualties we took at that point –
seven dead and thirty-three wounded was the count at the end of
the day – but I do know that the companies never stopped or even
broke stride; they "kept ga'n", and I must be a bit of a romantic,
too, I suppose, for whenever I think back on those few minutes
when the whizz-bangs caught us, and see again those unfaltering
green lines swinging steadily on, one word comes into my Scottish
head: Englishmen.

Then suddenly we were through, and the shelling stopped as
abruptly as it had begun. Hutton had been right: the closer we
got, the better. Only a few hundred yards of broken ground separated us from the line of ruined buildings beyond which the gradual
slope began, and the Japanese guns, on the reverse slope, must
already be at maximum depression – in other words, they couldn't
shoot low enough to hit us. Then there was small arms firing to

---

* Arroyo dos Molinos was a little hamlet in Spain, and there, during the
Peninsular War, this regiment achieved a distinction unique among British Army
battle honours: in an encounter with their opposite number in the French infantry
of the Line, Napoleon's 34th Regiment, they captured the enemy unit entire, even
down to their regimental band, our drum major wresting the staff from the hand
of his French counterpart. The Arroyo drums became the regiment's most prized
possession, and "Arroyo dos Molinos" was worn on the regimental cap badge
until amalgamation did what Napoleon's infantry had failed to do. But our
magnificent march, John Peel, remains.

the right, and we were ordered to take up firing positions in a cluster of low hillocks; I believe, but am not certain, that the right-hand company had hit bunkers, and our advance checked while they were cleared. Anyway, we were halted long enough for an incident which I blush to record, because it was too damned silly for words, but since I am writing a faithful record I can't very well omit it.

We were lying among the hillocks, watching our front and listening to the firing on the flank and the occasional whit! of a shot overhead, cursing the blazing heat and lamenting that we had no chaggles with us, when Grandarse asked Wattie for a drink from his bottle, a request answered in that comradely spirit for which Nine Section was celebrated.

"W'at's wrang wi' thi own fookin' bottle?"

"It's roond back on us, ye gormless Egremont twat! It's lyin' atop me bloody arse, that's w'at's wrang wid it!"

"Well, oonfasten the bloody thing!"

"Look, bollock-brain, if Ah oondoo the bloody straps Ah'll nivver git them doon oop again!" Grandarse, being portly, might well have had difficulty re-threading the two straps from which his bottle hung below the small of his back. "Ye want us runnin' at bloody Japs wid me bundook* in one hand an' me bottle in t'other?"

"Awreet – Ah'll oondoo it for thee mesel'. Then we'll baith git a drink – oot o' thy bottle!"

"Ye miserable sod, w'at difference does it mek w'ee's bottle we soop frae?"

"That's w'at Ah'm sayin'! W'at fer should we use my bottle 'stead o' thine? Y'are always on the scroonge, you! Guzzlin' big-bellied git!"

"Reet!" roared Grandarse. "Stick yer effin' bottle oop yer goonga, an' Ah hope it gi'es thee piles!"

"Ah, give ower, ye bloody bairns!" snapped Forster. "There's a fookin' well ower theer, wid watter in't. Use that, an' stop nat-terin', an' keep thi bottle till efter."

This sounded sensible, since water was liable to be precious by

* rifle

the end of the day, and the well was in plain view just outside our position, a circular mud wall enclosing the well-head. Grandarse, however, was hygiene conscious.

"It'll be full o' shit, like that 'un we used last week, an' foond there wez twa deid Japs in't. Bloated tae boogery, they were."

"Weel, ye took no 'arm!" said Forster. "The purification pills does the trick. Ye've got toons o' the bloody things!"

"We 'evn't got a chaggle," objected Grandarse. "We'll 'ev tae use oor 'ats tae git watter. Weel, then, ye 'ev to shek pills tae dissolve them – 'oo the hell ye gonna dae that in a bush-hat?"

That seemed to dispose of that, until Wattie had his great idea.

"Tell thee w'at! Why doan' we put t'pills in oor gobs, an' dissolve boogers that way! Then we can wesh 'em doon wid the pani,* easy!"

"Aw, piss off!" derided Grandarse. "Stick 'em in oor gobs!" He gave a great guffaw. "'Ey, that minds us o' w'en Jocky Rootledge wez constipated. Ye mind Jocky, back in't 5th Battalion? A reet wooden booger. Weel, 'e ga's till the M.O., an' the orderly gi'es 'im a suppository. 'W'at dae Ah dee wid this?' sez Jocky – 'e wez a reet iggerent cloon, tho'. 'Insert it in your rectum, my man,' 'sez the M.O. 'In me w'at?' sez Jocky. 'Stick it oop yer arse,' sez the orderly. 'Doan't give me yer bloody lip,' sez Jocky, an' 'e larruped 'im, an' brok' 'is jaw, an' got 'issel' twenty-eight days!"

"Fook Jocky Rootledge! Ye gan fer the pani or nut?" said Forster. "Ah's gittin' thoorsty listenin' tae ye!"

"Ah'm gehm," said Wattie, and after consultation with Peel I made a quick dash for the well to examine its condition. I peered over the wall into the murky depths, and while it wasn't company's own water, I'd seen worse. The surface was about six feet down, covered with a bright green scum no doubt rich in vitamins, but the pills should take care of that. I called to Wattie and Grandarse to brings their pills, and they scuttled across. Grandarse still had doubts about swallowing the pills along with the water, but Wattie brayed at him, insisting it was all one how they got inside him.

"Dissolve the bloody things in yer spit, man!"

* water

"Ah've got nee spit! Me mooth's like a Toorkish russler's jock-strap! Awreet, then – let's git crackin'!"

The difficulty was to reach the water. I lowered my hat on the end of a rifle sling, but the thing refused to sink through the emerald crust, however much I bounced and swung it.

"W'at's in this fookin' well – sheep dip?" demanded Grandarse. "Aw, booger it – Ah've 'ed this. It'll joost give us the fookin' cholera, any roads."

"We've got the pills!" cried Wattie, panting like the hart. "Coom on, man, gi'e's that sling!"

He plumbed away, blaspheming, without success. I had already decided that whoever drank from that well, it wasn't going to be me. We'd better pack it in, I said.

"Nivver!" cried Wattie, straining over the wall. "Sink, ye sod! Ah, hell! Ah'll git thee, thoo varmint! Giddoon!" But even he had to give up at last. "There's nowt for it," he croaked. "One of us'll efta ga doon." They both looked at me. "It'll efta be thee, Jock."

Now I know this was the point where I should have put my foot down, and indeed I did demur, quite forcibly, but Grandarse whined that he was dee-eye-drated, and I was his only hope. Which was true, for Wattie weighed thirteen stone, and Grandarse himself would have needed a cattle sling. Anyway, there was no sign of our having to advance soon, and it is difficult for a feckless youth to resist the pleadings of his elders, even when he knows they're idiots. And a good lance-corporal should look after his men. Or perhaps I'd got a touch of the sun. So a few seconds later I was hanging upside down just above the green surface, preparing to scoop with my hat, while Wattie and Grandarse, mumbling as they chewed purification pills, held my legs. To do this, they had to stand erect, oblivious of the fact that Jap was still in the vicinity.

In that confined space I didn't hear the machine-gun opening up, but I was aware of shots smacking into the well-head, splinters raining down, startled bellows from overhead, and of my legs being released. And that, my dears, is how grandpa came to fall down a well during the last great battle of World War Two.

I took the water smoothly, sliding in rather than falling, and fortunately the shaft was wide enough for me to turn underwater and come up head first, coughing and clawing waterweed out of my eyes. After the initial shock it was quite pleasantly cool, and I trod water while muffled shots sounded from the world above, and Grandarse announced my plight – he sounded as though he was speaking with his face pressed to earth; the section was evidently firing, and either they or the well-head were being fired upon in return. But it was difficult to tell, and the thought crossed my mind that *if* Jap counter-attacked successfully, I was going to be embarrassed. There wasn't a hope of climbing out, and I was just wondering how long I could tread water in heavy boots, when a bush-hatted head appeared above.

"W'at the hell are you daein'?" demanded Sergeant Hutton.

I try to be civil to superiors, but there are limits.

"I'm attacking Pyawbwe by submarine!" I shouted. "What the hell does it look like I'm doing? That bloody idiot Grandarse dropped me!"

"Jesus wept! Toorn yer back an' they're divin' doon bloody wells!" His head vanished, and I heard him bawling to the section to git rifle-slings an' git that gormless Scotch git oot afore 'e droons. The firing had stopped, and presently they were all hanging over the lip, helpless with mirth, asking if I needed purification pills and was the watter loovly and nut tae piss in it or they'd play war wid us.* To all of which I did not deign to reply.

They hauled me out with the help of rifle slings, and Hutton returned raging.

"Git the hell oot o' this afore Long John sees ye! You, Jock – it's dozy boogers like you that toorns ma hair grey! Christ, Corporal Peel, if ye can't keep a better grip on yer section – ah, the hell! Git formed oop! We're advancin'!"

The lines were moving on again, Nine Section consisting of eight men and a pillar of cloud, or rather steam, under a sodden bush-hat. I squelched for only a few minutes, for such was the heat that when the next check occurred, a Jap sniper opening up on the left and sending us diving for cover, I was bone dry again – and raging thirsty. But for the next hour there was little time to drink or to worry about what bugs I might have absorbed during my immer-

---

* A curious expression which I believe is peculiar to Carlisle. To "play war" is to scold violently.

sion; this was the sticky time with the company on our right in trouble, and Long John saved the day by fighting us forward to outflank the objective and help the other company on to it. I should remember it clearly, but the fact is that my memories are too uncertain to attempt a coherent narrative; I can only suppose that Nine Section played no significant part beyond giving covering fire; that I do remember, and a trivial incident when I was lying prone behind a little bund taking occasional shots at a rock which I'd been told concealed a sniper, and a man with a wireless set came tumbling down on me. I'd known him back home, and he addressed me not as Jock, but by name: "Aye-aye, Geordie, what fettle?" and asked me where Long John was. I thought he was ahead and left, so he muttered "He who hesitates is lost" and darted away with his wireless set, zig-zagging while I gave the rock five rounds rapid. He made it, and we have pints together every September with Long John and others.

And some time later we were all on our feet and going like hell for the ruins with the rusted railway line running through them; we went into them shooting, and there was an iron wagon by the tracks, half-derailed, and beyond it was the long slope, with Japanese running across it.

Nick jumped into the wagon, and I was on his heels. It was open on the far side, like a picture window; it might have been designed as a firing point for kneeling marksmen. All around the wagon men were yelling with excitement, throwing themselves down on the rubble and blazing away at those running figures, some of whom must have turned to fire at us, for two or three shots clanged against the wagon. But most of them were running, and all we had to do was pick our targets.

This was something new. In my previous contacts with the enemy, everything had been split-second in crisis, with nothing to do but react at speed, snap-shooting, grabbing for a grenade, throwing it, shooting again. There had been no time to think; it had been scramble and shoot and hope, trying to keep cool and yet move and act like lightning – in a way like a goal-mouth scramble or a rally at the net in tennis or a loose scrum near the line when the ball is like soap and there are bodies flying everywhere.

But in that railway wagon it was more like the moment when you're clear with the ball and know you have a few yards to move in and a few seconds to think about it. There wasn't much time, but enough: to pick a target, hang for an instant on the aim to make sure, take the first pressure according to the manual – and then the second.

It was exciting; no other word for it, and no explanation needed, for honest folk. We all have kindly impulses, fostered by two thousand years of Christian teaching, gentle Jesus, and love they neighbour, but we have the killer instinct, too, the murderous impulse of the hunter . . . but one must not say so. The young men going out to the Gulf felt obliged to tell the cameras that they felt nothing personal against the Iraqis, and wished them no harm – but I know, for I have felt it, that when an Iraqi came in their sights, the blood-lust would take them hot and strong. Never mind the excuse that this is what a soldier is trained for, that it is his duty, that like 007 he is licensed to kill; the truth is that he gets a kick out of it – which may be one reason why, when he is asked later: "Did you ever kill a Jap (or a German or an Iraqi)?" he will often dodge the question. Other reasons include a decent reticence, an understandable wish not to dwell on unpleasant memories, a reluctance to be thought a line-shooter or a psychopath, and a sense that the question is in doubtful taste. (The best answer, incidentally, is "Why do you want to know?" That makes them think.)

Such considerations don't arise when the human target appears in the V of the backsight. You're just thankful for the chance and concentrate on keeping the aim steady – which is not easy when you're excited, and fearful that they'll get away. First pressure and second pressure is all very well for the first five shots, but by the time I was at the bottom of my magazine I must have been snatch-ing at the trigger, and Nick was pausing between shots to observe: "Ye're firin' low an' left, Jock – that's it!" And then suddenly pointing, as he reloaded, to a fallen figure and shouting: "Git that booger – he's nobbut wounded!"

There are many grey areas around the Geneva convention, I suppose: I know a sergeant from another platoon at one stage yelled: "Ower theer! They're gittin' the wounded away!" and directed a Bren gun accordingly. A moment later he stumbled into the wagon beside us, shaking his head violently and striking his ears. "Ah's gone deef! Ah can't 'ear a bloody thing!" And he couldn't; even a rifle fired within a few feet of him was inaudible. (It turned out to be a medical curiosity: a shell had burst close to him on the advance, but his hearing had been fine until he was directing fire up the slope, and had gone stone deaf in an instant. A few hours later his hearing came back equally suddenly.)

Then it must have been all over, for the firing stopped and the section was reassembling among the ruins by the railway line, no one missing, no one wounded, everyone with that dazed, weary look that men wear after battle. We must have reached our objective for the day, for that was where we dug in, not far from the railway track – the derailed wagon which Nick and I had occupied became the section H.Q. I brewed up, and it was evening, and patrols were moving across the gentle slope to our front, sweeping the ground. We were hacking out our slit-trenches in the stony earth and boiling out our rifles when Corporal Peel came back from Company H.Q. and told me to take a couple of men and have a look at a small square building away on our left front, just to make sure it was unoccupied.

The last thing I needed just then was a half-mile hike over broken ground. For some days I'd been suffering from that military curse, foot-rot; it had been getting worse all day, and my feet felt like fiery sponges. But there it was; I took Morton, who had a tommy-gun, and Wedge, and we set off for the building, scanning right and left for wounded Japs. There weren't any; indeed, on this flank there was only an occasional body sprawled on the rocky earth with the flies buzzing in the dying sunlight. The patrols had swept the area, but not as far as the little square building which stood about three hundred yards away on level ground where the slope petered out.

It looked deserted enough, four broken walls and no roof, and while it was just the spot for a sniper, with a good field of fire on our forward positions, I doubted if Jap was in residence. I was in that resentful, foot-sore state where I could convince myself that this was a ridiculous, unnecessary chore; it wasn't reasonable, after we'd had our ration of war for the day, that there should be any more to come. That is how stupid you can be when you're tired. Away to our right there was the occasional sound of a shot, and once a rattle of Bren fire, but I approached that house knowing it would be empty, with no more precaution than signing to Wedge and Morton to watch the sides while I went in through the ruined doorway.

He was there, though, and if he hadn't been wounded he'd have had me. I had taken a cautious step over the broken door-frame, and was glancing left when I heard the clatter to my right and he was rearing up from behind a pile of rubble, grabbing for his rifle, and I fired and he gave the kind of "ouch!" that you make when you stub your toe and fell face down on the tangle of broken masonry. I whipped another round up the spout, jumping back to get my shoulders against the wall, but there was no one else in the little ruined room. His body was settling, twitching a little, then he was still. Strange, I can't remember his face at all, but I can still see his head as he lay prone, with the grey stubble on his skull, and beside it was a small wooden plaque which I have in a drawer somewhere: it's about the size of a visiting card, with what looks like a sacred figure among sunrays stamped on it, and a little hole which suggests it was worn on a string. One of his puttees was off, and there was a bloody rag wrapped round his wounded leg.

The shot brought the other two at the double, Morton crying: "Is 'e dead?" I said he was, and Morton stepped forward and put a single shot into his back. I witnessed a similar incident, later, when a "dead" Jap came to life after a *burst* from a Thompson hit him, but this one did no more than jerk with the shot. We turned him over to see if he was carrying anything, but he seemed to be just a private soldier.

I had to take a moment to draw breath, feeling shaken at the unexpectness of the thing and my own folly (never think he *can't* be there, that's when the bastard's sure to be there), and then we took a brief scout about fifty yards beyond the building – going the second mile, if you like. But that was far enough; shock followed by relief doesn't cure burning feet, and I was tired enough to weep. How tired I didn't realise until we were retracing our steps past the ruined building, and from far behind us there was a shot which passed overhead – the kind of distant speculative effort I'd heard when I was first fired on, years ago, at Meiktila. I'd been quite impressed, then; now, with my soles hot and raging, and having had the fright of my life from the wounded Jap, and being bloody weary and hungry and thirsty and sick to death of everything, I just pulled up and looked back and gave vent to my feelings with a great roar of: "Oh, bugger off!" Two more shots came, passing harmlessly above us, and I noticed that Wedge and Morton didn't even duck. It wasn't coolness under fire; it's just that sometimes you're so brassed off that you couldn't care less, and he was so far away he couldn't have hit a barn door with the knocker.

Two hours later everything was fine. It had been a long, dirty day, but it ended well, in a drowsy feeling of contentment. I reported finding the Jap to Peel, and I seem to remember that an o.p. was being set up in the little building, and I know we had no stags to stand because all through the night our patrols were busy in the no man's land in front of our positions. Peel thought that we were almost alone in having reached our objective, and that the attacks on the other sides of the town hadn't gone so well, but tomorrow would see the finish of it.

I remember standing in a group round the'fire, sipping hot tea and smoking happily, having bathed my feet and smothered them in the M.O.'s foot-powder, listening to the ribaldries, and all the shelling and the shooting on the slope and my plunge down that blasted well (oh, God, why did You give me such a talent for the ridiculous?), and the horrid moment when I heard the clatter in that little room and fired by pure reflex action, and the distant sniper – they all seemed a long time ago, and I was too dozzened to care about them.

We walked slowly back to the rusted railway wagon where we would sleep head to toe along its length, and some were already settling into their blankets while others stood in the warm gloom chatting; Wattie and Wedge were arguing about the North Star, and Grandarse was yawning that he was aboot tired, and Parker was telling us about Shanghai before the war, and Peel was saying he didn't think we would be going in again tomorrow. As on the night after the temple wood duffy, there was no talk of the battle, but neither was there the silence that had been cast then by the deaths of Gale and Little. We sensed that it had been a good day;* we had got there and killed a lot of Japanese for only ten wounded in the company; Long John had played a stormer, and the company was pleased with its commander and with itself. It was bedtime, and all well; the fight was done, and the drought and rage of extreme toil, the breathlessness and the faintness, had been soothed by supper, tea, and tobacco, and the happy warriors were settling down.

"'Ey, Dook," said Forster, "git thee arse off the pillow!"

"My arse isn't on your pillow, Foshie," said the Duke. "It's my feet."

"Weel, they stink bloody rotten! They want boilin' oot!"

"I suppose you think your feet smell like Madame Dubarry's tits!" said the Duke, mildly incensed, and there was a long pause. Then:

"W'ee's tits did ye say?" asked Grandarse.

"Madame Dubarry's."

"W'ee th' 'ell's she?" asked Wattie.

"A French king's tart," said Peel. "Didn't you see the picture?"

"Mistress of one of the Louie's, if you must know," said the Duke, yawning. "Which one, Jock – fourteenth, fifteenth?"

"Dunno. Think of a number."

"Shurroop, ye eddicated gits! W'at picter, Tommo?"

"Dubarry was a Lady. Lucille Ball was in it, and that Red Skelton feller."

"By God!" rasped Forster. "Loo-seel Ball! Ah could dae wi' that alangside us. Ah'd give 'er soom stick!"

"Lucky Miss Ball, to be in California," murmured the Duke.

"She's awreet. Ah fancy Susanna Foster meself," said Wedge, with dreamy reverence. "By, she's a loovly lass, that! Sings, an' a' – she can't 'alf twilt† it!"

"I remember her," said the Duke. "Blonde, sort of ice maiden. C above Top C, very hard, clear voice. Nice legs."

---

* It had been a brilliant one. To the battalion's credit, it alone, out of the four attacks launched on the town, fully achieved its objective, killing 151 Japanese for the loss of seven dead and 33 wounded. The company's figures were 92 Japanese for the loss of only 10 wounded.

† Literally, to beat, chastise (Cumbrian), hence to perform with vigour

"Nivver mind bloody legs!" cried Grandarse, keeping to the essentials. "Warraboot this French bint's tits, Dook? Waddid they smell like?"

"How the hell should I know? I was merely making a comparison with Foshie's revolting feet. Go to sleep!"

"An' dream of great tits of 'istory," chuckled Parker.

"They reckon Susanna Foster's legs is better'n Marlene Dietrich's or Betty Grable's," said Wedge. "See 'er in *Phantom o' th' Opera* –"

"Ah seen that fillum, an' nivver saw 'er bloody legs!" objected Wattie. "She wes wearin' lang goons a' the time!"

"Well, aye, man! It wes a 'istorical picter, in th' old days, in Paris –"

"Famous for various Louies, Madame Dubarry, and tits," groaned the Duke. "Why don't I keep my mouth shut?"

"That was the film abaht the feller in the sewer, with a mask on 'is face, 'cos 'e'd been given the acid –"

"Claude Rains," said Wedge.

"Claude Rains?" cried Grandarse, on a new tack. "That minds us! 'Ey, Jock – did ye ivver read that book, The Cat's Revenge, by Claude Balls?"

"I know," I said, "and The Nail in the Banisters, by R. Stornoway."

Forster, naturally, knew many more titles, too obscene to mention, and that started them on limericks, each one concluded by the singing, in unison, of "That was a cute little rhyme, sing us another one, just like the other one, sing us another one, do-o-oo!" It must have lulled me to sleep, for when I was awakened by Grandarse's snoring and had elbowed him into silence, the rest of the wagon was in heavy-breathing repose, except for Wedge, who was muttering that Susanna Foster could have been a great opera singer but she made more money in Hollywood, and any roads she was better-looking than Lucille Ball or Madame Doo-whatsit . . .

PYAWBWE FELL NEXT DAY without a shot fired. A patrol from the battalion went into the town centre at dawn, but Jap was dead or gone away. There were more than 1100 of his bodies on the ground, and thirteen guns abandoned; his army had finally, to quote Slim, been torn apart, and while the remnants would fight on desperately in the jungly swamp of southern Burma in the monsoon, they were never a coherent force again. Which makes a private soldier wonder why Tokyo, surveying its battered lines from Burma to the Pacific, didn't acknowledge that all hope was gone, and call it a day. But governments, of course, never do. They're not lying with a shattered leg in the wreckage of a little room, too far gone to hear the footsteps outside the door.

It must have been on that following day that we shifted our pits, for I remember a slow sweep across open rubble-strewn ground where the Japs had died in their tracks, and their corpses were lying where they had fallen, in stiff grotesque attitudes. I don't remember any vultures or kites; our advance may have scared them off. One body had its stomach ripped open, and the swollen intestine protruded like a great balloon; someone pricked it with his bayonet, idly, and there was a most disgusting stench.

"Aw, Jesus – pack it oop!" cried Grandarse, and Nick looked about him and upbraided the dead in withering terms.

"Ye stupid sods! Ye stupid Japanni sods! Look at the fookin' state of ye! Ye wadn't listen – an' yer all fookin' deid! Tojo's way! Ye dumb bastards! Ye coulda bin suppin' chah an' screwin' geeshas in yer fookin' lal paper 'ooses – an' look at ye! Ah doan't knaw." He shook his head. "All the way frae fookin' Japan!"

If it sounds shocking, it didn't at the time. Nick had a bitter sense of humour, but I'm sure that on this occasion he was simply saying what he thought. He didn't pity the Japs; none of us did. If anything, he was angry, not only at the folly that those bodies

represented, but because only yesterday they had been al
trying to kill us, and if he had added: "An' serve ye ri___ _
wouldn't have been surprised – or disagreed.

There is much talk today of guilt as an aftermath of war – guilt
over killing the enemy, and even guilt for surviving. Much depends
on the circumstances, but I doubt if many of Fourteenth Army
lose much sleep over dead Japanese. For one thing, they were a
no-surrender enemy and if we hadn't killed them they would surely
have killed us. But there was more to it than that. It may appal a
generation who have been dragooned into considering racism the
ultimate crime, but I believe there was a feeling (there was in me)
that the Jap was farther down the human scale than the European.
It is a feeling that I see reflected today in institutions and people
who would deny hotly that they are subconscious racists – the
presence of TV cameras ensured a superficial concern for the Kurd-
ish refugees and Bangladeshi flood victims, but we all know that
the Western reaction would have been immeasurably greater if a
similar diasaster had occurred in Australia or Canada or Europe;
some people seem to count more than others, with liberals as well
as reactionaries, and it is folly to pretend that racial kinship and
likeness are not at the bottom of it.

As to the Japanese of fifty years ago, there is no question that
he was viewed in an entirely different light from our European
enemies. Would the atomic bomb have been dropped on Berlin,
or Rome, or Vienna? No doubt newspaper reports and broadcasts
had encouraged us, civilians and military, to regard him as an evil,
misshapen, buck-toothed barbarian who looked and behaved like
something sub-Stone Age; the experiences of Allied prisoners of
war demonstrated that the reports had not lied and reinforced the
view that the only good Jap was a dead one. And we were right,
then.

It is difficult for me to equate the Japanese of the 'forties with
those neat, eager, apparently polite young men whom I see in
airports and tourist centres, bustling, smiling, and clicking their
Leicas. But old feelings persist, and I prefer not to sit beside them.
Nor will I buy a Japanese car (for one thing, I think that German
cars are better). And if I am a foolish and bigoted old man, I can
only plead the excuse that apologists are forever advancing on

behalf of modern criminals – like them, I am a victim of my environment and upbringing; I need understanding. So, I suspect, do most of my old comrades who gave the best years of their lives (and sometimes life itself) to decreasing the population of Japan. Do not reproach them with it, but be thankful.

As to old grudges and hatreds . . . well, one cannot help what one feels, and guilt and regret just don't come into it. At the same time, I remember watching, a year or two ago, televised interviews with old Japanese soldiers who had fought in the war, and being conscious, despite myself, of a sort of . . . not sympathy, but a curious sort of recognition of the wrinkled old bastards, sitting in their gardens in their sports shirts, blinking cheerfully in the sunlight, reminiscing in throat-clearing croaks about battles long ago. It crossed my mind: were any of you on the Pyawbwe slope, and lived to tell the tale? Well, if they did, at this time of day I don't mind.

We were at Pyawbwe a week, but it seemed longer, possibly because all of a sudden there was nothing very active to do – no stags, no patrols, no fatigues even. We were waiting for the war to catch up with us, and there was time to get a decent all-over bath, to collect our big packs from the trucks and rummage through them, to write letters at leisure, to re-read and abandon the short story I'd begun the night Jap broke through the wire, to give kit and weapons a thorough going-over – in my case, to take possession of a tommy-gun, much against my will. I had grown to love my old snub-nosed Lee Enfield, and resented having to part with it, but it was usual for a section 2i/c to carry a Thompson if one were available, so I accepted the thing and detested it. It was ugly, ungainly, I hadn't been trained in its use or taught to regard it as a wife, and it couldn't have come within ten feet of a falling plate at two hundred yards. Its whole purpose was automatic, and my view was that if single aimed shots had been good enough for the Duke of Wellington, they were good enough for me. For some reason I felt like a bully, just carrying it, and it rusted like an old bed-frame. I threw it in a Sittang creek, eventually, but in the meantime I had to go about like Lance-corporal Capone.

I associate that week at Pyawbwe with the first return to something like normal life since the campaign began. A mobile cinema arrived and showed us a film, *Northern Pursuit*, in which Errol Flynn was a dashing Mountie foiling Nazi agents in Canada – I assume he foiled them, for the projector broke down halfway, to howls of rage from the groundlings. Flynn was in terribly bad odour at that time, for having appeared in a movie called *Objective Burma* which had given great offence in Britain because it had concentrated on America's part in the Burma campaign; it had been withdrawn from U.K. cinemas after outraged baying from the popular press and, I believe, politicians. That being so, a Flynn movie might have seemed an odd choice for a Fourteenth Army audience, but it wasn't: Flynn, his absence from the war notwithstanding, was popular with the forces, who admired his lifestyle and wished they'd had half his bother. And we would have liked to see *Objective Burma* for ourselves, if only in the hope of discovering inaccuracies and being able to hurl abuse at the screen. In that we would have been disappointed; I saw it years later, and it was an above-average war picture which may well have been a fair reflection of the Stilwell–Merrill operations in the north for all I know. The Americans did play a supporting role in the Burma land war, and if they wanted to make a movie about it, good luck to them.

We liked war movies, British or American, but I realise that their popularity in war-time may seem strange nowadays, when super-sensitivity is the rule. I suppose it is natural enough to postpone the TV showing of an air disaster movie when there is a real air crash in the news, or even to withhold an American prison drama of the 'forties at a time when rioters are hurling slates from the roof of a British jail. But when the showing of *Carry On up the Khyber* was cancelled during the Gulf crisis because it showed comic British troops opposed to comic Muslims, one couldn't help recalling the delight with which war-time audiences hailed movies in which George Formby and Will Hay, among others, made merry of the struggle against the Nazis. No one took the war less seriously because of such entertainments; they did not offend taste, and far from undermining morale, they strengthened it. Times, and perhaps the sense of humour, have changed.

Half of *Northern Pursuit* was not our only relaxation; a great bundle of magazines was distributed, and one of them contained, to the delight of Wedge, a full-page pin-up of the idolised Susanna Foster displaying her celebrated legs; he affixed it to the rusted side of the railway wagon and contemplated it with deep-breathing worship, and even Grandarse was moved to admit that she was "not a bad bit stoof" which from him was the equivalent of a poem from Herrick.

I got two paperbacks from home which I had requested: *Henry V*, which we had done in my last year at school and for which I had developed a deep affection, and *Three Men in a Boat* – not that I was a devotee of Jerome's, but I had felt that comedy and a reminder of the beauties of the English countryside wouldn't come amiss. I had also thought that it might be acceptable when passed round the section, but I didn't expect any takers for Shakespeare, intellectual snob that I was. The result was instructive.

I was lying on my groundsheet, renewing acquaintance with Jerome and the tin of pineapple, when Sergeant Hutton squatted down beside me.

"W'at ye readin', then? W'at's this? 'Enry Vee – bloody 'ell, by William Shekspeer!" He gave me a withering look, and leafed over a page. "Enter Chorus. O for a muse of fire that wad . . . Fook me!" He riffled the pages. "Aye, weel, we'll 'ev a look." And such is the way of sergeants, he removed it without by-your-leave; that's one that won't be away long, I thought.

I was wrong. Three days later it had not been returned, and having exhausted Jerome and the magazines I was making do with the Fourteenth Army newspaper, *SEAC*, famous for its little cartoon character, Professor Flitt,* a jungle infantryman who commented memorably on the passing scene. And I was reading a verse by the paper's film critic

> I really do not care a heck
> For handsome Mr Gregory Peck,
> But I would knock off work at four
> To see Miss Dorothy Lamour

---

* Or was it spelled Phlitt?

when Hutton loafed up and tossed *Henry V* down beside me and seated himself on the section grub-box. A silence followed, and I asked if he had liked it. He indicated the book.

"Was Shekspeer ivver in th'Army?"

I said that most scholars thought not, but that there were blanks in his life, so it was possible that, like his friend Ben Jonson, he had served in the Low Countries, or even in Italy. Hutton shook his head.

"If 'e wesn't in th'Army, Ah'll stand tappin'.* 'E knaws too bloody much aboot it, man."

This was fascinating. Hutton was a military hard case who had probably left school long before 14, and his speech and manner suggested that his normal and infrequent reading consisted of company orders and the sports headlines. But Shakespeare had talked to him across the centuries – admittedly on his own subject. I suggested hesitantly that the Bard might have picked up a good deal just from talking to military men; Hutton brushed the notion aside.

"Nivver! Ye knaw them three – Bates, an' them, talkin' afore the battle? Ye doan't git that frae lissenin' in pubs, son. Naw, 'e's bin theer." He gave me the hard, aggressive stare of the Cumbrian who is not to be contradicted. "That's my opinion, any roads. An' them oothers – the Frenchmen, the nawblemen, tryin' to kid on that they couldn't care less, w'en they're shittin' blue lights? Girraway! An' the Constable tekkin' the piss oot o' watsisname –"

"The Dauphin."

"Aye." He shook his head in admiration. "Naw, ye've 'eerd it a' afore – in different wurrds, like. Them fower officers, the Englishman an' the Scotsman an' the Irishman an' the Welshman – Ah mean, 'e's got their chat off, 'esn't 'e? Ye could tell w'ich wez w'ich, widoot bein' told. That Welsh booger!" He laughed aloud, a thing he rarely did. "Talk till the bloody coos coom yam, the Taffies!" He frowned. "Naw, Ah nivver rid owt be Shekspeer afore – Ah mean, ye 'ear the name, like . . ." He shrugged eloquently. "Mind, there's times Ah doan't knaw w'at th' 'ell 'e's talkin' aboot –"

* "I'm a Dutchman", probably from "tap", meaning mad.

"You and me both," I said, wondering uneasily if there were more passages obscure to me than there were to him. He sat for a moment and then misquoted (and I'm not sure that Shakespeare's version is better):

"There's nut many dies weel that dies in a battle. By Christ, 'e's reet theer. It's a good bit, that." He got up. "Thanks for the lend on't, Jock."

I said that if he'd liked it, he would like *Henry IV*, too. "Falstaff's bloody funny, and you'd like Hotspur –"

" 'Ev ye got it?"

I apologised that I hadn't, and promised to write for it. By way of a trailer I told him as much as I remembered of Hotspur's "When the fight was done" speech, but I'm no Sean Connery, and although he nodded politely I could see I was a poor substitute for the written word.

He went off, leaving me to reflect that I had learned something more about *Henry V*, and Shakespeare. In his own way Hutton was as expert a commentator as Dover Wilson or Peter Alexander; he was a lot closer to Bates and Court and Williams (and Captains Jamy and Fluellen) than they could ever hope to be. And I still wonder if Shakespeare *was* in the Army.

My other strongest memory of Pyawbwe is of getting to know the Gurkhas, whose pits were close to ours, and to whom I made regular visits to trade rations. As Grandarse said, they would have sold their souls for tinned herrings in tomato sauce, or for sardines, and I only had to stroll across to their positions with a couple of the oval tins in my hand to be greeted with huge smiles and squeals of "Hey, Jock – chapatti, dood, cheeny! Shabash!*" And out would come the sugar and condensed milk, or the big flat chapattis which they baked on their company fire, by way of exchange, the deal being cemented by the offer of cigarettes on my part and the acceptance of a huge mug of their sickly sweet tea, to be drunk sitting in the middle of a grinning chattering group of those wonderful little men. There is nothing like tea in the afternoon, whether it is in snug comfort at home on a winter's day, or on the terrace of Reid's or in the cool white peace of the old Raffles in

* Bravo!

Singapore, or the Hong Kong Peninsula (even if they did put onion with the salmon sandwiches), or in an English tea-shop – but having tea with the Gurkhas is something special, for they radiate a cheer and good-fellowship that has to be experienced, and once you have, you understand why British soldiers have always held them in an affection that is pretty close to love.

Exuberance is a poor word for their social behaviour. Except for a few exchanges in broken Urdu we could not converse, but having heard me addressed as Jock they knew I was Scotch, which sent them into peals of delight, with half a dozen of them scurrying away to bring their company piper, who regaled me with "Scotland the Brave" and "Cock o' the North" while sundry of his comrades marched up and down, scowling horribly in what I took to be Caledonian imitation. One of them got so carried away that he suddenly leaped in front of me, grimacing and yelling: "Hey, Jock – Japanni *mat karo!*" (which very loosely translates as "Death to the Japanese!") and went into a violent pantomime in which he clove the air with his kukri, to enthusiastic applause, and then enacted the dying enemy, writhing on the ground screaming: "Banzai *bus!* Banzai *bus!*" and feigning death while his friends sat round and hurled abuse at his corpse. After which they all collapsed in laughter, and we had some more tea.

A Gurkha subaltern whom I met later told me that commanding a platoon of them was like leading a group of perfectly-disciplined ten-year-olds, and I believe him. Watching them playing football, for example, was like watching very small children, for they had not the least idea of playing the game; they had no interest in teams or goals or anything of the sort. Their one idea was to chase the ball in a screaming, laughing mob, booting it as far as possible and running after it with their little skulls gleaming and pigtails bobbing, to boot it again. Unless chance directed the ball back to where they started, they were liable to vanish into the distance, yelling: "Futtbal! Futtbal!" – and the extraordinary thing was that they did it properly dressed, with their puttees on and shirts buttoned at the wrists.

Their only other recreation that I saw was the catapult – the Y-and-elastic toy which the Americans call a slingshot. Many

Gurkhas carried them in their hip-pockets, and if you were suddenly stung *a tergo* and heard a smothered giggle from behind a tree, it was worth stopping and shouting: "*Idderao,* Johnny! *Ham dekko,** you little bugger!" just for the pleasure of seeing the small face come peeping cautiously out, followed by the marksman himself, wearing a sheepish grin and holding up his catapult by way of explanation, as if you didn't know. So far as I could see they confined themselves to British targets (there seemed to be no great love lost between them and the Indian regiments, especially the Sikhs), and we took it as a compliment. No one would have dreamed of taking offence; it would have been downright cruel, for the Gurkha was as eager to please as a playful grandchild. The thought of quarrelling with one of them never even occurred – for one thing, you'd be better picking a fight with a king cobra.

That was a thing that was often hard to remember: that this delightful little man, with his ungainly walk and protruding backside and impish grin, who barely came up to your shoulder and was one of nature's born comedians, was also probably the most fatal fighting man on earth. Their reckless courage was legendary, and I imagine that in proportion to their numbers they must have won more Victoria Crosses than any other race in the Army. I was never among them during an action, but I was once privileged to watch, from a distance, a company of them attacking a Japanese position. There was a Highland unit on their left, advancing with that slow, deliberate 110-paces-to-the-minute tread which used to be the trademark of the kilted regiments; the Gurkhas had to trot to keep up, little green figures with their bush-hats at the rakish Gurkha angle, each man with his rifle at the trail in his left hand and his drawn kukri in his right. Over .the last few yards the Highlanders suddenly accelerated, but any noise they made was drowned by the ear-splitting scream of the little hillmen going like demented dwarves, brandishing their knives as they scampered into the trees – and I was profoundly glad that I was not Japanese. One of the Highlanders told me later that when they came out again they found the ground before

* "Come here, Johnny! I can see you!"

the position littered with Gurkha rifles: most of them had gone in with kukris alone.

There was another occasion when a Gurkha platoon close to us held a position against two companies of Japanese who wouldn't take no for answer, but kept coming time and again, yelling "Banzai!"; the Gurkhas just stood fast and stopped them until the position was littered with Jap dead. When the Gurkhas were finally withdrawn it was discovered that they hadn't a single round of ammunition among them.

I knew only one Gurkha really well, a fellow-cadet at Officers' Training School after the war. Unlike the Gurkhas I'd known in Burma, he was far from child-like, being as bright intellectually as anyone in the cadet company, but if he had a sharpness and dignity beyond the jolly little killers of the 17th Division, he was quite as genial and given to merriment. Like many Gurkhas, he answered to the name of Thapa (the h is silent), and played in front of me in the company soccer team, a quicksilver terrier of an inside man who was everywhere at once, clapping his hands and clucking "Jock-Jock-Jock-Jock-Jock!" like a hysterical hen if I didn't give him the ball fast enough, savaging opponents twice his weight and giggling as he held the goalkeeper's jersey at corner kicks (he was one who had learned the rules, and then some).

Naturally, he was a general favourite in that company of young men, half of us British, the other half drawn from most of the warrior races of India; Thapa was the only Gurkha, but there was also a black Nigerian and I think one or two Malays – it was a remarkable international mix with one common goal, a commission in H.M. Forces, and I wish some of our race relations experts could have seen us, and heard the entirely uninhibited mess discussions on politics (this was shortly before Indian independence and, just for interest, a majority of the Indian cadets were against it), religion, sport, military shop, social gossip, world affairs, and so on. Indeed, I wish I had tapes of them myself: our average age would be in the early twenties, ranging from pink schoolboys from England to a gnarled Pathan (he must have been all of twenty-nine) with three rows of ribbons, and we talked and argued with a freedom that would have had a T.V. discussion host reaching for his panic button. One result of this was that I saw a most disturbing phenomenon: an angry Gurkha.

We were talking politics, and a clever and articulate Congress Party supporter, who happened to be extremely swarthy, got very emotional. "You British," he cried, "with the help of this type of people –" here he indicated Thapa and a couple of Sikhs "– have been exploiting this land for centurees! You have bled India white!"

One of the Sikhs murmured behind his gin and tonic: "It hasn't had much visible effect on you," which was well below the belt, but it might have passed if the Nigerian hadn't laughed fit to rattle the chandelier. Thapa elbowed him, muttering to him to shut up, and the Congress boy, mistaking the gesture, rounded on Thapa and was ill-advised enough to call him "a monkey bastard".

Thapa's grin vanished as though it had been wiped off. He didn't say anything, just stared at the other, and then suddenly turned and *ran* out of the mess. Some of us went after him, calling him to come back, but he ran full tilt to his quarters, where we found him unearthing his kukri from a tin trunk while his native bearer gibbered in a corner. Thapa was mouthing dreadful things about sons of owls and swine, and it took four of us to wrestle him down while some brave soul stood on his wrist and secured the kukri. Then we sat on him until the Senior Under Officer arrived, by which time he had stopped struggling and we judged it safe to let him go. But he was still grey with rage, and when the S.U.O. had finished tearing strips off him he flatly announced his intention of killing the Congress boy at the earliest opportunity; there was no doubt whatever that he meant it. We reasoned with him, literally for hours, pointing out that he'd certainly swing for it; that meant nothing, and it was only when the S.U.O., inspired, assured him that as a murderer he hadn't a hope of a commission, that he showed signs of weakening. Finally, round about lights out, he gave his word of honour not to avenge the insult provided the Congress wallah apologised – which I'm bound to say the latter did with a good grace. But Thapa would not shake hands, or even look at him thereafter, and he was never quite the same cheery companion again. I suppose he's dead now – Gurkhas are not noted for longevity – and I sometimes wonder where the Congress boy is, and the laughing Nigerian, and the Sikh whose snide crack started it all.

With the Army reduced to a shadow of its old self, there are many fewer Gurkhas in British service nowadays, and they look subtly different from the happy little toughs of forty years ago: they are taller and better shaped, and the broad grinning faces I remember have given way to more refined and serious features. The race can hardly have changed in so short a time, and I wonder if they are being recruited with a view to size. Or perhaps I'm just imagining the change; even half a century ago a Gurkha on parade was as regimental and poker-faced a soldier as any, and it was only up the road, with his catapult in his pocket and his pigtail and kukri bouncing as he trotted along, that you got the big grin and the cheery wave and the high-pitched yell of "*Shabash*, Jock! Rangoon *jao!*" That's how I remember him, and always will.

Towards the end of our week at Pyawbwe I went for a walk at random, to think about things. A letter from my parents had referred to the imminent collapse of Germany, and the possibility of the whole war being over soon – it must have been natural at home to suppose that once Hitler was out of the way, the whole Axis would collapse, but the thought hadn't even crossed Nine Section's mind. We were in our own hot little world, our own private war, and it wouldn't be over until we reached Rangoon, 300 miles due south, with Jap in between. It might well not be over even then; there would still be Malaya and Siam to clear, as far as Bangkok and Singapore. In Delhi and London they might know that the Japanese position in Burma was beyond repair, but that didn't mean a great deal at our level; he had been bad to shift in the first 100 miles south of the Irrawaddy, and with three times that distance still to go, the outlook wasn't promising. It's all in the point of view: armchair strategists can look at the last stages of a campaign and say there's nothing left but mopping-up, but if you're holding the mop it's different. The last Jap in the last bunker on the last day can be just as fatal to you personally as the biggest battle at the height of the campaign, and you don't look or think much beyond him – wherever he is.

Perhaps you have to be an old soldier, watching the T.V. news telling you that the Iraqis are on the run and another couple of days will do it and hip-hip-hooray it'll be a glorious victory and the boys will be home before you know it, to feel mounting anger as you watch pictures of the tanks rolling and staff officers looking confident at press conferences and studio pundits pontificating – because you know, even if the complacent commentators don't, that some poor sod is still at the sharp end hoping to God that that bunker is empty and that the ground before it isn't mined. (Forgive me if all my sympathy is with Jamy and Fluellen and Bates, Court, and Williams. After all, what else are the commentators going to say?)

So, in April '45 we didn't think of the war ending; it would happen some day, but in the meantime what was the name of the next Jap stronghold down the road, and would our company have to take it? (It's strange, thinking back and remembering, you find yourself falling into the habits of forty-five years ago – bitch, bitch, bitch, moan, moan, moan. That's how soldiers are; before you know it I'll have developed sore feet just sitting at my typewriter.)

As I walked that afternoon, I was digesting the fact that my parents had reached that stage of desperate hope when the end is in sight. Churchill's broad, sunlit uplands were coming into view, and the closer that prospect seemed, the more they must have worried, and asked themselves for the thousandth time what cruel fate had determined that while other campaigns were ended or ending, and other people's children could be accounted safe, their wandering boy should be caught up on the last front of all. It must have been a bitter thought, but they kept it to themselves; their last letter had been full of optimism, and even talk of what I might do after the war. Re-sit my exams in the hope of getting into medicine? That, I knew, was what they wanted, and in my first year in the Army I had gone along with it, even to the extent of getting Highers papers from the education office and brooding disconsolately over Livy and quadratics and volumetric analysis, whatever that was. I hadn't the heart to tell them, now, that I had about as much chance of getting into medicine as I had of beating

Joe Davis at snooker. It wasn't that war had blunted my brain and blighted my hopes; it was just sheer bloody laziness, reinforced by distaste at the thought of peering at boils and rectums. (Or should it be recta? Which reminded me of the old military joke about the fellow who was wounded in the backside. "Rectum? Bloody near killed him!")

No, I had only one ambition now: to get my commission. It was sheer naked pride, nothing else. I thought, with all the conceit of youth, that I was good enough. Better equipped, too, than those contemporaries who had passed where I had failed, and would now be dispersing from their OCTUs with their new pips, wondering what active service would be like, and could they lead people in action. I knew what it was like, now, and that if I shouted: "Come on, Grandarse, Parker, Nick, Forster!" they would follow, even if I did fall down a well along the way. Yes, I would pass the next board if I had to kill the psychiatrist to do it, and get through OCTU, and with Burma in my pay-book I'd apply for the Gurkhas (oh, lord, I'd have to learn Gurkhali as well as Urdu) or the Dogras, or if I opted for British service, the Gordons, my family's regiment, or the Black Watch ... provided the war lasted long enough, for I supposed that once it was over there would be no demand for new subalterns – which shows how little I knew.

In a way, my problem was the reverse of Dr Grantly's, who didn't want his father to die, but since he was going to anyway, couldn't he get a move on so that Grantly could succeed to the bishopric before the Government fell? My thought was that the war was going to end (and the sooner the better, obviously), but since it wouldn't be tomorrow, couldn't it last at least until I hoisted my first pip? Assuming I survived it, of course. Well, it wasn't up to me; I would just have to wait until the tumult and the shouting were fading, and remind Long John of my ambition.

So I reflected, as I wandered through the rubble-strewn outskirts of Pyawbwe, pausing by the railroad track where the Sappers or the R.E.M.E. had got a hand-cart scooting along the rusted rails as a preliminary to opening the line again. I strolled on and sat down for a smoke and quiet survey of our positions, and the town buildings in the distance. I was in a shady spot, with my back to a half-ruined wall, watching the gekkos on the rocks, one moment motionless, and in the next motionless again after a lightning scuttle too fast for the eye to follow. Only when I got up did I realise that the wall I'd been leaning on enclosed the little room where that wounded Jap had been a week ago.

I took a look inside. There was the pile of rubbish where he'd been lying – had he been asleep, or half-unconscious with his wound, when we approached? Possibly; he hadn't known I was there until I was inside the door, when he'd grabbed for his rifle. If he'd been wide awake he'd have had it in his hands, covering the doorway, waiting. In which case I probably wouldn't have been standing here now, speculating about the Gordons and the Gurkhas. Wedge and Morton would have got him.

I went back to the pits thinking

> Two thousand pounds of education
> Drops to a ten-rupee jezzail

and wondering how much my education had cost, and how many rupees it would take to buy a Japanese .300 rifle.

Nine Section weren't at the pits; they had walked across to the main highway, a battered bit of tarmac which wouldn't have qualified as a B road at home. Men were marching down it, past our positions and towards the town, long lines of jungle green and bush-hats, one section on the right margin of the road, the next on the left, the third on the right, and so on – that way you don't eat the dust of the section in front. They were swinging along in battle order, looking just like us, except that they were a little less shop-soiled, and they were whistling in unison "Blaydon Races".

I'm ready to swear to that tune in court, and it has been in my mind for forty years that they must have been Northumberland Fusiliers, our friends from over the fells, or perhaps Durham Light Infantry, for who else would whistle the Geordie national anthem? But I search the official history's index in vain for those two regiments, and for the Sherwood Foresters – I looked for them because I have a vague memory that as I joined the section to watch the march past, Parker was quoting:

The Notts and Jocks are a lousy lot
They lost their Colours in Aldershot

which is a well-known libel on the men of Sherwood. So what regiment they were remains a mystery – but everyone knew what division they belonged to, and Nine Section let the light of its collective countenance shine on them.

"'Ey, Wedge, w'eer are ye, ye moanin' booger?" cried Nixon. "Ye've bin askin' after them ev'ry neet – weel, theer th'are, at lang last, so tek a good look! The Flamin' Arseholes!"

Wedge contemplated them with the kind of rapture he reserved for Miss Foster's pin-up. "Fifth Div," said he, like a man whose ship has finally come in. "Fifth Div."

"'Igh bloody time, an' a'," said Grandarse. "They was meant tae coom through us in Meiktila. Mind? We wes th'anvil, an' they wes meant tae be the fookin' 'ammer. Idle boogers!" He raised his voice. "'Ey, w'at th' 'ell kept ye?"

The corporal of a passing section raised two derisory fingers. "Six months leave in Paint Jungle – what the hell d'you think? We were waiting for you lot to get out the way!"

"Cheeky booger!" cried Grandarse, grinning. "Aye, weel, Rangoon's doon that way, lad! Joost keep ga'n, an' if ye drop owt, doan't fret – we'll pick it oop!" The corporal waved, and then they were past, and "Blaydon Races" was faint in the distance.

To a military psychologist, Grandarse's brief, good-natured exchange with the corporal might have been significant. 5th Div had been meant to relieve us at Meiktila, and it hadn't happened – no fault of 5th Div's, just the necessities of war which had brought us south in a hurry to throw Jap out of Pyawbwe. But if you're Grandarse (or better still, Forster), here is fine fuel for grievance; in no time, you're convinced that you fought 5th Div's battle for them, and belly-ache accordingly – and not just at the time, either. I can hear it, in some ex-Service club forty years on: "Aye, bloody 5th Div! Should 'ev coom through us at Meiktila, but did they boogery! Aye, so we 'ed tae carry the can at Pyawbwe – by Christ, Ah sweated that day, Ah'll tell thee! W'at? An' w'eer were the Flamin' Arseholes, eh? Awreet, Jonty, Ah'll 'ev a pint –

aye, an' a small rum. Good lad. But doan't talk tae me aboot bloody 5th Div . . . etc., etc."*

This being the case, you'd have expected Grandarse to be hurling dog's abuse at 5th Div when they finally came through – but all he came out with was mild pleasantry; he seemed quite glad to see them, and sped them on their way with good wishes. And not just because they were taking the lead and the next stage of the fighting. No, Grandarse was looking farther ahead by now; he had his eyes on a distant goal, which he was confident could be attained, thanks to the system whereby we and 5th Div worked in tandem, first one taking the lead, then the other. I shall let Grandarse himself explain:

"It's like this, sista. 'Oo far are we frae Rangoon? Three 'oonerd mile – reet. Noo, if 5th Div 'ed coom through us at Meiktila, we'd ha' bin coomin' through them again joost aboot noo. 'Stead o' w'ich, they're coomin through us. Noo then, Ah reckon they'll be kept in froont till they're aboot 'alf-way t'Rangoon – an' then we'll leapfrog them an' git theer foorst. See w'at Ah'm gittin' at? If they'd coom through at Meiktila, like they wes meant to, *they*'d ha' bin foorst tae Rangoon. As it is, the boogers 'ev 'ad it! We'll be the ones that tek Rangoon!"

Barrack-room logic at its ripest, plus a fair measure of wishful thinking, but it explained why he had forgotten his fancied grievance against 5th Div. The truth was, however he might gripe and moan, however he might revile the military hierarchy from Hutton to Mountbatten, however he might hate the war and the Far East and wish to God he was shot of them – in spite of all this, Grandarse wanted Rangoon. He wasn't alone: the whole 17th

* I must make it clear, before indignant veterans of the splendid 5th Indian Division call me to account, that the above paragraph was written in ignorance, and gives a false impression. Troops of 5th Div did in fact arrive in Meiktila two weeks before we left the town; in other words, they relieved us as Cowan had promised. However, we of Nine Section, with our limited horizon, were unaware of this; we didn't *see* 5th Div troops at Meiktila, and nobody told us – or possibly we weren't listening. We had assumed, wrongly, that 5th Div would *pass through* us at Meiktila, and when this didn't happen and we were sent south to attack Pyawbwe, we were aggrieved. Only now, 46 years late, have I discovered (from the official history) that we were under a misapprehension, and I apologise on the section's behalf for our uncharitable thoughts at the time, and for whatever Grandarse may have said since.

Division wanted Rangoon, with a fervour that had been growing steadily since we crossed the Irrawaddy. In a way, the far-off city had assumed an almost mystic quality, like the High Barbaree or Never-Never or Tir-nan-og; it was the ultimate prize of a long and dreadful war, and once it was taken Burma would be part of military history. Perhaps Slim's speech by the lake had had something to do with it; perhaps there was a hope that the big boats would sail thence indeed.

Whatever the reason, the Black Cats had come to regard Rangoon as a personal prize. After all, 17th Div, God Almighty's Own, was the oldest formation in Fourteenth Army, had borne the heat at Imphal, had led the way south of the Irrawaddy and broken Jap in the Dry Belt. No one would have dreamed of minimising what other divisions had done – but no one had a better right to the first sight of the gilded Shwe Dagon pagoda and the Gulf of Martaban. Or as Grandarse put it:

"Ah 'evn't coom this fookin' far for nowt."

"You're just a bloody glory-hunter, you," said the Duke. "You'll be shouting 'Gung ho!' in a minute. Want to tell your grandchildren how you took Rangoon, do you?"

"W'at for not? All Ah'm sayin' is, we're entitled – not the bloody Flamin' Arseholes or the Cross Keys or owt like them," said Grandarse stubbornly. "Any roads, bar Mandalay, it's the only place in bleedin' Boorma that any booger's ivver 'eard of."

WHEN I WAS ABOUT fourteen I sat three exams in mathematics, and scored 27 per cent in algebra, 10 in arithmetic, and 0 in geometry. It was below par even for me, and that third mark in particular rankled so much that I actually did some work for a change, mastered the simpler theorems, pinned Pythagoras (and his corollary) to the mat, and became something of an authority on the angles within a circle. It didn't get me within a rod, pole, or perch of passing Lower Maths (O-level, I suppose it is now-adays), but it was a fatal application just the same – or so I sometimes think, on the basis of if-I-hadn't-done-so-and-so, such-and-such-would-never-have-happened, which is a futile specu-lation at the best of times. Still, if I hadn't learned those circle theorems, I'm pretty sure that things would have been different one night south of Pyawbwe.

We left the town in mid-April, and spent the next two weeks jaunting peacefully down the road on the heels of 5th Div, who were clearing the way to Rangoon. According to one military history, they encountered only "slight opposition" – one of those phrases which cause me unreasonable annoyance, because while it may be slight to a historian, it certainly wasn't to the man on the spot, whoever he may have been. But whatever trouble they struck, we were a long way behind, taking in the scenery which was increasingly fertile and occasionally jungly, lush and green in the hot spring sunlight after the arid paddy of the Dry Belt. It was as pleasant as a journey can be in the back of a rattling 3-ton truck when you have nothing to do but bask in the heat, punish the water chaggles, watch Grandarse perspiring, and envy Stanley's ability to sleep like a babe with the Bren clasped upright between his knees and his head cradled on the flash eliminator; monot-onous it might be, but it beat the hell out of marching and fighting. Only very young soldiers and head-cases object to boredom in war-time. Back in Ranchi, before the campaign began, I had been silly enough to remark to Parker that I was brassed off waiting to get into action, and he had grinned pityingly and replied: "You won't be sayin' that in a month or two." Now, after Meiktila and Pyawbwe, I knew how right he'd been, and understood Nine Section's content as the long dull miles rolled slowly past. I could even endure a neighbour's composition of "South of Meiktila", hummed to himself in a soft, maddening murmur:

> Then the lads on the mortars got weavin',
> They had the Japs on the run.
> South of Meik-til-la,
> Down Pee-aw-bee way-y-y . . .

over and over, ad nauseam, as he polished his awful lyrics – no doubt W. S. Gilbert and Oscar Hammerstein used to do the same sort of thing, but without the risk of being hurled bodily over the tailboard around Milestone 200. As I said earlier, it has since found its way into an anthology of Second World War songs, but no one sang along at the time; it was too hot, and too excruciating.

Although 5th Div were taking the strain, we dug in and stood stag at night as carefully as we would have done if we'd been up front. Jap might have been thoroughly hammered at Meiktila and Pyawbwe, and his armies split and scattered,* but he was still there, both sides of a bridgehead no wider than the road itself which 5th Div and ourselves were driving into southern Burma. High command may have known how badly his military machine had been thrown into confusion, but we didn't, and it was a dead certainty that he had more men in his three armies, spread from the Salween river in the east to the jungly hills of the Pegu Yomas in the west, than the 17th and 5th Divs combined. So each night the road south of Pyawbwe, for a hundred miles and more, was a series of armed camps waiting to be counter-attacked and taking no chances.

---

* If anything illustrates how comprehensive his defeat was, it is a comparison of times and distances. From the Irrawaddy to Pyawbwe is about 100 miles, and it had taken us the best part of two months to cover; the next 260 miles down the Rangoon road were done in twelve days.

Digging in was much easier now. In the Dry Belt the excavation of a slit-trench four feet by four by two had been a back-breaking struggle with pick and shovel against ground as hard as flint and full of stones, and the entrenching tool had been as much use as a tea-spoon; once Grandarse, a skilled navvy among other things, had taken pity on my incompetence and plucked me one-handed out of my half-finished pit and completed it himself with huge smashing strokes of the pick. ("It's nowt tae dee wid stren'th, Jock; it's knawin' 'oo tae swing a pick, sista, an' thoo's got nae mair idea than parson's grandmither. Coom oot!")

In the softer dark earth of the south even I could dig a pit in under an hour, and at one place where we stayed two nights, and the earth was a firm sandy clay, the section amused itself constructing a network of tunnels connecting pit to pit – quite unnecessary, but fun to do. It was the best position we ever had, for there was a fine field of fire across flat open ground to the jungle edge, a nearby tank* where we bathed, and our brigade box enclosed a little village on the road where we could get mangoes and the magnificent jungle bananas, which are a brilliant scarlet in colour and three times the size of the ones that you buy in supermarkets.†

Our pits were on the edge of the perimeter, facing west; somewhere beyond the jungly fringe ahead lay the Pegu Yomas, where Jap was reportedly getting his breath back, and patrols had brought in rumours of enemy movement in that direction. We operated the normal two-hour stags, and for added strength a platoon of Jat machine-gunners from the Frontier Force Rifles set up their guns between our pits. The Jats are a tough lot, from the Punjab, tall, light-skinned, and not unlike the Baluch hillmen of our brigade; being originally from Central Asia they looked as much like East Europeans as Orientals, with their narrow moustached faces and thin straight noses. Nick watched approvingly as they mounted their heavy Vickers pieces and took careful sightings across the open ground before setting the guns on what was called "fixed line". The object was that, with the guns angled so that

* pond
† I may be mistaken about getting these exotic Burmese fruits at this stage of the campaign (late spring), but they were a staple of diet later on.

their lines of fire intersected, the gunners could simply keep their fingers on the button in the event of a night attack, and a blanket of fire that nothing could get through would cover our whole front.

"That'll gi'e the boogers a belly-ache, John," said Nick, and the Jat havildar* grinned wickedly. "*Tik hai,†*" said he. "Japanni wallah come this way – *bus!*" He fed a belt of ammo into his Vickers, took a last squint along the sights, and accepted one of Parker's cigarettes, which he smoked in the approved sepoy fashion – the butt between the pinkie and third finger of the clenched fist, the smoke being inhaled through the mouthpiece formed by the curled forefinger and thumb. A variation is to cup both hands together to form an air-tight pocket, but either way will make your head swim, and you won't want to smoke for a week. It was nothing new to the section, but now several of them were moved to try it again, and the peaceful dusk was shattered by their gasps and retchings.

"Obviously one inhales more air," wheezed the Duke, "but why that should make the dose more powerful I can't imagine. You'd think it would dilute it."

"Christ, it's like smeukin' owd socks an' black ploog!" croaked Wattie, racked with coughing. "It's woors'n Capstan Full Stren'th!"

"Ye could git the habit, mind," said Grandarse, hawking and weeping. "By God, it's got a kick till it!"

"Daft boogers," said Nick, who smoked a pipe.

"Can't see meself gettin' used to it," said Parker. "Makes me wonder why I ever started the bleedin' things!"

"Never fancied 'em, mesel," said Wedge primly. "Saved me money."

"Git hired, ye clean-livin' git!" said Morton, having coughed himself to a standstill. "Ye'll joost spend it on drink."

"Route marching in Blightly started me," I said. "Everyone lit up at the ten-minute halts, and I felt out of it, so I began cadging fags, and then buying my own."

* sergeant
† all right, good

"Ah'll bet ye took yer time aboot buyin'!" snapped Forster. "Mean Scotch ha'porth. Coom on, then, gi'es one! W'at the 'ell's this – doo Morrier? Wid a bloody cotton wool tip? That's a tart's cigarette, man!"

"Give it back if you don't want it," I said.

"Piss off an' gi'es a light. Bloody 'ell, Ah might as weel be smeukin' fresh air!"

Filtered cigarettes were rare in those days, and considered effete. Lung cancer, passive smoking, and health warnings were unheard of, almost everyone smoked, and those who deplored the habit did so as much on moral as physical grounds – there was a sense, among the godly and school authorities and my aunts, that it was sinful, not because it fouled the atmosphere or damaged the health, but rather because it betokened a low character.

"It boogers yer wind," conceded Wattie, inhaling with satisfaction. "Thoo, Grandarse, tha'lt nivver win Grasmere the rate thoo's puffin' awa'."

"Knackers," retorted Grandarse. "Ah'll win Grasmere. Fags nivver done me nae 'arm. Ah joost smeuk it in an' fart it oot, an' Ah's in grand fettle." He demonstrated thunderously, guffawing, and those nearest recoiled in disgust. The Duke, still inhaling thoughtfully through his fist, ignored him.

"There must be a scientific reason why the mixture of air and smoke has such a wallop," said he. "Something to do with the diffusion of gases, wouldn't you say, Jock?"

"Ask Grandarse. He's the great diffuser."

"I'm sure we did it in physics . . . what's Boyle's law?"

"Watt's pots never boyle."

"Hee-bloody-haw! Is that your own?"

"No. *1066 and All That.*"

"That just about sums up my education," said the Duke glumly. "Christ, the things I've forgotten in five years! Used to know all about gases, once . . . maybe I'm thinking of Avogadro's hypothesis, whatever that was." He shook his head. "I dunno why my parents bothered. Thirteen years of wasted time, apart from cricket. D'you know, I doubt if I could parse a sentence nowadays, and I'm buggered if I know what a gerund is. Supposing I ever did."

"A gerund*ive* is a pass*ive* adject*ive* – but don't ask me to define either of them."

"As for bloody geometry," said the Duke, "I can't even remember what an isosceles –"

"They're at it again!" cried Forster. "Lissen' 'em! Eddicated fookers – Ah doan't think! Doan't knaw their arses f'ae 'oles in't grun', eether on 'em! Shawin' off wid a' the shit they didn't larn at their snob skeuls!" He got up, stabbing an aggressive forefinger at the Duke. "Lissen you, clivver-clogs! Ye doan't knaw owt woorth knawin'! You or that Scotch twat – 'ey, Jock, gi'es anoother fag, ye mingy sod!" He puffed it alight and blew smoke at the Duke. "Ye should ha' gone till elementary skeul, you! Might ha' got soom sense lathered intil ye!"

"You think I didn't get leathered?" asked the Duke.

Forster made an unbelievable noise of derision. "If ye did, it didn't larn ye owt! Bloody took-shops! Ah nivver saw a bloody took-shop, but Ah've larned things you'll nivver knaw!"

"I can well believe it," drawled the Duke, and the tone and the look were like a red rag to Forster. He stiffened, spat, and leaned forward.

"Can ye, noo? Ye're that bloody smart, aren't ye? Awreet – you that's so bloody full o' science an' shit – tell us: if yer drivin' a bus, an' ye cross yer 'ands on't wheel – w'at 'appens?"

"I've never driven a bus –"

"Naw! Not you! Nivver woorked in yer fookin' life!"

"– but I imagine you cross your hands to make a sharp turn."

"That's w'at ye think, eh?"

"What does happen if you cross your hands on the wheel, Foshie?" I asked.

"Ye git fired! Sacked! Kicked oot on yer arse!" His voice was shaking; all of a sudden, where I thought he had been merely needling, he was pale with anger. "Ah knaw, 'cos that's w'at 'appened tae me! The fookin' inspector saw us, an' Ah got me cards, theer an' then! Oot on't bloody street, November sivventh, nineteen-thurty-bloody-fower! W'ile you an' Dook were at yer fookin' posh skeuls, larnin' nowt an' stoofin' thasels in took-shop! On't bloody dole! But you – w'at the 'ell dae you knaw aboot that!"

Abruptly he turned on his heel and threw himself down beside his pit, drawing violently at his cigarette. Grandarse raised his head, surprised; the Duke was chewing his lip. If any two men in the section detested each other, he and Forster did, but it had never been so open before; at the same time, there was that in Forster's outburst which gave the Duke pause. Forster sour, Forster sneering, Forster scrounging and subverting, we knew – but not Forster in a storm of bitter indignation.

"It's 'ell in the trenches," said Parker philosophically. Then the Duke said, in a quiet voice:

"That's a bit rough, I must say. They sacked you just for that?"

"Aye! Joost fer that! Roof, be Christ!"

"Well," said the Duke, "I'm sorry, Foshie, but I don't see what it's got to do with what we were talking about –"

"Naw, you bloody wouldn't!" He was quieter, but still plainly full of bile. "You 'evn't a wife an' two bairns an' fook-all but the dole to live on!"

"Give ower, man," said Nick.

"Give ower me arse! Stook-oop bastard meks me sick!"

The Duke sat up, slightly pink, and since Peel wasn't present I brought the ponderous weight of my one stripe into play.

"Cut it out, Foshie. Forget it, Duke –"

"Foshie," said the Duke, "if you've got something up your nose, blow it out. It's not my fault you were on the dole –"

"Ah nivver said it wez!" Forster rolled up on one elbow. "But Ah'll tell thee this, Dook – if Ah'd 'ed thy chances, Ah'd nivver ha' bin on't bloody dole neether! Ah'd ha' made summat o' me bloody sel'! Nut like you, that nivver knew 'oo weel off tha wez! An' bloody Jock theer! A' you twa knaw is w'at ye doan't fookin' knaw, the pair on ye!" He glared and turned away, grinding out his half-finished cigarette. For a man who had been known to crawl all over the truck looking for abandoned dog-ends, this was proof of strong emotion indeed.

The Duke opened his mouth and closed it again. Parker made a restraining gesture towards him and winked at me. "'Oo's fer a brew-up, then? Wot say, Jock – 'ow abaht workin' yore well-known magic an' treatin' us to a fragrant steamin' pialla? Arraboy

– wiv my permish you'll get a commish! Got the grub-box there, Dook? Let's 'ave a dekko at wot we got, then, eh?"

It petered out there, as most section quarrels did that stopped short of blows, with the older hands changing the subject and the principals lapsing into tight-lipped silence: damp it down and let it lie. I brewed up, with Parker pattering, and presently the tensions disappeared; by the time we were on to the second pialla Forster was grinning sourly again and cadging another of my du Mauriers, while the Duke, across the fire, was talking to Wedge and Stanley about K-rations as opposed to compo. But from time to time he would glance in Forster's direction.

Finally we turned in, which consisted of rolling up in our blankets beside our pits, but I wasn't like sleep at all. It was one of those tropic nights that travel agents dream about, warm and still, with a huge Burmese moon high in the deep purple sky, so silver-bright that it lit up the perimeter and the whole open ground to the feathery jungle edge. With the Jat guns and their crews in among us, the perimeter was thick with blanket-wrapped bodies; everyone was down except the men standing stag, two every thirty yards or so in their slit-trenches, and the Jat duty gunners sitting by their weapons. I was having a last (unlawful, since it was after dark) cigarette, shielding the glow in my cupped hands, when a figure approached from the far end of our section position: it was the Duke, his blanket round his shoulders, picking his way through the sleepers.

"Can't kip," said he, squatting down. "Too bloody riled. I should have pushed that griping sod's face in. Shouldn't I?"

"No point. He was just letting off steam."

"Yeah – in my direction, as usual. He's a needling bastard. I can do without it." He pulled his blanket closer. "Anyway, I'm buggered if I'll tailor my conversation to suit him. What the hell did I say, anyway?"

If he couldn't see what had irritated Forster, there was no point in telling him; it wouldn't have been easy, and I wasn't inclined to try.

"God knows. Maybe he's got a touch of malaria; he's looking pretty yellow."

"Who isn't? Anyway, as a matter of principle, I want to finish our discussion. So say something educated to me, will you?" I stared. "Anything, go on!"

"Have you been hoarding your rum ration?" I wondered.

"No. I just want a minute's civilised conversation in which every other word isn't 'fook'. So humour me. Or tell me to piss off, if you can't be bothered. Anything'll do, so long as it isn't about the bloody Army, or Burma, or Japs – just for a moment, before, I was remembering school, and it was a pleasant change."

Being curious, I asked: "What school was that?"

"Oh, you've never heard of it." The moon was on his face, and I saw the wry grin. "Little place in the West Country, run by a retired I.C.S. wallah who liked to imagine he was a housemaster at a big public school. He had us playing the Eton field game, no kidding. But it was all right." He shivered, huddling in his blanket. "Come on, for God's sake – conjugate something, or tell me the principal exports of Bolivia. Or the Corn Laws. Or valency tables. Any damned thing."

He was in a curious state; if action had been imminent I'd have said he was edgy. It came to me that I really didn't know the Duke at all; we were so used to his languid, damn-you-me-lad style that it never occurred to us that there might be someone else behind it. However, if he wanted eccentric diversion . . .

"You mentioned isosceles triangles . . . will it do if I prove Pythagoras for you?"

"Jesus," he said, "the square on the hypotenuse. I'll bet you can't."

I did it with a bayonet, on the earth beside my pit – which may have been how Pythagoras himself did it originally, for all I know. I went wrong once, having forgotten where you drop the perpendicular, but in the end there it was, and the Duke's satisfaction was such that I went on, flown with success, to prove that an angle at the centre of a circle is twice an angle at the circumference. He followed it so intently that I felt slightly worried: after all, it's hardly normal to be utterly absorbed in triangles and circles when the surrounding night may be stiff with Japanese. When I confessed that that was as far as my mathematical genius went, he seemed contented enough, and settled himself to sleep, having thanked me between yawns. I asked if he wasn't going back to his own pit, and he said he couldn't be bothered.

"You ought to have your bundook with you," I told him.

"Oh, don't get regimental on me, Jock; I'm tired." He yawned again. "D'you think Foshie did get fired for crossing his hands on the wheel?"

"Yes. He isn't likely to forget it, either."

"Well, I didn't fire him. What's he got against me?"

"He's got something against everybody. Get your head down."

I was just dropping off when he spoke again. "Can't stand him. Pity. He's a bloody good soldier . . . bar his belly-aching . . ."

That was all I heard. For the next four hours I must have been dead to the world, and when I woke it was to the deafening rattle of a Vickers and people yelling; there was the inevitable split second of bewildered panic and then I was rolling into my pit and grabbing my Thompson simultaneously, shouting for Stanley and his number two. They tumbled in beside me and Stanley got the Bren to his shoulder as we watched our front – not that we could see a thing, for the moon was down and even the nearest pits were lost in the gloom. The guns of the Jats on either side were chattering, sending tracers scudding out into the darkness, and then someone roared "Cease fire!" and in an instant there was nothing but the echoes dying away, a subdued call for quiet, and the drift of cordite. Suddenly a Verey was fired, and then another, and we were staring out across the empty ground lit by the flickering crimson flares. But there were no Japs to be seen, no movement at all, and no sound but the puzzled muttering along the line of pits, and the clatter of the Jats changing the belts on their guns.

We stood to until dawn, half an hour later, and when the light grew someone spotted the body lying a few yards in front of the pit to our immediate right. It was the Duke. He had been cut almost in half by the Vickers fire.

It soon became plain what had happened. Someone had got up to go to the latrine, and in the dark had trod on one of the sleeping Jats, who had cried out – not loudly, but still loud enough to wake a third party, who had asked what was up. A fourth man had said something like: "It's just one of the Jats", and a fifth man, probably half-awake, had misheard the last word of the sentence and exclaimed: "Japs?" In an instant someone else had shouted "Japs!", and there was a mad scramble for the pits, with the Jat gunners starting to blaze away – and at some point the Duke must have come awake, remembered that he was away from his pit and his rifle, and made a bee-line for them. Only it was pitch dark, and he had run the wrong way.

I can't be certain when we buried him, but I imagine it must have been the same afternoon. It was quick and simple, as usual: we dug a slit-trench beside a line of bamboo saplings, the platoon gathered round, the blanket-wrapped corpse was lowered in on log lines, Long John read the burial service and saluted, and we shovelled in the soil.

I should be able to describe the section's reaction, but I can't because all my attention was taken up by Forster. He was one of the men on the log-lines, and as he withdrew the cord and stood back I saw his face, and the hair rose on my neck. He looked like a madman, glaring at the grave as he coiled the line, and when we dismissed he stalked off a few paces and then turned back, mouthing and looking from one to the other of us. Then he started talking, in a bitter cursing stream, demanding to know why the burial had been conducted with such haste, and with so little reverence for the dead, and without proper ceremony. I can't reproduce what he said, possibly because it came out in a semi-coherent flood, and possibly because I found it shocking and unreal. If I were writing fiction I might have a stab at it – if I didn't dismiss the scene as too far-fetched – but I'm recording fact, and that was how Forster reacted. Some things I remember: the phrase "shoovelled in as if 'e wez cattle!", and a furious demand to know what the Duke's family would have thought if they could have seen it, and more in the same strain.

What the section thought, God knows. They just dispersed, and only Sergeant Hutton, presumably in an effort to quieten Forster down, assured him that in due time the Duke would be properly reinterred in a military ceremony. Forster fell silent at that, and presently moved off to one side, and Hutton left him to it.

I was heart-sick sorry for the man. He and the Duke had disliked each other as bitterly as men can, but they had seen a lot of hard service together, and their last exchange had seen Forster at his obscenely vitriolic worst. Now the Duke was dead, in circumstances far crueller than if he'd bought his lot in a duffy, and Forster was in a private hell of his own, made all the worse for his being the kind of hard man whose emotions are stark and simple, and not subject to rationalisation. His remorse had come out in the only way he knew, looking for something to vent itself on, and finding the perfunctory burial – which, as he knew perfectly well, was standard procedure in a swift-moving war.

Forster, and his comrades, had seen too much death to be outwardly moved by it, whatever they felt. His was the only reaction I ever saw which verged on the theatrical, and he had special cause. But there was nothing to be done but let him come out of it in his own time, and I was walking away when he turned and fell into step beside me. He seemed to have settled a little, but I was uncomfortably aware that he was still glaring and breathing hard. Why he chose my company, I don't know, unless it was that he felt I had been a particular friend of the Duke's – which I hadn't been, in fact. But abruptly he stopped, and I automatically stopped with him. He looked back at the grave, and then rasped out:

"Wadda *you* think aboot it, then?" I answered with care.

"It'll be all right, Foshie," I said. "You heard Hutton – they'll do it properly, later on." I should have left it there, I suppose, but I honestly felt compassion for him, and in my folly I dropped an enormous brick on the road to hell. I can only say it was kindly meant, and his question had taken me by surprise. Anyway, I blurted out:

"He thought you were a bloody good soldier."

He frowned at me, his lantern jaw working. "Ye w'at?"

"The Duke. He said it to me, last night, after . . . just before we went to sleep. He said you were a bloody good soldier."

He blinked, looked down at the rope still coiled in his hand, and then back at the grave again. For a long moment he said nothing, and for no reason that I can think of I took out my cigarettes and offered him one. He lit it with his hands cupped against the slight breeze, inhaled, blew out smoke, and gave me his most unpleasant grin, without any mirth in it at all.

"Doan't give us yer shit, Jock," he sneered, and walked away.

I have nothing to add, either in comment or attempted explanation, after forty-five years. That is what happened, and that's all.

WITH ONLY 140 MILES TO GO to Rangoon, Grandarse was triumphantly vindicated: we leapfrogged over 5th Div at a place called Pyu, and now the road was clear except for the last Jap bastion at Pegu, 100 miles farther south – and the monsoon was still a fortnight away. Delight and excitement ran through the division, and when "Punch" Cowan's jeep was seen on the road, with the Black Cat fluttering on its bonnet, he passed to the kind of reception that generals must dream about, with his men cheering and hammering on the sides of the trucks. We hadn't seen him since the start of the year, at Ranchi, and I remember thinking, as he drove through somewhere about Penwegon, how old he looked, with his silver hair and the hooked nose that gave him his nickname. But he was grinning like a schoolboy; we were almost there.

There were portents, too, of impending final victory. Parties of British and American prisoners of war, turned loose by the retreating Japs, were being reported, and one day an American flier wandered into our position (I've no idea of the date). He had been several months in Japanese hands and had escaped somewhere near Rangoon and set out north; he was in a fair old state, and when the master-gyppo put porridge and a fried breakfast in front of him he burst into tears and, according to an eye-witness, buried his head in the bosom of the nearest soldier and kept repeating "Oh, boys, boys!" while they assured him he was awreet, noo. Hatred of the Japs rose a notch higher – and this was before we knew about the horrors of the River Kwai and the Moulmein railway.

The battalion took a prisoner, too, about ten miles north of Pegu, in a combined attack with the Gurkhas on a Jap position from which the enemy withdrew during the opening barrage, leaving one unfortunate who was found hiding under a blanket.

My one memory of Pegu town is of a dirty pot-holed road leading to a metal-girdered bridge across a swollen brown river.

Jap was well dug in, and there was some stiff fighting for the town, but we took no part in it and were still on the wrong side of the river when the leading elements of the division had fought their way over. But it would only be a matter of hours before we were all across, guns, tanks, and men; Jap was reported to be pulling out, the last few miles to Rangoon would be wide open, and there would be nothing to do but motor down to the sea and the golden Shwe Dagon, that "bonny kirk a' set wi' rubies braw", and wait (in our imagination) for the big boats to India and home.

Then, two weeks early, the monsoon broke.

The section were in a jungly clearing, brewing up, when it began. There had been a few showers in the previous week, and it had been one of those dull, steamy days when breathing is an effort and the sweat runs off you in buckets, but the official wisdom was that we would be snug in Rangoon before the real downpour set in. I was in the act of bending over the brew-tin, stirring in the leaves, when the first big drops landed in the boiling water, and I looked up in the gathering dusk at a sky that had suddenly turned dark grey and seemed to be descending slowly. There were cries of disgust and alarm, and repetition of the section's favourite four-letter word, and then it hit.

If you haven't seen the monsoon burst, it's difficult to imagine. There are the first huge drops, growing heavier and heavier, and then God opens the sluices and the jets of a million high-pressure hoses are being directed straight down, and the deluge comes with a great roar, crashing against the leaves and rebounding from the earth for perhaps a minute – after that the earth is under a skin of water which looks as though it's being churned up by buckshot. Before you know it you are sodden and streaming, the fire's out, the level in the brew tin is rising visibly, and the whole clearing is a welter of soaked blaspheming men trying to snatch arms and equipment from the streams coursing underfoot. The din is deafening, partly from the storm and partly from Grandarse's stentorian bellowings: "Git the tent afore we droon! Coom on, ye idle boogers, gi'es a hand!"

The tent, a massive mildewed slab of canvas and cord, was in the truck, and it took four men to drag it out and carry it to the clearing. Fortunately the ground was uneven, and there were a few raised areas on which to pitch it once we had got it unfolded, something which had not been done since its issue long before. In the interval, and especially since the first showers, it had become home to assorted jungle crawlies, spiders, leeches, and worms – and to as splendid a specimen of the mirapod of the class Chilopoda as I ever hope to see.

The giant centipede is exactly like the little amber beastie found in civilised gardens, except that he is literally twenty times bigger. This baby was just short of sixteen inches, with a body as thick as a golf ball, and when he scuttled out with his pincers to the fore and his myriad legs going like the oars of a galley, the section dispersed at speed. He snaked out on to the muddy ground and took stock of his position, and I for one was on the top of the grub-box with a single bound.

"Doan't ga near it!" shouted Morton, as if anyone wanted to. "The boogers is poisonous! If 'e nips ye, ye've 'ad it!"

"That's cobblers!" said Nick, keeping his distance. "There's nowt tae worry aboot unless 'e gits on ye – doan't try tae broosh 'im off backwards or 'e'll dig 'is claws intil ye, an' there's 'oondreds on 'em, an' they'll fester! 'It 'im oop the arse an' 'e'll fa' off 'eid foorst!"

" 'It 'im oop the arse yersel'!" cried Wattie. "By, will ye look at the oogly sod! That's it, Tommo lad, 'it 'im wid yer dah!"

Corporal Peel had drawn his machete and was approaching the brute warily, for when it scuttled it moved like lightning. He took a swipe and missed, jumping back as Little-Many-Legs shot in his direction, and then it changed its mind and scurried to the grub-box, nestling in at one side while I left precipitately at the other. But I'm proud to say that even in my haste I hadn't lost sight of the interests of zoology.

"*Tairo* – hold on!" I cried. "Don't kill it! It must be about two feet long – my God, I'll bet it's a record! If we can bottle the bugger, and preserve it in petrol, it could be sent home to a museum. We might even", I added hopefully, appealing to their better instincts, "flog it. No kidding, the Imperial Science people would give their back teeth for it!"

I can only say that it seemed a good idea at the time, but the weight of opinion was against me, crying "Barmy booger!" and suggesting that I catch and bottle it myself. By then it was too late; Peel had bisected it neatly, but the top part continued to wriggle until he hit it again, after which it was beyond repair. I still think it was a pity, because when I measured the pieces next morning (without touching them) they amounted to almost three times the amount of tropical centipede previously known to science, six inches being the norm according to the encyclopedia. It was a genuine monster, and possibly lethal, for all centipedes are poisonous to some degree, and if size is anything to go by that one was in the cobra class.

But the vandals destroyed it, and it seemed to me a judgment on them when the tent proved to be rotten at the seams, falling apart when we stretched it. We stood about in the pouring rain, damning the government, and to make matters worse the truck, in or under which we could have found shelter, was sent off on some equipment-ferrying business or other. So we spent the night under bushes, sleeping in six inches or so of warmish water, all except Grandarse, who lay out in the open, beaming contentedly up at the downpour and exclaiming: "Aye, gran' growin' weather!" Strange to tell, I never slept better; in a hot climate there's something soothing about sodden clothing and a blanket that's nine parts water, so long as you don't sleep on your face, because that way you drown.

It rained steadily for about a week, but in the first twelve hours the Pegu river had risen to an uncrossable level, and the bridge approaches turned into a morass in which no vehicles could operate; the airfields were rained out of commission, and the drive south came to a squelching halt. We began a month on half rations, which I have to say I don't remember, so it can't have been a great privation, presumably because we eked out our issue food with bananas, mangoes, and whatever else that company of expert foragers could win from the waterlogged countryside. But short rations and the incessant downpour and the impossibility of keeping dry were small matters beside the news which dropped like a bombshell on the division just two days after the rains started.

We were not going to Rangoon. It had been taken by seaborne assault while we were held up in the monsoon mud. The old division that had endured the retreat three years before, had been in the thick of the great battle that stopped Jap at the gates of India, and had led the way south, was denied the ultimate prize at the last minute. I couldn't complain, I was a newcomer, but even I felt disappointed, and to the old sweats like Nick and Grandarse and Forster, who had soldiered through the Burma war, it seemed like a betrayal, and hit them harder than their commanders ever knew. It may seem a small, selfish thing; the taking of Rangoon was what mattered, not who took it. But soldiers have a strong primitive sense of fairness: no one had promised them Rangoon, but they felt there had been an understanding, and it had been broken.

And that wasn't the half of it: as though to add injury to insult, we were ordered back up the road which we had just come down, to deal with whatever was left of the Japanese armies. In blunt terms, no big boats, just a return to the war.

How other parts of the division reacted, I can't say, but for a little while the atmosphere in Nine Section was mutinous, in the everyday rather than the military sense. No one publicly flung down his hat and belt and announced, in the immortal words of the Army Act: "I'll soldier no more, you may say what you please." But looking back, in the knowledge that British troops *did* mutiny more than once in the last war, I can say that I'd have hated to see the section any closer to the edge than they were that morning. It was just talk, but it was ugly while it lasted, and I report it for what it was worth.

We had found ourselves a basha to live in by now, a neat little one-roomed wooden bungalow on stilts which raised it above the level of the flooded ground, and when Peel came in with the word that we were going north again there was a long moment of disbelief in which the only sound was the steady roaring of rain on the palm thatch. We just stared at each other, and then the swearing and raging began, and Forster threw aside the rifle he had been cleaning and shouted:

"They're nut gittin' me up yon fookin' road again! Ah's nut gan! Noo, then! Booger the lot on them!" He fulminated on, while everyone else sat glum and paying no heed, for it was only the Foshie we knew and loved giving vent to his feelings, but when he suddenly rounded on us, demanding: "Is thoo lot gonna stand for

it, then? Ista?" I was startled to hear Grandarse, from whom I'd
have expected a shrug of resignation, say in a grim harsh voice:
"It's a bad do. By Christ, it's a bad do!"

"Bad do?" cried Forster. "It's a bloody stab in't back! That's
w'at 'tis! Well, they can stoof it – bastard Louie Mountbatten an'
a'!"

"It's not fair," said Stanley, and everyone looked at him, for
Stanley was not given to opinions. "They told us we were goin'
to Rangoon," he went on, going red under the general scrutiny.
"That's what they said."

"Lyin' bastards!" said Wattie. "They'll tell ye owt, an' then
drop ye in't shit! Ah've aboot 'ed it, me!" And he stood up, looking
about as though for support.

"An' me!" roared Forster. "Well, Ah's nut gan! Nut one fookin'
step!"

I expected someone to say: "Wrap up, Foshie!" or "Give it a
rest", but no one spoke except Wedge, reminding us bitterly that
we'd been told we'd be relieved at Meiktila by 5th Div, and the
boogers had never arrived, and Morton who repeated with furious
oaths what Stanley had said: we'd been promised we were going
to Rangoon.

"Well, you ain't, my son," said Parker flatly. "So you can forget
it."

"Bollocks!" This was Forster again. "You can fergit it, Parker,
but Ah's nut!" He wheeled suddenly on Peel, who had been quietly
donning his webbing and ignoring the outbursts. "Ah'm tellin' ye,
Tommo – they've 'ed me! *Bus!* That's the whole sub-muckin'!
Balls to 'em! Noo, then!"

Peel slung his rifle and picked up his pack. "Don't waste tha
breath tellin' me," he said. "Long John's just ower the road. Go
an' tell him." He turned to the door, said: "We fall in in ten
minutes," and went out, sensible man.

"Ah's nut fallin' in!" Forster bawled after him, and more
ordures of speech followed, culminating in: "They can stick us
away if they want till – Ah's nut gan, an' that's flat! Noo, then!"

To my dismay, Wattie said: "Fook it," and turned to Grandarse.
"W'at aboot you, owd feller?"

That was the moment when I wished that Peel hadn't left, for while one could ignore Forster, Wattie was another matter, and Grandarse was wearing a lowering, sullen look I hadn't seen before. It was all nonsense, of course – no one was going to defy orders, and once Forster's spleen had spent itself all would be well – but at the time it was beginning to sound serious – Grandarse's silence being the most serious sign of all.

"Aye – w'at say, then, Grandarse?" Forster sounded eager. "Coom on, lad – w'at say?"

Nick, who had not spoken until now, knocked out his pipe and got up. "Doan't talk sae bloody wet, Forster. Ye want tae shut yer gob an' give yer arse a chance."

"You!" shouted Forster. "Git up tae me, ye mangy lal sod, an' Ah'll blitz ye! Noo, an' Ah'm warnin' ye!" He let go another stream of filth – and suddenly I'd had enough of him. I was the n.c.o., I'd probably been spoiling for a go at him ever since the Duke's burial, or perhaps I had a touch of fever, as many of us did at that time. Whatever the reason – and it was probably just that he was being so unbearably noisy and obscene – I raised my voice.

"Shut your bloody trap, Forster! No one's listening!"

He looked at me in genuine astonishment. "W'at the 'ell's it got tae dee wid thee? Y'evn't got yer bloody knees broon yet!"

That did it. "That's why I've got a stripe and you haven't!" I said. "And I don't mind losing it for the pleasure of breaking your lousy neck!" Leadership is an art, you see.

"That's me old Jock!" crowed Parker. "Kick 'is nuts in! Wiv my permish –"

He got no further because Forster called me a really disgusting name and I went for him in a blind rage and landed a lethal right on the brim of his hat, at which point fortunately Nick and Parker draped themselves round me – I say fortunately because someone would certainly have got hurt, and it might well have been me. And as they were heaving me away, and Forster was spitting vengeance, Grandarse got to his feet, and said in mild irritation:

"Haud on a minnit. Ah can't 'ear mesel' think!" He stood staring at the floor, and then gave a great despondent sigh: "Aw, it's nae fookin' use. There's nowt we can dee aboot it." He began to put on his equipment, Stanley picked up the Bren, and Wattie, after a moment's hesitation, said "Aw, shite!" and began to gather his gear together. I contented myself with saying: "Any time you like, Foshie", and he told me to piss off, in a Pickwickian way, and a few minutes later we were falling in outside in the downpour, after another glorious anti-climax. To quote a phrase I learned from the late Bill Shankly when he was managing Carlisle United, everyone had talked a good game.

Rangoon was never mentioned again, but it was a while before Nine Section got over their disappointment and returned to their normal state of belly-aching discontent. You can see their point; within a week of Rangoon's fall came the news of Hitler's death and the German surrender, crowds at home were giving way to the delirium of VE Day, and we were going back up the road to resume the debate with a Japanese enemy whom we'd hoped never to see again. I mentioned earlier the fiasco of the officer who announced the end of the European war just as we were about to start an attack; that could be laughed off, but the prospect of a longer haul was less amusing.

The fact that the end was definitely in sight was a mixed consolation; as in a game, where there's a peculiar cruelty about losing a last-minute deciding goal, so it is in war; no one wants to buy it at any time, but it seems doubly hard to buy it late in the day, especially from an adversary who by any normal standards should have packed in long ago.

For it was common knowledge now, even at rifle-pit level, that as an organised force Jap was finished. His armies had been cut in two and scattered at Meiktila, Pyawbwe, and Mandalay, and when 5th and 17th Divisions began leapfrogging to Pegu the last hope for the broken enemy was escape to Siam. Those to the east of the road could head south between the Salween and Sittang rivers, but those to the west, cut off by our drive to Pegu, could only take refuge in the jungly hills of the Pegu Yomas and wait for a chance to break across the road before heading south in turn.

For the next three months, being Jap and not knowing when he was beaten, he kept trying, and Fourteenth Army kept getting in his way. By the end of that time he would be on his chinstrap, short of food, out of ammo, plagued with malaria, dysentery, jungle sores, and foul weather, and sometimes barely able to stand, let alone walk, but he was still dangerous, and he kept coming. I dare say Japanese historians regard the last phase of the Burma war as something best forgotten; speaking as objectively as I can, I'd say that from what I saw of them, and what I heard, the remnants of the Japanese 15th, 28th, and 33rd Armies did their country proud. I shouldn't be surprised if some of them were still holed up around the Sittang Bend, waiting to die for their emperor.

It's a time which I cannot hope to write about systematically, because it lacks the big points of reference which I think of as milestones, and which have enabled me to give some narrative form, however erratic, to my story so far. With the help of written histories I have been able to trace Nine Section's progress through Meiktila and Pyawbwe to Pegu, but after that there were no major actions for us, no obvious objectives, and for me no plotted course to follow. For most of the time from May to August we were engaged on the Rangoon road and its surrounds, trying to stop Jap breaking across it, which meant a deal of shuttling up and down, manning road-stops, occupying outlying villages, laying ambushes which often came to nothing, constantly patrolling in search of Jap and rumours of Jap, and getting wet enough to grow fins, for by now great stretches of the country were under water. In those three months the battalion shrank to about half its former size, through repatriation, bore a distinguished part in the final destruction of the Japanese 28th Army when it tried to make its big break across the road in late July (at which time I was with another unit), and accounted for 119 enemy dead in the last two weeks of the war. All this is a matter of record, but my memories of those three months are random and confused; I have plenty of my coloured "film strips", of incidents lasting anything from a few seconds to a few days, but there is not room for them all, and often I have no clear recollection of when or where they happened, or how they fitted into the overall scheme of things. I can only plead my erratic memory; when I consider the things I must have known and have forgotten, I can only shake my head.

For example: at some point the battalion was reorganised into three new companies – and I don't even know which one I belonged to. Two of the companies consisted of the longer-served men with low demobilisation numbers who were due for repatriation; my demob number was 57, God help me, so presumably I was in the third. I was sent on leave to Calcutta, but I can't remember when, or the details of how I got there and back. On my return I was detached to another unit because of my alleged specialist knowledge (ha!), and did not return to the battalion until just before VJ Day. So, having catalogued my deficiencies of memory, I shall record what I'm sure of.

For some weeks after turning back from Pegu we were in and around a godforsaken village on the Rangoon road called Penwegon, foraying occasionally to outlying places, but always coming back to the section billet, which was a fine bungalow with a verandah, more or less surrounded by water. There I received from my father, God bless him, a copy of Bernard Fergusson's account of the Chindit expedition, *Beyond the Chindwin* – just the reading I didn't need, but Long John seemed to enjoy it. And it was on a patrol from Penwegon that Morton had hallucinations about midget Japanese commanded by Sir Walter Womersley, Minister of Pensions, and repulsed them with his kukri. We thought at the time that he was suffering a mild bout of jungle happiness, but it may have been fever; I had a touch of malaria at Penwegon and lost a couple of days out of my life. The M.O., whom I shall call McMenemy, accused me of not taking my mepacrin tablets (which was a military offence), but when I pointed out that, like everyone else, I was a rich yellow in colour from swallowing the bloody things, he admitted grudgingly that they were not an infallible prophylactic. Half the section was feverish to some degree, and scoured by dysentery in its various forms ("Ah 'm crappin' ivvery colour bar blue" was Grandarse's diagnosis). We blamed the monsoon, which certainly had one alarming effect: it puckered the skin in a revoltingly puffy fashion, and brought forth a great plague of jungle sores on wrists and ankles. McMenemy painted them purple and gave us constipating draughts, and when the company radio picked up Bing Crosby singing

> And where will you take her, Reynaldo?
> I'll take her to San Pedro.
> And where will she live in San Pedro?
> In my little house on the bay.

it was immediately parodied as

> And where will you take him, McMenemy?
> I'll take him to the sick bay.
> And what will he do in the sick bay?
> Eat mepacrin all bloody day.

He was a good and popular M.O., noted for going in with the troops in attacks, during one of which, on a village, he was observed running ahead with a rifle, hopefully crying: "Pig-pig-pig-pig-pig."

We were kept busy at Penwegon, but there was still time for occasional recreation. A makeshift cinema had been set up in a disused rice mill, and showed two British films, *Champagne Charlie* and Noel Coward's *This Happy Breed*, both featuring Stanley Holloway (what British film of that time didn't?), and even if most of the dialogue was inaudible, with hundreds of tons of monsoon water battering the roof, the screen images were welcome reminders of home for men sweating on repatriation. A few of Nine Section preferred more esoteric diversions, like cock-fighting, to which the villagers of Penwegon were devoted, and which must be about the only cultural link between Burma and West Cumberland. I never saw a cock-fight myself, but I remember Grandarse counting his rupees and crying: "Awoy, Wattie, ista coomin' tae the main?" – an expression I wouldn't have expected to encounter outside the pages of Georgette Heyer. But then, Cumbrians are a breed apart from the rest of England, in sport as in other things; who else still wrestles on the green and whistles in the trail hounds from their fellside races and pursues foxes *on foot* for astonishing distances up and down the lake hills? Since the war a Cumberland farmer has stood for Parliament on a platform for the legalisation of cock-fighting and the docking of horses' tails; he lost his deposit, but his election meetings were packed out, and he left behind one of the great Parliamentary slogans: "Git the spurs oot, an' let's git crackin'!" Grandarse probably voted for him.

It may have been at Penwegon, but I rather fancy it was at a road-stop farther south and later on, that Corporal Peel received a deserved promotion to sergeant in another platoon, and since no corporal appeared to replace him, Nine Section found themselves groaning under the iron heel of their lance-corporal, a fate which they bore with commendable indifference, but which filled me with dismay, for this was Responsibility (unpaid, too), and I didn't welcome my first independent exercise of it.

Less than ten miles from the road and running parallel with it lay the Sittang river, now a dread name in Japanese memory, since it saw the final extinction of their armies; those from the north fled down along it, and for those to the west of the road it was the great barrier as they tried to escape east. I don't think I was ever across it, but we patrolled towards and along its west bank, saw scores of enemy bodies, bloated and disfigured, coming down in the swift-flowing current, and from time to time set up temporary posts between it and the road, and it was from one of these that I had my first taste of leading the section on patrol, probably some time in late June or early July.

We had a new platoon officer by this time, and he briefed me and other patrol leaders in a hut in a miserable hamlet not far from the west bank. I've forgotten his name, but not his moustache, which was luxuriant and apparently endowed with a life of its own, for it heaved and undulated even when he wasn't talking. Sergeant Hutton, who was taking another patrol (across the Sittang, I think), stood at his elbow as I was instructed to take the section to a village several miles down the river, settle in for the night, scout the country round the following day, wait overnight at the village, and come home the morning after. In the event of sighting or hearing of any significant Japanese activity I was to send a runner back at speed, and wait.

It was routine stuff, but I was quite sure it was being entrusted to me only because there was no one more experienced to send. With the battalion short of officers and n.c.o.s, and the platoon operating independently, the new subaltern was having to make do with what he had, and (doubtless on Hutton's advice) I was being given the cushiest of the three patrols, to an area where there was little likelihood of encountering Jap; the other hazard, Burmese bands engaged in the national pastime of brigandage, might be anywhere; the battalion had already had to deal with some of them.

My chief worry was not the bandits out there, but the ones at my back. When you've just escaped from your teens you have doubts about your ability to control and direct that kind of hard-bitten gang for two days in the field, there and back across twenty-odd miles of roughish country. However, the officer, who was possibly even more nervous than I was, seemed to take me for granted; he gave me a map and a compass and wished me luck, and Hutton cuffed my shoulder and said: "Awreet, son? Tek time, stick wid the river, an' ye'll be fine. Aye, and see if ye can pick oop a few eggs, eh?"

He was a psychologist, was Hutton; the mention of eggs made it seem a less desperate venture, somehow.

We struck across country in the rain to the river, which twists and turns a good deal in those parts. Sticking to it, as Hutton had advised, would add miles to our journey, but it was insurance against getting lost. The country was fairly open, but there were jungly patches and I wanted to avoid them as much as possible, so I kept the brown oily flood in view and before we'd gone more than a couple of miles we had made contact with the enemy – only one of him, fortunately, a short, bespectacled figure festooned with equipment, hanging about disconsolately and looking thoroughly lost. Forster, who was on point, covered him, and the Jap unslung his rifle and sat down. By the time I came up Forster had relieved him of his watch and was rifling his pack; the Jap sat blinking and looking wet.

I had no Japanese beyond "Banzai" and "Sayonara", and when Parker tried him in Chinese he just gaped in a forlorn way; the contents of his pack suggested he was a medical orderly – certainly he was the least combatant Jap I'd ever seen. He looked about sixteen, and unlike most of his countrymen at that time was carry-ing a fair bit of fat. There was nothing for it but to send him back to the platoon, where he would be passed on for interrogation, and I was tempted to detail Forster, my most insubordinate element, as escort, but he was too useful altogether, so I sent Wedge. They trudged off, the Jap stolid and bandy-legged, with Wedge talking to him in Birminghamese. I said nothing about the watch, partly out of weakness, partly because while I disapprove of robbing prisoners, Forster had taken him and was entitled.

We marched on, and after an hour came to our first obstacle, a chaung (not marked on my map) which ran across our front and emptied into the main river. It was sluggish but deep, and I was just wondering whether to try it farther inland or swim across when Wattie pointed out that there was a canoe-like craft beached on the bank were the two streams met.

The Sittang, according to the gazetteer, is unnavigable in this region, and I'm not arguing, if its monsoon tributaries are anything to go by. The canoe made it across the chaung and back three times, but foundered on its final trip, and Parker and I had to flounder ashore. Fortunately it wasn't far, and the current was even slower than it looked, possibly because, to quote the gazetteer, the waters hereabout "carry a great deal of silt in suspension": it was like wading through dirty custard.

We squelched on along the bank, and as the rain slackened and the sun became visible through the mist and cloud across the river, my spirits rose. We'd taken a prisoner, such as he was, and the fact that he was alone suggested that there was no large Jap presence in the neighbourhood, or he'd have been with them. That left the dacoits, who were reported to be using discarded Japanese weapons in their attacks on villages, and I've no doubt that as we marched I was remembering:

> Bo dah Thone was a warrior bold,
> His sword and his Snider were bossed with gold

and reflecting that this was the very territory where

> He shot at the strong, and he slashed at the weak,
> From the Salween scrub to the Chindwin teak:
> He crucified noble, he sacrificed mean,
> He filled old ladies with kerosene.
> And the newspapers over the water cried:
> "A patriot fights for his countryside!"

It had been one of my father's favourites; I could picture him reciting as he showed me how to maintain a camp-fire, Masai fashion, feeding a log into the embers on a hillside in Glen Elven. He had never imagined that the listening small boy would some day encounter the real thing.

That happened when we reached the village just on nightfall. It lay on the far side of a jungly stretch through which a narrow track twisted and turned so abominably that I began to have visions of losing our way altogether. The track had an alarming habit of petering out in swamp or undergrowth, and we hacked and splashed, being bitten witless by leeches and mosquitos. Once we found the way blocked by a stream unlike any I've ever seen: it looked exactly like milk, and there were dark snake-like shapes moving in its depths.

"Watter-snakes," said Grandarse. "Bastard things."

"Are they poisonous?"

"Ah nivver foond oot," said Grandarse, "an' Ah's bloody sure Ah's nut gan to noo."

So we turned aside until a tangle of roots and creepers enabled us to cross, ploughed on into the undergrowth, and I was just starting to have pups at the prospect of bedding down in that green mess for the night when we came out of it, and saw the lights of a village less than half a mile away.

Wattie scouted it and reported. "Nee Japs, but there's soom foony-lookin' boogers in theer, Ah'll tell thee." There were, too, ten or twelve of them, Burmans all right, but not your average peasant – there were plenty of those, women, children, and old folk, quietly going about their business, but my attention was fixed on the Dirty Dozen, taking their ease round a fire before the biggest basha in the place and looking like fantasy pirates, some with scarves round their heads, others in straw hats, and all bristling with enough assorted cutlery to start a shop – dahs, swords, knives – and several undoubted Jap rifles.

They were dacoits, no question, but far from terrorising the village they seemed to belong to it, judging from the way the children were playing among them. No doubt the proper course would have been to disarm them and take them in for questioning, but I could think of four good reasons against it: there was nothing amiss but their villainous appearance, they weren't disturbing the peace, there were too many of them for comfort, and I'm not

Sanders of the River. Also, they greeted us with the Burman's
unfailing courtesy, rising as one man with nods and becks and evil
grins, and I was wishing I knew the Burmese for "good evening"
when the local headman appeared.

He was a jovial old buck in a spotless white robe, a brass medal
of George V on his imposing stomach, and a staff of office which
he flourished in welcome. He spoke excellent English, ushered us
to the fire, ordered up refreshments, and established his bona fides
by singing "Keep the Home Fires Burning" in a thunderous bari-
tone; he had learned it, he said, in France with the Burma Rifles
in the First World War, and did an encore while his gang of
cut-throats beat time and hummed along, offered us cheroots,
passed the mangoes, and cast envious glances at our Bren gun.

They were armed, the headman said, against possible attack by
dacoits who were taking advantage of the troubled times to plun-
der far and wide; several villages nearby had suffered from their
depredations. He translated this into Burmese for the benefit of
his other listeners, and the gang round the fire shook their heads
in concern. Then, of course, there were the unspeakable Japanese
– none of whom, fortunately, were in the vicinity at present, but
if we wanted any help in slaughtering stragglers his lads would be
charmed to assist, in return for a few grenades and any spare small
arms we might have about us.

It was so reassuring that I didn't sleep a wink – not that I could
have even if I'd wanted to, for we all bedded down on mats on
the long verandah of the headman's house with his numerous
family, Granny being discreetly positioned between the brutal sol-
diery and the younger females, and she snored like the Last Trump.
What with that and being eaten alive by mosquitos and my sus-
picions of the bandits in the next basha, I spent most of the night
pacing the village street in my monsoon cape, reflecting that if I
had studied just a little harder I would have been snug in student
digs in Hillhead with nothing to worry about but lectures and
exams in anatomy – and just that thought was enough to make my
present lot seem very heaven, wet and mosquito-plagued though it
might be. There would be time enough for desk-work and the
humdrum business of making a living in civvy street, and then this
little outpost at the back of beyond would be like a dreamland,

long ago and far away. How many times, in the late 'forties and 'fifties, did one see a sober citizen in his office throw aside his pencil and stare at the window and exclaim: "Oh, God, I wish the war was still on!" It is a strange echo now: who could possibly want to be at war? Nobody in his right mind, and of course the sober citizen wasn't longing for battle and sudden death, but remembering the freedom of service life, the strange sights and smells of places just like this, the uncertainty of tomorrow, and the romance of distant lands and seas. They have their hazards, but once you've trodden the wild ways you never quite get them out of your system.

You never get malaria out of it, either, and while mine hasn't troubled me for years, that's no fault of the buzzing pests which infested that village in their billions. By morning my face was swollen beyond recognition, and most of the section, and the younger villagers, had been badly bitten. Granny and the older generation, being made of leather, were apparently anopheles-proof; she clucked in dismay at my appearance, and gave me a fine old herbal (I hope it was herbal) ointment to rub on, which if anything made it worse.

The armed Burmese had slipped away during the night, the headman was nowhere to be seen, and I didn't know whether to be worried or not. The hell with them. My hated tommy-gun had collected another fine patina of rust in the soggy atmosphere, and I oiled and cursed over it while Grandarse bargained for provisions with the villagers, airing his Burmese with "*Jet-oo lo jinde?*", which means "Have you any eggs?" They inquired by signs how many he wanted, which was what he'd been waiting to be asked for weeks. He beamed and cried: "Shit!", which is the word for "eight" – needless to say, he went on to purchase eight cheroots and eight mangoes and eight bananas; any other number would have seemed tame to him.

We scouted in a two-mile arc beyond the village without seeing a soul, or anything but misty plain and scrub. We brewed up at noon in the shelter of a palm-grove, and were making our way back reluctantly for another night in Mosquito City when we hit on something that altered the whole nature of the patrol. In a ramshackle basha hidden away in a little chaung we surprised four

Indian soldiers in their underclothes; their uniforms and equipment were gone, but two of them still had rifles which they snatched up at sight of us, only to drop them as hurriedly when we covered them.

There was no doubt what they were: Jifs, deserters to the Japanese. One of them, who seemed to be the leader, had a little Japanese pamphlet on him, which might have been some sort of identity card, but in answer to questions they stubbornly pretended not to understand, which was nonsense: an Indian soldier with absolutely no English at all was a rare bird. My Urdu was good enough to ask their names, ranks, and regiments, but all I got was a blank stare. They just weren't talking. The question was what to do with them, and Forster had the answer.

"Shoot the boogers," said he.

"Don't be a bloody idiot!" I snapped, all the angrier for not knowing what to do next.

"Ah's nut the bloody idiot!" he retorted. "W'at ye gan dee wid them, then?"

That was the difficulty. If there had been one or even two of them, we could have kept them prisoners through the night and the next day of the patrol, but four was too many, even disarmed. They were dead men when the Army got them, a court-martial would see to that, and they knew it; they would certainly try something, and God alone knew what that might lead to. And I didn't know what to do. The crisis had come, in totally unexpected form.

Grandarse suddenly thrust one of them against the wall and put his bayonet to his throat. "W'ee the 'ell are ye, ye bastard!" he shouted, and the man just glared and closed his mouth, tight.

"He's a fookin' Jif!" said Forster. "They're worse'n the bloody Japs! Shut the boogers, Ah say! Christ, Ah'll dee it!"

"Shut up or you're under arrest!" I said, which is the weak n.c.o.'s last resort, but I was rattled and couldn't see the simple, obvious solution. It had all happened too quickly, and I could only look at the four brown faces in silence, for no one else was saying a word. They were ordinary *jawans*,* skinny and helpless-looking

_____
* soldiers

in their shorts and singlets – how they'd lost their uniforms, when they'd deserted, what they were doing there, I still don't know. They were watching me, ugly and sullen, but not scared. Of course, shooting them was out of the question ... but listening to the silence I had a horrid feeling that if I *did* give the unthinkable order, the section would obey it – Forster for certain, Wattie and Morton probably, perhaps even Grandarse and Nick; they might not do it themselves, but they would not object to its happening. If you think that atrocious – well, it is, by civilised lights, but they don't shine, much, in war-time. (They mustn't, or you'll lose.) The section were hard men, used to killing as a matter of course, and these were traitors who wouldn't have hesitated if the positions had been reversed.

I may be wrong, but I'm pretty sure those Jifs would have been dead if I'd given the word I had no intention of giving. I'd heard the section, only a week or so earlier, discussing the deaths of some Japs who'd been found asleep in a basha out towards the Pegu Yomas – the soldier who'd found them had woken them up, and *then* shot them, and the feeling of Nine Section had been that it didn't matter, but on the whole he had done the proper thing, because it wasn't right to shoot men asleep.

"Weel, we gonna *sarf karo** 'em or nut?" challenged Forster, looking around, and Parker spoke for the first time. "Can't keep 'em overnight, corp," and the last word made it plain that he was leaving it to me. He regarded me impassively, the old professional. Then he added: "Can't shoot 'em, either," and I knew the relief of not being alone.

"W'at for nut?" demanded Forster.

"They're bloody Jifs, man," said Wattie.

"'Oo we gonna look efter 'em?" Grandarse was addressing me.

"We'll take 'em in today," I said, voicing the conclusion I'd have reached earlier if I'd had my wits about me. "We can have 'em back before dark."

"Warraboot the patrol? Thowt we wez meant tae ga back tomorrer."

"I'll worry about that," I said, and that settled it. We tied their

---

* Literally, to clean, hence to clean up, to kill

hands with log-lines, and I went outside and took a bearing to get us home by the shortest route. Forster had to have the last word.

"If they'd bin fookin' Japs," he announced loudly, "we'd nivver ha' thowt twice. Bleedin' Jifs! Ah doan't knaw!"

It may seem that I am making much of a trivial incident, or trying to show how enlightened a Christian I was. I'm not enlightened, and believe that the best way with enemies is the short one, and at least part of the reason for not letting Forster have his way was that I'd have been called to account, and probably court-martialled, when the story got out, as it inevitably would. But although it had been a thirty-second crisis at most, it had been a vital moment for me: I can look back now and say that there was only one possible outcome, but for half a minute I'd felt the weight – and I never knew any doubts about being in command again.

Coming home on a straight line we hit the chaung about a mile from the river, and found it shallow enough to wade – once the rain stops, water levels can fall at astonishing speeds. We ran into a Baluch patrol who were coming out as we returned, and from the looks directed at our prisoners it was plain that the Jifs had been lucky to be taken by a British unit. We reached the platoon area as night fell, and to my relief the subaltern approved my decision to cut the patrol short. Sergeant Hutton was less impressed: he obviously considered Grandarse's eggs a poor haul. I was just glad it was over, and that I was carrying a Lee Enfield again. I had appropriated one of the two taken from the Jifs, and my tommy-gun has long since rusted away at the bottom of a tributary to the Sittang.

Polling in the 1945 General Election took place between July 5 and 12, and resulted in an overwhelming defeat for Churchill and the Conservatives at the hands of the Labour Party, an outcome which astonished the world, but not the British Army. Servicemen under the age of 21 were not entitled to vote.

"''Ey, Grandarse – 'oo d'ye spell Iredell?"

"'Oo the hell dae Ah knaw? W'ee's Iredell?"

"Liberal candidate in Carel.* Ah's writin' yam tae see w'at 'e's on aboot."

"Weel, Ah doan't belang bloody Carel. Ah belang Peerith,† an' Ah doan't ken w'at constituency it's in, an' Ah doan't care 'cos Ah's nut votin', neether."

"Ye ought to vote, man."

"W'at for? The Labour man doesn't stand a fookin' chance, an' Ah'm boogered if Ah'll vote Tory. Them boogers 'es bin in ower lang."

"Weel, vote Liberal, then."

"Git hired! Ah doan't knaw booger-all aboot politics, but Ah knaw the Liberal's ca'd Roberts, an' 'is family's temperance, so knackers till them. They 'ed a cellar oot at Naworth, boorstin' wid the best drink in the coonty, an' the teetotal boogers poured the lot on't doon drain! Think Ah'd vote for them? Man, they say if ye coom oop at Brampton Court the foorst thing owd Roberts says is: 'Was there a haroma of drink haboot the haccused, constable?', an' if the constable says 'Aye, yer woorship, 'e wez pissed rotten', then ye've 'ad it. Sod them."

* Carlisle
† Penrith

"*Ye doan't deserve the vote, you. Does any booger knaw 'oo tae spell Iredell?*"

"*Give ower, man, ye're wastin' yer time. They'll nivver put a Liberal in for Carel. It'll be owd General Spears, the Tory – 'im that wez in't desert wid Lawrence of Arabia. 'E's bin tellin' folk there's twenty million Arabs waitin' on the resoolt o' the Carel election. Daft booger. They reckon 'e'll git back, tho'.*"

"*Nut if Ah can 'elp it. Ah's bloody votin' Labour, an' Ah doan't give a monkey's left goolie w'ee the candidate is. It can be bloody George Formby, 'e'll git my vote.*"

"*Reckon Labour'll gi'e thee tha job back on't booses, Foshie?*"

"*Booger the booses. Ah want Choorchill oot, an' his whole fookin' gang. Ah remember the 'thirties, marra, if thoo doesn't. Ah want rid of the bloody Tories, see, an' the lah-di-dahs, an' the lot o' them. They got us into this fookin' war, didn't they?*"

"*Weel, Ah'm votin' Labour to git rid o' bloody old Womersley. Ah reckon we'll be better wi' Labour.*"

"*Girraway, it'll mek nee bloody difference – nut till the woorkin' man, any roads. Them that's better off'll still be better off, nee matter w'ee gits in. W'ee's the Labour man in Carel, Foshie?*"

"*Ah've joost bin tellin' ye, Ah doan't knaw! But 'e's gittin' the nod frae me, anyway.*"

"*His name's Edgar Grierson.*"

"*W'at, 'im that woorked in't Co-op? 'E won't git many votes in Stanwix. 'Oo the hell dae you knaw, Jock – ye're not owd enuff to vote, you!*"

"That's right, Foshie. I just know who the candidates are. You big grown-ups 'll decide who the government is."

"*Ye're bloody reet we will. Weel, Ah'm glad ye 'evn't got the vote, Jock, 'cos ye'd joost vote Tory, wadn't ye – you that wants tae be an officer!*"

"No, I'd vote for Edgar Grierson."

"*Girraway! Ah can see ye!*"

"*W'y'd ye vote Labour, Jock? Shooroop, Foshie! W'y, man?*"

"Because my father's Edgar's doctor, and he used to take me to football when I was small –"

"*Ye're small yet, soony boy!*"

"– and Mrs Grierson made bloody good high teas."

"Typical! That's yer eddicated man, Grandarse! Votin' wid 'is bloody belly!"

"So you vote for him, Foshie. He's all right – and a bloody sight more honest than most politicians. He was in this regiment, too, in the Great War."

"W'at? A bloody officer! Bollocks till 'im, then!"

"No, a private. In the trenches."

"'E'll do me, then. Booger them an' their class distinction."

They voted with high hopes, for a better, fairer Britain, and to some extent they got it. Mostly it was a vote to get "them" out – "them" being not just the Conservatives, but all that it was believed they stood for: wealth and privilege and authority as personified by civilian employers and Army officers (who, I suspect, were as likely to vote Labour as Tory, especially the younger men). It was a strange election for me – old enough to lead a section in war, but not old enough to vote. I had no complaints; I wasn't fit to vote, for I took no interest in politics, and my support for Grierson (who got in, I'm delighted to say, and Westminster never saw a better man) was entirely personal. Mind you, better that than voting for a party. And the truth was that while I knew how to be a soldier, and had some idea of how to lead a section, I knew nothing of working for a living, of being a farm labourer, or a factory hand, or being on the dole, or being fired for crossing my hands on the wheel. No, it was their election, not mine. They had earned it.

With the exception of Parker, who I suspect voted Tory if he voted at all (free lances are a conservative lot), and one or two of the rustics, who may have voted Liberal, they were Labour to a man, but not necessarily socialists as the term is understood now. Their socialism was of a simple kind: they had known the 'thirties, and they didn't want it again: the dole queue, the street corner, the true poverty of that time. They wanted jobs, and security, and a better future for their children than they had had – and they got that, and were thankful for it. It was what they had fought for, over and beyond the pressing need of ensuring that Britain did not become a Nazi slave state.

Still, the Britain they see in their old age is hardly "the land fit for heroes" that they envisaged – if that land existed in their imaginations, it was probably a place where the pre-war values co-existed with decent wages and housing. It was a reasonable, perfectly possible dream, and for a time it existed, more or less. And then it changed, in the name of progress and improvement and enlightenment, which meant the destruction of much that they had fought for and held dear, and the betrayal of familiar things that they had loved. Some of them, to superficial minds, will seem terribly trivial, even ludicrously so – things like county names, and shillings and pence, and the King James Version, and yards and feet and inches – yet they matter to a nation.

They did not fight for a Britain which would be dishonestly railroaded into Europe against the people's will; they did not fight for a Britain where successive governments, by their weakness and folly, would encourage crime and violence on an unprecedented scale; they did not fight for a Britain where thugs and psychopaths could murder and maim and torture and never have a finger laid on them for it; they did not fight for a Britain whose leaders would be too cowardly to declare war on terrorism; they did not fight for a Britain whose Parliament would, time and again, betray its trust by legislating against the wishes of the country; they did not fight for a Britain where children could be snatched from their homes and parents by night on nothing more than the good old Inquisition principle of secret information; they did not fight for a Britain whose Churches and schools would be undermined by fashionable reformers; they did not fight for a Britain where free choice could be anathematised as "discriminisation"; they did not fight for a Britain where to hold by truths and values which have been thought good and worthy for a thousand years would be to run the risk of being called "fascist" – that, really, is the greatest and most pitiful irony of all.

No, it is not what they fought for – but being realists they accept what they cannot alter, and reserve their protests for the noise pollution of modern music in their pubs.

CALCUTTA IS STILL my favourite city, probably because I haven't been there since 1945 and remember it as it looked to me then, which was something like a paradise market. Nowadays the name conjures up images of poverty, starvation, disease, and squalor, of Mother Theresa and that fine old retired British officer who runs his own field kitchen in the slums. It wasn't much better, I dare say, when I saw it in the twilight of the Raj, but I was there on seven days' leave, and as every holiday-maker knows, even in this enlightened age, you don't spend an eagerly-awaited vacation seeking out the plague-spots which exist within a mile of your hotel.

Not that you had to look far for them in "Cal": the beggars displayed their sores and hideous deformities on the main streets, you could find corpses on the station platforms, and a tram-ride to Howrah would take you through slums and hovels populated by uncountable filthy multitudes who didn't so much live as swarm. One look would have convinced the most zealous reformer of the sheer impossibility of doing anything with that vast, prolifer-ating Augean stable, and if you had been any time in India you were hardened to it. There was something else, too, which if it did not transform the second city of Empire, lifted it at least a little from the depths. Everybody smiled.

That may be at the root of Britain's three-century love affair with India. Nowadays it is taught (usually by people who never saw the Raj) that our passion for the sub-continent was mere pride of possession, arrogant satisfaction of conquest, and lust of exploitation, leavened only by a missionary zeal to improve. No doubt those feelings existed, among some, but they don't account for the undying affection that so many of the island race felt for that wonderful country and its people. Nor do all its great marvels:

the beauty of the land and its buildings, the endless variety of its customs and cultures, the wonder of its art and philosophy and ancient civilisation, the glory of its matchless regiments. They may inspire awe, even reverence, but they don't quite explain why thousands of soldiers and merchants and administrators and traders left their hearts there, to say nothing of their mortal remains. One can babble about the magic of India, and convey nothing: I can only say that when I look back at it my lasting memory is of smiling faces, laughter in the bazaar, tiny naked children grinning as they clamoured for buckshee – and it wasn't an act, for they still laughed and joked and play-acted if they didn't get it. There was a life, a spirit about India that was irrepressible, and it outweighed all the faults and miseries and cruelties and corruptions. That, I think, is why the British loved it, and some of us will never get it out of our systems, even in an age when Indian and Pakistani immigration is about as welcome in Britain as the British were in India.

We must have been somewhere on the Rangoon road when we were told that we were to go on leave, and I have only mental snapshots of the journey: the long straight highway through the Rangoon suburbs, with their pleasant bungalows and green gardens looking as though there had never been a war; the Shwe Dagon pagoda gleaming in the moonlight – they said the Japs had stripped away its gold leaf, but it still shone for me; sleeping on a marble floor under the counter of "Honkers and Shankers" (the Hong Kong and Shanghai Bank building), which was the only billet available; reading *Gone with the Wind* in the stifling 'tween-decks of the troop transport, or staring overside at the flying fishes and the sinister weaving shapes of the sharks in the cobalt depths of the Bay of Bengal; running up between the chocolate and green banks of the muddy Hooghly river; driving past the imposing buildings and Victorian statuary of the great city; and the final arrival in the cool vaulted chambers of the Museum, with the beds set out among the glass display cases. If a museum seems an unlikely base for a furlough – well, you may keep the Beverly Wilshire and the Hotel du Cap and the Waldorf Astoria and the Savoy and even the Grand in Rome; I have been content (more or less) in all of them, but the Museum, Calcutta, is the only establishment to which I would give six stars and as many rosettes as you like.

No doubt my view was coloured by youth and the bewilderment of change. After six months of chlorinated water and compo, baking and freezing by turns in the Dry Belt and being permanently sodden in the monsoon, feeling like a walking delicatessen for leeches and mosquitos and ticks, and with the occasional possibility of being killed – suddenly there was the peace and unimaginable luxury of a frame-and-rope native bed with a real pillow (no sheets in the British Army, though) beneath gently-stirring punkahs, and the certainty of sleep untroubled by stags or o.p.s or night attacks or yells of "Stand to!" Jap was five hundred miles away, and in his place there were bearers to keep the place tidy, and *dhobis* to launder our clothes, and *dersis* to make and mend, and downstairs a cool and airy canteen where they'd never heard of bully stew or K-rations and the service was supervised by amazing memsahibs who addressed the native staff and each other like gym mistresses thundering encouragement across the fields of Cheltenham. They were volunteers charged with the welfare and refreshment of the troops, and by God we were going to be well-fed and comfortable or they'd know the reason why.

Each man received a brand-new suit of jungle green, starched and pressed, and on each the *dersis* sewed the shoulder-flash of the black cat arching its back, and we dug out our regimental badges and polished them and set them in our bush-hats, and we counted the thick wads of little blue notes – six months' back pay, even if it's only eighteen rupees a week, soon mounts up in a country where you buy and sell in tinned fish and mangoes, and I didn't need to touch my brag winnings in Lloyd's – and we beamed at each other across the table in the tired, happy knowledge that we had nothing to do for seven days but loaf and spend time and money and gape contentedly at the real world again.

From what I read and television tells me, soldiers on leave have different priorities nowadays. It was with stunned disbelief that I read that U.S. forces in the Gulf were to receive "counselling" on how to "relate" to members of the opposite sex after a few months in the desert; the idea of G.I.s needing this kind of instruction must have convulsed their predecessors, and I'm sure it came as a shock to the present generation of the American military, too. But it shows how the modern official mind works, and what it expects servicemen to do when they are turned loose in the fleshpots.

Maybe sex is more important nowadays than it used to be. Or maybe we were a more restrained, inhibited, pious, and timid generation. But I was interested to note that Nine Section, who for months had been deprived of female society, and had remarked on the fact from time to time, showed no tendency to behave like Casanova gone berserk. They eyed what talent there was in the bars of Chowringhee, danced with abandon at the service clubs, and chatted up the Wrens, Waafs, ATS, and nurses, and that was about it, apparently. Parker was an exception; by his own admission it was on this leave that he contracted his umpteenth dose of Cupid's measles, and rolled off to the M.O. almost as a matter of course – catching a social disease, incidentally, was not a military crime, but concealing it was. And it may well have been that the risk of infection was the great restrainer; there were no simple cures at that time, and that for clap was reputed to be excruciatingly painful; syphilis, which was rumoured to be incurable, was regarded much as AIDS is today. So, apart from the feeling, quite widespread in my generation, that illicit sex was a bad thing, frowned on by church, school, and family, there was considerable caution, and it was natural that Grandarse, solemnly regarding a coloured poster in the billet which showed two sultry houris smiling invitingly above the caption "Do you want it – we've got it", should sigh heavily and observe: "Aye, weel, Ah'd sooner 'ev a pint anyways." The Army propagandised unceasingly, with lectures, short-arm inspections, and terrifyingly explicit films; one poster, I remember, showed a statuesque blonde, surrounded by leering Japanese, with the caption: "Is this the face that loved a thousand Nips?" I wouldn't have thought that many of the light ladies of Calcutta had had the opportunity to bestow their favours on the Japanese, but there you are. Another discouragement, I should add, was that the average Indian and Eurasian prostitute was not notable for charm or beauty.

I'm not trying to pretend that my military generation were any saintlier than soldiers ever are. As a harassed orderly officer in

North Africa I had to raid more brothels, endure the screaming protests of more furious harlots, and see more frustrated amorists into the paddy-wagon, than I care to count, and I remember the blue and khaki queues outside the bawdy-houses of the Cairo Birkah, the more impatient customers already in their shirt-tails with their trousers neatly folded over their arms. Certainly a proportion of the services behaved like demented rabbits, but I would guess they were a minority.

Forster was an interesting case. On our first night in Calcutta he spruced himself up with Lifebuoy, flourished the prophylactic kit which he had drawn from the M.O.'s office, admired himself in the mirror, sketched out a programme of debauchery which would have frightened Caligula, and strode forth like Ferdinand the Bull. Three hours later he was back, full of gloating accounts of his sexual heroics, and unaware that in the interval Grandarse and I had been sitting three rows behind him in the Lighthouse cinema, watching Laurel and Hardy.

It sounds terribly tame, I suppose, but our chief occupations in those seven days consisted of eating and drinking to excess, wandering in the bazaars, drinking again, going to the cinema, riding in the tram-cars, or, if we felt expensive, in one of the coolie-drawn rickshaws, having yet another pint at Jimmy's Kitchen (the Bristol, where the sea captains went, and the big hotels frequented by the officers, were not for us), and best of all, simply strolling and surveying on one of the great streets of the world: Chowringhee.

No doubt if I could see it now I'd be disillusioned, but in my memory it makes Piccadilly and the Via Veneto and the Champs-Elysées and Rodeo Drive and Princes Street and Broadway look like ordinary streets with undistinguished shops. Chowringhee was Bond Street and Change Alley and the Arabian Nights all in one, with a touch of Park Lane to one side where the broad Maidan with its trees and distant buildings was separated from the street itself by the clanging tramway line. The roadway was crowded with every kind of vehicle imaginable, from limousines and the famous taxis driven by bearded burly Sikhs to bicycles and horse-drawn carriages and the flying two-person tongas with their long shafts between which the lean brown tonga-wallahs, naked but for loincloths, raced along, clanking their tiny bells; at speed they would leave the ground, being borne along by the impetus of the high-wheeled vehicle before hitting the tarmac again with their bare soles, covering the ground in giant strides to become airborne again.

But Chowringhee pavement, on the built-up side of the wide road, was where the excitement and enchantment were. There, it seemed, you could meet every race and type in India, and every uniform of the Allies in the Orient: beggars and generals, fakirs and merchants, memsahibs and pan-spitting layabouts, massive native policemen with their metal-shod staves and American fliers with their hats tilted back and the inevitable pack of Camels in their breast-pockets, a Naval officer in brilliant white with his sword on one hand and his bride on the other hurrying through a laughing crowd from their hotel, and a wild man with hair to his waist and his near-naked body smeared with paint and ashes pushing across their path as he stared ahead with empty eyes, sacred white cows with garlands ambling along (to whom you gave way) and red-capped military policemen with cold nasty expressions (to whom, being Fourteenth Army and knowing it, you did not). I never saw anyone lying on a bed of nails on Chowringhee, but I did see a snake-charmer, a rope-trick prac-titioner, and a Bhil knife-thrower who cut the ace of diamonds out of a playing card with four knives thrown simultaneously, two from either hand.

The shops and booths and canopied stalls of the pavement would have taken a lifetime to examine, for they seemed to be packed with everything of East and West, crowded in among the larger buildings and hotels and cafés. You might pass a great pillared entrance with broad steps guarded by splendidly-accoutred Sikhs standing like statues, and next to it a tiny booth dispensing chapattis and curries to a jostling pack of babus, with limbless mendicants crawling among their feet, and beyond that a bookstall where complete sets of Scott and Dickens and Hardy and Jeffery Farnol stood shoulder to shoulder in immaculate rows with Milton and Shakespeare and Burns and Ella Wheeler Wilcox and Edgar Rice Burroughs, with a prim little Eurasian clerk at the receipt of custom, his lips moving as he solved the *Times of*

India crossword and lashed out with his cane at any beggars who touched his stool. And then an ivory shop, where you could watch the workmen carving those amazing ball-within-a-ball ornaments and intricately-decorated tusks and perfect little Taj Mahals that would fit under a thimble, and a leather boutique that would have shamed Cordoba, where they would trace your foot on a piece of paper and build a shoe around it, all within an hour, for ten rupees (and they lasted me as many years), and the little Tiger Cinema with its wickerwork armchairs and a twenty-foot coloured cut-out of Betty Grable in *Pin-Up Girl* above its marquee, and a tattooist where Wedge, the lunatic, had a cobra imprinted on his arm, coiled round from wrist to elbow, with a scroll saying "Mother", and the swinging doors of the Nip Inn, packed to capacity with beer-soaked servicemen, and white-helmeted American M.P.s parked outside in their jeep, swinging their truncheons and waiting and hoping, and if you turned the corner you were in Hogg Market, that great clamorous emporium with its quiet corners where nothing was bought without being haggled for, and within a few minutes you had acquired, without quite understanding how, a silver cigarette case beautifully enamelled with peacocks and a map of India with all the names misspelled, for another ten chips, and a beautiful razor-edged kukri for eight (or twelve, depending on who won the toss, you or the grinning bandit of a stall-holder), and a roll of silk, and had your photograph taken under a sign reading "Karsh of Calcutta" ("Please to hold still, sahib, you are moving extremely and the result will be oll fuzzee and unsatisfactoree!"), and been shaved by a squatting *nappy-wallah* who used no lather but your own sweat and left your skin like glass.

After which there was nothing for it but to rest in Ferrazini's and linger over a Desert Sunrise, which was about a gallon of ice creams and syrups of every flavour and colour. And a Turkish coffee.

It was all new and exotic and dazzling to us, in those days before package travelling, when Britain was in the grip of war-time austerity; what is now commonplace was a novelty. For example, I had never had a shoeshine until Calcutta; I had never eaten a steak until we treated ourselves at Jimmy's Kitchen to a mysterious thing called a T-Bone, with chips. Nor had I known the exhilaration of being massaged by an Indian barber, all across the shoulders and down the arms to the fingers, each joint of which he cracked resoundingly, and produced a feeling of well-being beyond anything I had experienced.

Being eccentric, I had to hunt out the Black Hole of Calcutta, and found it (in Strand Road, if memory serves), a low archway just above pavement level through which you could look into the infamous dark dungeon; I wonder if the little plaque to the 23 who died inside it is still there; knowing the Indians, I imagine it is.

But sightseeing and riding in tongas and rubber-necking at the wonders of Chowringhee was all very well; what I was starved of was reading, and the booksellers made enough out of me to retire. They had a simple system: you bought a book for ten rupees and when you had read it they bought it back for seven. I have mentioned the works of Jeffery Farnol, and I think I know why he was so available in Calcutta; whatever his literary merits, he was the great romantic conjurer of Old England, painting his word-pictures of leafy lanes and bosky woods and green fields and pints of ale and rosy-cheeked milkmaids and saturnine squires and all those never-never things that were so far away from the heat and dust and smells of India. I went through him like a devouring flame, and counted him cheap at the price.

The movies then being what T.V. is nowadays, we spent hours in the Lighthouse and the Tiger and the other cinemas, but (and this is unusual for me, for my memory for old films is prodigious) I can give the title of only one of the dozen or so pictures I must have seen in Calcutta, and that is *Chal, Chal Re Navjavan* ("March, March the Youth") which I went to out of sheer curiosity, never having seen an Indian movie. From its title I imagine it must have been aimed at those supporting the Indian independence movement, but it consisted largely of winsome young females in saris riding bicycles and glancing coyly at intense young men; there were interminable shots of blossoms and lily ponds, all to the accompaniment of zithers and keening half-tone singing, and after about ten minutes Grandarse exclaimed: "Booger this for a lark, Ah's gan for anoother dekko at Grable," and left. That is my total recall of Calcutta cinemas, except for the item which probably displaced all the Hollywood features from my memory, and that was the newsreel which accompanied them: the first pictures to come out of Belsen concentration camp.

We were not a squeamish group in Nine Section; if anyone had seen war in the raw, we had, but that newsreel left us numb. If we hadn't seen those ghastly walking skeletons and great heaps of emaciated bodies, I don't think we'd have believed it. Even now it doesn't seem possible that human behaviour could sink to such depths. Some people left the cinema, and one woman was physically sick. I stood in the foyer afterwards reflecting that if Robert Burns had seen those pictures he would have revised his famous lines about man's inhumanity to man making countless thousands mourn, and substituted a much stronger verb.

"If Ah'd my way," said Forster, over his beer, "ye knaw w'at Ah'd dee? Ah'd roond oop ivvery fookin' Hun in Germany, an Ah'd boorn the boogers alive. Noo, then!"

This was weighed, and Stanley asked, what about women and children?

"The whole bloody sub-cheese, the lot!"

"Not on," said Parker. "You'd be just as bad as the bleedin' Nazis."

"Don't talk cock!" retorted Forster, and produced an analogy of which I'd not have thought him capable. "Ye tellin' me, if soom booger commits a moorder, an' Ah hing 'im for't, that Ah'm as bad as 'e is? Ga'n git stoofed!"

This was at a time when the death penalty was not an issue, except among a few intellectuals, so the ethical point was not pursued. The practical one was, though.

"Wimmen an' kids didn't starve them poor boogers tae death," said Nick.

"Naw!" insisted Forster. "But 'oo aboot w'en the kids grow oop? Think they'll be any better? Look at yer bloody 'Itler Youth, man! They're a' the same! Christ, man, fowk like them isn't fit tae live! That's my opinion."

"Tell ye w'at Ah'd dee," said Nick. "Ah'd hing the boogers that did it, an' chop the goolies off a' the Jerry men, an' gi' the German wimmen till the Rooshans – by God, that'd larn the bitches! –"

187

"Sod that," said Parker. "I'm shot if I'd do them red bastards any favours."

"– an' Ah'd send a' the kids till Australia, an' nivver let on tae them w'ee they were, or w'eer they cam' frae."

"Stone me! What's Australia done? An' wot's the point?"

"Gi' the kids a chance tae grow oop decent. Australia's a big place – an' a bloody lang way frae Germany."

"Fat bloody chance they'd grow up decent!" scoffed Forster. "Look, man – my owd Dad got blew tae boogery in Flanders, lost a leg, nivver wez any use efter. Weel, the fookin' Jerries started *that!* Aye, an' w'en we'd lathered 'em, we let 'em be – an' w'at 'appened? Fookin' 'Itler 'appened – an' the likes o' them that did w'at ye've joost seen in't newsreel! An' ye'd gi' the swine anoother chance? They'll dee it again, mark my woords! Ah'd wipe oot the bloody lot – *bus!* Durty Hun bastards!" He sat drumming his fingers. "An' Ah'll tell ye this, Nick! They're lower than bloody Jap, the Germans! Theer, noo! Jap's a fookin' gentleman compared wid that lot!" Irrelevantly, for him, he added: "An' they ca' theirsels Christians!"

"Doan't talk sae wet, Foshie," said Grandarse patiently. "Ye can't wipe oot a whole coontry, man. W'eer ye ganna stop, eh? Ye ganna kill Conrad Veet?" He meant Conrad Veidt.

"Conrad w'ee? W'at the hell ye talkin' aboot, man?"

"Conrad Veet, the film star. 'E's a Jerry."

"Conrad Veet's a British subject," said Wedge, the authority. "Marlene Dietrich's German, an' all."

"Can't give Marlene to the Russians," sighed Parker. "Wasted on 'em. Give 'er to me, Foshie. I'll volunteer."

"Ah's nut talkin' aboot Conrad Veet and Marlene bloody Dietrich!" cried Forster, enraged at this levity. "'E's a reet slimy-lookin' sod, mind – prob'ly a Fifth Columnist. Ah'm talkin' aboot the Huns in Germany! Coom on, man," he appealed to Parker. "Ye seen that film – mek ye spew yer guts oop! Ye ganna let them off?" He stared angrily round the table. "Are ye?"

"It won't be up to us, Foshie," I said. "Even if it was, Grandarse is right – you can't wipe out a nation. At least, I don't think you can." My grasshopper mind had immediately skipped to the Picts. I wasn't sure about the Aztecs and Incas.

"Ah'd 'ev a bloody good try," said Forster. "An' Ah tell ye w'ee else would – the Russkis. Let them loose on Germany – by Christ, they'd sort it oot!"

There was no support for this. Whatever the view of the Soviet Union among C. P. Snow's men of the left, there was a definite feeling at the grass roots of the British Army – or what I saw of it – that after Berlin and Tokyo, "next stop Moscow" would be not a bad idea. I remembered a conversation I'd heard on a bus just after war broke out, and an elderly working man saying: "Ah telt oor boy, w'en 'e joined oop: Nivver mind 'Itler, son, but if ye meet that booger Staylin, put a bay'net oop 'is arse." Labour voters they might be, but for Communism few of them had any use.

Forster's solution to the German problem, if I may call it that, was held by most of the section to be impractical – which is not to say that it was received unsympathetically. The spirit of revenge was strong, especially after the horrors of Belsen and the other camps were revealed, and it was realised what the Germans had been doing and why. I imagine that the Nuremberg trials (which seemed to me, even at the time, to be proceedings of doubtful wisdom) were staged to satisfy this feeling, but there may have been loftier motives. My own instinct would have been to shoot the leading Nazis out of hand, and the devil with legal forms, but I concede that that wouldn't have been as simple as it sounds.

Our beery discussion sounds terribly naïve now, but at that time the term "war criminal" had not been coined; even the concept was unknown to us. After all, no one in 1945 was pursuing war criminals from the First World War, let alone the Boer War of forty-five years ago, and we could not have envisaged that war crimes from *our* war would still be being prosecuted forty-five years into the future. And the notion that the House of Commons in 1991 would be violating a vital principle of British justice by legislating to prosecute people who had committed no crime in British jurisdiction, would have been laughed out of the room. (Pursuit of a just feud, outside the law, would have been another matter; that we would have understood, none better.)

But if we had known the concept of war crimes, we would have thought of them as exclusively German and Japanese. After all, we were the winners, and it would have seemed incredible, then, that the day would ever come when a former British Prime Minister, and a Secretary-General of the United Nations (which didn't exist then) would be "linked" to allegations of atrocities, however distant. And the thought that any of *us*, Nine Section, could ever have had the finger pointed at us . . . really.

Yet, having followed the Waldheim affair and the brouhaha over the Cossacks, and being aware of how fashionable perspectives (to say nothing of common sense) have changed in half a century, I am fairly sure that the section, myself included, could well be charged with war crimes, if anyone wanted to take the trouble. It seems to be established that knowing of a war crime, and winking at it, is to be guilty, at least as an accessory, or by association. Of course, we survivors of Nine Section are of no eminence or importance, and no one can grind a political axe by pursuing us, and they'd have a hell of a job collecting evidence at this time of day, so Nick and Grandarse and the rest of us can probably sleep in peace. But by today's standards, we're dead to rights.

There was a village, no matter where, which contained a curious building, roofed but open at the sides, and its floor was about forty feet by twenty, and made of concrete. Down the length of the floor ran a central trench, also of concrete, perhaps eight feet wide by six deep, rather like a very big garage inspection pit. The building was used as a prison hospital for sick and wounded Japanese, who were laid on stretchers and palliasses down both sides, but not in the central trench. They were guarded, night and day, by picquets drawn from various units. I was never on guard myself, but I was in the building a couple of times, and saw the Japanese, who may have numbered anything from twenty to fifty; I can't be sure. They were all in pretty poor shape.

One morning, after an Indian unit had been on guard, there were no Japanese to be seen in the building, and the central trench was full of rocks. The Japanese were found underneath them, dead. They had been thrown into the trench in the night, and the rocks hurled down on them.

I heard this from one of the section, in the presence of my comrades. We didn't go to the building, so I had only that man's word for it, but from what I heard later from other sources, there was no doubt his report was accurate. I know it happened, although I never saw the evidence.

What had happened was a "war crime", no question. So, what should I have done? Investigated, like a good n.c.o.? Informed my superior – and gone higher if necessary? Written to my M.P.?

It did not even cross my mind to do any of these things. I probably grimaced, remarked "Hard buggers, those jawans", shrugged, and forgot about it. If I had made an issue of it with higher authority, I'd have been regarded as eccentric. I'd have regarded *myself* as eccentric. By the standards which I have heard applied recently to those who turned a blind eye to similar incidents, and by all the canons of popular moralists of 1991, I should have made a stir, demanded an inquiry, and not rested until the offenders were brought to book. I didn't, not because of any conscious decision on the point, or weighing of pro's and con's, but simply because it didn't matter to me. It had happened, beyond repair, and I felt no dereliction of duty, military or moral, in ignoring it. I still don't.

That is not to say that I condone major war crimes, or would take any but a short way with those who commit them. I know that the killing (or murder, which is what it was) of those Japanese was well beyond the civilised borderline. But being of my generation, in the year 1945, towards the end of a war of a peculiarly vicious, close-quarter kind, against an enemy who wouldn't have known the Geneva Convention if it fell on him, I never gave it a second thought. And if I had, the notion of crying for redress against the perpetrators (my own comrades-in-arms, Indian soldiers who had gone the mile for us, and we for them), on behalf of a pack of Japs, would have been obnoxious, dishonourable even.

To the modern mind, accustomed to hearing soldiers asked, after a terrorist has been killed in Ulster: "Was it necessary to open fire? Could he not have been taken prisoner?", and to being bombarded with emotive phrases like "shoot to kill", and being lectured about "reasonable force", my attitude may seem shocking. But we did not share today's obsession with guilt, or its manic desire to find someone (preferably in uniform) to blame, or from whom to seek compensation; we were not over-worried about virtue for mere appearance's sake. We were in the business of killing Japanese; it was what we were trained for; it was our livelihood, in a very real sense.

I am not justifying, but explaining, when I say those were the days when, if a selection board chairman asked (and he did): "Wouldn't you like to stick a bayonet in a German's guts, eh?", he was not expecting an answer drawn from the Sermon on the Mount. An American movie of the time, I remember, showed a Japanese plane exploding in flames, and an American air gunner (I think it was George Tobias) chortling: "Fried Jap going down!" The audience chuckled (and last year a film commentator singled out the clip for a shocked comment). That was the atmosphere of the time, and it would be a bold man who said it was a *wrong* atmosphere for the time, however ugly it may look now. I can see that the incident I mentioned earlier, about Japanese soldiers being wakened, and *then* shot, must seem barbaric now – yes, they probably could have been taken prisoner; excessive force was used, and that too was probably a war crime. But they do come in different sizes, and it is possible to react with revulsion and rage to Belsen, and at the same time to regard the killing of those Jap stretcher cases as a matter of little account. And to anyone who disputes that, I can only say: Get yourself to the sharp end, against an enemy like the Japanese, encounter a similar incident . . . and let me know how you get on.

We saw another newsreel in Calcutta, showing American troops dealing with bunkers in the Pacific. They had flame-throwers, both one-man portable jobs and the big-calibre variety fired from tanks. Both were highly effective, and we saw Japs staggering from bunkers enveloped in flame, literally burning alive. We speculated on what our reaction would have been to the issue of flame-throwers, and Sergeant Hutton's opinion was universally approved:

"They wadn't git me carryin' one o' them bloody things. Nut that Ah give a monkey's 'oo many Japs they boorn; they can send the lot oop in flames. But Ah wadn't 'ev five gallons of aviation fuel strapped tae my arse – w'at appens if a tracer 'it's it?"

I PARTED COMPANY with Nine Section on coming back from leave. It would have happened anyway, with the battalion reorganisation, for they were mostly old soldiers due for repatriation and demob, and I was not, but there was a more immediate reason. My application to go before a War Office Selection Board to see if I was fit for officer training had been granted by the colonel, and when the next board assembled, in a few weeks' time, I would be sent up to Meiktila to be flown out to face the examiners. Splendid news which put the wind right up me, for while if I passed I would go straight on to one of the Indian military academies, failure would mean returning to the battalion with my tail between my legs.

In the meantime I was not to be attached to a platoon, but to company H.Q., where I was to make myself generally useful.

So I packed up my traps in the section billet, to cries of "Bloody 'ell, w'at's the Army comin' to?", "Wiv my permish you'll get a commish!", "If ye think Ah'll ivver gi'e you a salute, ye're arse is oot the winder!" and trudged across to company H.Q., not feeling a wrench, exactly, but suddenly lonely. We'd been together, a close-knit, interdependent unit, for six months of war, and now I would never march with them again, or stand stags with them, or look round for them in action. The bond that had formed wasn't quite one of friendship, although I'd liked them, Forster excepted – no one could like Foshie, for all the sterling qualities among his less agreeable traits. (The Duke had been right: he was a good soldier, sour, carnaptious, and derisive, but when you hesitated at the bunker entrance or the branch in the track, and glanced sideways, he would be there, sucking his teeth and looking wicked, on the balls of his feet, sniffing for Jap.)

The others I had learned to respect and admire and be thankful for, but it had been trust more than affection. Sometimes, in a field game, you find a player with whom you fit like hand in glove; you've never seen or spoken to him before, but you have an instant understanding and work together almost by instinct, and when you shake hands at the end you're surprised to find that you don't really know each other at all, except in one narrow field, and part company. Liking doesn't really come into it; you just remember, with occasional regret, how well you combined. That was how it was with Nine Section; if there was an emotional tie, it was one of gratitude.

I would have felt the parting more if it had been absolute, but they were just down the road, and I found myself dropping in at their basha to cadge a pialla of tea and listen to them beefing about their new section leader, a full corporal, and Irish at that; I felt an unworthy glow on discovering that they didn't like him.

"Regimental Paddy!" was Nick's verdict. "Mind you, there's summat tae be said for the booger – at least 'e's full growed an' auld enoof tae vote, nut like soom that ye git parked on ye – knaw w'at Ah mean, Jock?"

"Aye, yoong lance-jacks, an' the like o' them," said Grandarse. "Scotch lance-jacks is the woorst, Ah always say. Clivver boogers, full o' bullshit."

"Haggis-bashin' bastards," agreed Wattie. "Burgoo-belters."

"Scotchies, Ah've shit 'em," said Forster. "Aye gittin' aboov theresels, wantin' commissions, don't-ye-know-old-boy. One thing, we've bin gittin' a decent brew-up since we got rid o' you, Jock."

"Lying sod," I said. "Who's taken over?"

"General Slim sends us doon a dixie ivvery day frae Meiktila," said Nick. "Wid a note on't lid: 'Drink oop, lads, ye'll a' git killed'." He emptied the contents of his pialla in disgust. "W'ee's bin pishin' in't brew-tin, for Christ's sek?"

"W'at they got ye on these days, Jock?" asked Morton. "Ablutions?"

"Ablutions orficer, that's wot 'e's gonna be," said Parker. "Right, Jockie boy? Wiv my permish you can 'ave two pips an' a latrine bucket, an' spend the duration diggin' shitahses for the Pioneers. You won't know the difference from Nine Section – *semper in excreta*."

In fact, what they had me on at Company H.Q. was filling in wherever a spare lance-corporal was needed, and I was kept fairly active in an irritatingly piecemeal way. Unknown to anybody, the war was into its last month, although there was no sign of this along the Rangoon road. Jap's final effort to break across to the east was at its height; they were coming out of the Pegu Yomas like gang-busters, and there was action all the way from Pegu to Penwegon and beyond. Patrols and ambushes were being stepped up, his attacks were being driven back or fought to a standstill, and apart from the main thrusts the country was crawling, literally, with stragglers, many of them half-dead with disease and starvation. They were wandering in the jungle, drifting down the rivers, lying in the chaungs, too spent to do anything but wait to die or be captured; even the "comfort girls" who marched with the Jap armies were being rounded up. But the remnants of 28th Army who were still on their feet were not giving up; their casualties were mounting into thousands, but they were making Fourteenth Army fight right down to the wire.

So while Nine Section were operating with their new corporal, I found myself going out in strange company, and missing them damnably. I was only out two or three times with different sections, and we accounted for the odd enemy, killed or captured, including the one I mentioned in the foreword who came screaming at us with a home-made spear, one against a dozen and he should have been dead weeks ago by the look of him.

"An' after this, it'll be Malaya," I heard a sergeant say. "God knaws 'oo many divisions Jap's still got doon theer – joongle a' the way tae Singapore, be Christ! They say we'll be gittin' mules again. Wrap oop an' roll on!"

Malaya, mules, and more Japanese – well, it wouldn't be my *indaba*,* unless I failed wosbie. Although even if I passed, what were the odds that I wouldn't be back as a second-lieutenant, commanding a platoon in Borneo or Sumatra, nine months hence? On VE Day it had seemed that our war, too, must soon be over, but now if anything it was hotting up, and people were talking of another campaign. With mules. And if anyone had told us that

* business

195

thousands of miles away in the Pacific an aircraft called Enola Gay was preparing to load up, it wouldn't have meant a thing.

Meanwhile, the war still had novelties in store, and as I recall them they seem quite apart from anything that had gone before; it's almost as though they took place in a different world, and I was a different person. That can only be because they happened away from the enclosed regular military life to which I had grown so accustomed; they were, in the proper sense of the word, eccentric, a curious detached interlude of my time in Burma.

It began with a summons to the company basha where I was ordered to hand in my pay-book, that AB 64 Part 1 which is the documentary proof of your military existence, and which you part with only in unusual circumstances. My new company commander, an abrupt but good-natured veteran, explained.

"There's a selection board meeting in two weeks' time, at Chittagong, so you'll be going up to Meiktila in a week or so. Nervous?" He grinned sympathetically. "I've heard they pass about one in three nowadays, but don't let that worry you – most of 'em probably never saw an angry Jap and haven't any qualifications except School Cert and three years' service in the stores." Which wasn't true, but was a fair reflection of a 17th Div infantry major's view of the rest of the military scene. "Got your AB 64? It'll have to go to your old company commander so that he can give you your character in writing. Leave it with the clerk."

That was enough to set the adrenalin pumping. I hadn't seen Long John for weeks, since he was with one of the other companies. It hadn't occurred to me that he would have to pass judgment on my general fitness, recording it forever in my pay-book, where it would be scrutinised by those cold, fish-like examiners. What would he say? Well, he was the one who'd promoted me – and on my first outing my section had looted half an air-drop, and on the second I'd fallen down a well. Was he aware of these things? I could hear the selection board president: "In a word, corporal, you showed your talent for leadership by failing to restrain your men from pillaging, and in the attack on Pyawbwe you hid underwater. H'm . . ." Common sense told me that Long John would confine himself to general observations . . . but what would they be? Sins of omission and commission rose up to confront me . . .

dear God, the best he could say was "Average", or at a pinch "Satisfactory", and what could be more damning than that?

"By the way," said the major, "d'you know anything about this anti-tank gun, the Piat?"

I said I did; I'd been trained in its use in England, although I'd never fired it.

"At least you'll know one end from t'other," he said, "which is more than anyone else does. We've had one in store for a bit, but no one's mentioned it until now. Corporal, give us that file marked Piat. Yes . . . there's been a request for one from—." He mentioned an unpronounceable village which I'd never heard of. "About twenty miles up the road, small unit near the river. They also want an instructor. Let's see, you've still got a week in hand . . . well, why not? Take it up, show 'em how it works, and either bring it back yourself or leave it with them and fetch a receipt. But make it clear that you've to be back here inside a week – here, I'll give you a chit for their O.C." He squinted at the file and gave a barking laugh. "A captain whose name, to judge from his bloody awful writing, is Grief. Well, he should know . . ."

Pleased at the prospect of change, and escaping from the orbit of a company sergeant-major who had proved himself a dab hand at finding work for idle lance-corporals to do, I went off to renew acquaintance with the projector, infantry, anti-tank, commonly called the Piat. It was the British counterpart of the American bazooka, and might have been designed by Heath Robinson after a drunken dinner of lobster au gratin. It's not easy to describe, and I may have forgotten some of its finer points, such as its exact measurements, but I'll do my best.

From memory, then, it consisted of about four feet of six-inch steel pipe, one end of which was partly cut out to leave a semicylindrical cradle about a foot long, in which you laid the bomb. At the other end of the pipe was a thick butt pad which fitted into your shoulder when you lay on the ground in a firing position, the body of the pipe being supported on a single expanding leg. The bomb, a sinister black object fifteen or so inches overall, had a circular tail fin containing a propellant cartridge, a bulging black body packed with high explosive, and a long spiked nose with a tiny cap which, when removed, revealed a gleaming detonator.

Within the body of the pipe was a gigantic spring which had to be cocked after each shot: you lay on your back and dragged the Piat on top of you, braced your feet against the projecting edges of the butt pad, and heaved like hell at something or other which I've forgotten. After immense creaking the spring clicked into place, and you crawled out from under, gamely ignoring your hernia, laid an uncapped bomb gently in the front cradle, resumed the lying firing position, aligned the barleycorn sight with the gleaming nose of the bomb, pressed the massive metal trigger beneath the pipe, thus releasing the coiled spring which drove a long steel plunger up the tail fin of the bomb, detonating the propellant cartridge, you and the Piat went ploughing backwards with the recoil, and the bomb went soaring away – about a hundred yards, I think, but it may have been farther. The whole contraption weighed about a ton, and the bombs came in cases of three; if you were Goliath you might have carried the Piat and two cases.

Like many British inventions, it looked improbable, unwieldy, and unsafe – and it worked. The principle was that when the bomb hit a tank, the long spiked nose penetrated the armour, and all the concentrated explosive in the bulging body rushed through into the tank's interior, brewing up everyone within. Where a Piat had hit, the only visible exterior damage was a small, neat hole, or so they tell me. I never fired it at a tank.

I drew it from the stores with four cases of bombs – all they had – refreshed my memory by stripping and reassembling it, and hopped a truck next morning. I also took my rifle and fifty rounds, as per regulations, plus my kukri and a couple of grenades; if there was trouble I wanted some real weaponry handy.

The monsoon had eased by now, and it was a pleasant hour's drive to the village where there was a battered jeep waiting, with a Burmese driver. We loaded the Piat aboard and bounced away along a sunlit track past paddy-fields which were calm silver lakes fringed by scrub and jungle, and another hour brought us to a little collection of huts half-hidden by undergrowth on the edge of nowhere, which was the operational base of the officer I always think of as "Captain Grief" – and I call him that now because he may still be about, and I don't want

him suing me or trying to kill me or, even worse, seeking me
out for a jovial reunion.

Civilian readers may think my description of him, especially his
conversation, exaggerated. It is not, and any old soldier will bear
me out, for he was a prize specimen of a type in which the British
Army has always been rich – I've no doubt he was at Hastings,
and will be there, eccentric as ever, when Gabriel sounds the last
rally: a genuine, guaranteed, paid-up head-case. Which is not to
say that he was clinically mad, just that he behaved as though he
was. You have heard of them: when touched with genius they
become Chinese Gordon or Lord Cochrane or, in the last war,
Wingate, that gifted guerrilla who revived the military beard,
carried an alarm clock to remind everyone what time it was,
scrubbed himself with a toothbrush, quoted Holy Writ, and was an
authority on Donald Duck – or so I have been reliably informed.
Splendid men, especially to keep away from.

Captain Grief may have been less gifted, but he had all the
Deolali hallmarks. He was driven apparently by some high-octane
spirit, full of restless energy and strange cries like: "Bags o' panic!"
and "Bash on regardless!" and even "Aha, Ermintrude, at last we
meet – over the bridge you go!", uttered with a glittering eye as
he paced up and down, clapping his hands. He was tall, rangy,
lantern-jawed, and eager as an unleashed hound. His dress consisted of an old tweed fishing cap, a dilapidated bush shirt, cor-
duroy trousers, and brothel-creeper boots, and my heart sank at
the sight of him, for I could read the signs: this was one who
would probably want the Piat mounted on a jeep, with me manning it in the passenger seat and himself at the wheel, roaring with
laughter at top speed and changing gear with his foot.

To be fair, he did have tranquil moments, in which he sat brooding, sighing frequently and talking to himself. But he was in full
cry when we drew up outside his basha.

"Come on, come on, come on!" he shouted, rubbing his hands
and beaming. "Let's get weaving! Is this the old *iskermoffit?* *" Let's
have a dekko!" Before I could get out he was ferreting in the back

* A corruption, I believe, of *iskar mafit* (Arabic), signifying in Army slang,
"the thing". "Yagger", of unknown origin, was synonymous.

for the Piat. "Stone me! Who's been robbing the Titanic's engine room? Got bags of ammo for it, have you, corporal? Bang on, good show! All right, stand at ease, stand easy, come in, have a pew, let's get to it! Tea, Sarn't Jones! Tea and your most welcoming smile for our friend here, Lance-corporal Whatsit – you don't mind if I call you Whatsit? It was my mother's name." He threw himself into a canvas chair, put his dreadful boots on the rickety table, and beamed at me. "So that thing's a tank-buster, is it? Right, put me in the picture! Take a refreshing sip, and shoot!"

I did, and he hung on every word, interrupting only occasionally with exclamations like "Spot on!" and "Just the old boot!". Then I lay on the floor and cocked it, showed him how the trigger worked, and demonstrated the sight, and he promptly tried for himself, recocking it with one swift jerk and whipping into a firing position in almost the same movement. I impressed on him that the bombs were sensitive, and he cried: "Piece o' cake!", untwirled the cap, and regarded the gleaming copper nose as though it were a rare gem.

"Bloody marvellous! Look at this, Jones – breathe on it and reach for your harp! Right, corporal, let's recap – this little *isker* pierces the target and all the good news rushes through, causing alarm and despondency to those on the other side? Great – woomf!" He flourished the bomb spear-fashion, while I made mewing noises and Jones, a stout little Welshman, watched resignedly. "Not to panic, people! Everything's under control! We replace the dinky little cap, so – gad, the skill in these two hands! Take it and press it between the leaves of your diary." He handed me the bomb. "What's the effective range?"

"I'm not sure, sir. A hundred yards, thereabouts."

"'Tis not so wide as a church door, but 'tis enough, 'twill serve!" said Grief happily. "Now, corporal, eyes down, look in – we can't use it against tanks, 'cos Jap hasn't any – and I wouldn't fancy it against low-flying aircraft, but since he hasn't got any of those left either, we're quids in! How about boats?"

"Boats, sir?"

"The very word I was looking for! Note it down, Jones. Yes, good ancient – boats! Floating vehicles, and I don't mean the Queen Mary. Wooden jobs, sampans, lifeboats, rafts, once-round-the-lighthouse-in-the-ruddy-Skylark things." He cupped a hand to his ear, expectantly. "Take your time, writing on one side of the paper only."

The line between affected eccentricity and jungle-happiness is a fine one, but I was sure by now that this was your normal wild man, and not permanently tap. Apart from his three pips he wore no insignia, and I wondered if he was a Sapper, which would account for a lot. The reckless confidence with which he handled H.E. was right in character – I once knew a Sapper who corrected a wobbly table by shoving a land-mine under one leg, and it was weeks before we discovered the thing was armed and ready to blow.

I said it should sink any small craft, but that if it burst in the open rather than a confined space its explosive force would be dissipated. He nodded gravely and said, in a heavy Deep South drawl: "Naow, ain't that a goddam sha-ame . . . In other words, not much of an anti-personnel job. Be honest, hold nothing back!"

I said it ought to do as much damage as a 36 grenade, perhaps more, and he brightened.

"You wouldn't want to be within fifteen yards, wearing your best battle-dress?"

"Not even wearing denims, sir," I said, entering into the spirit of the thing, and he regarded me with alarm.

"I doubt if there's a suit of denim this side of Cox's Bazaar," he said in a hushed voice. "Oh, well, it can't be helped." He gave a sudden explosive laugh, slapped his hands on the table, and was off again. "Right – Sarn't Jones, this is the form! We'll have a practice shoot, with good old Whatsit here pressing the doodah and shouting 'Fore!' Everyone on parade, no exceptions, summon 'em from the four corners – every man in the unit must be thoroughly clued up on this supreme example of the ballistic engineer's art, so that if our young friend should cop his lot, which –" he flashed me a cheerful smile and assumed another American accent "– which we shall do all in our power to ensure is a calamity that does not eventuate –" he became British again "– some other poor bugger will be able to fire the thing." He gave me a sad stare. "But we shall miss you, corporal. Yes . . . yes, we shall."

Jones asked when he wanted the parade, and Grief resumed his seat. "In one hour, neither more nor less! All mustered, Mr Colman, everybody out, bags o' bull, bags o' panic, tallest on the right, shortest on the left, and heigh-ho for the governor's gouty foot!" He waved in dismissal. "Find the good corporal a modest lodging, give him his fill of meat and drink, and put a sentry on his beastly bombs, twenty-four hours a day or longer if need be. Away, avaunt!"

You may have noticed that for all his idiotic persiflage, Captain Grief had mastered the basics of the Piat, handled it like an expert, asked sensible questions, and was wasting no time in having it demonstrated to his men, all of which was reassuring. True, as I gathered up the Piat and Jones collected the bomb-cases, he was lying back in his canvas seat, doing physical jerks with his arms and crooning, to the tune of "Mairsie doats":

> Liberty boats and Carley floats
> And little rubber dinghies
> Paddle your own canoe
> Up your flue . . .

but then, as I saluted before withdrawing, he suddenly sat upright and took me flat aback by saying, in a normal, quiet voice, and with a smile that was both sane and friendly:

"Hold on a minute – don't know what I've been thinking of. Corporal, I haven't even asked your name."

Relieved, I told him, and handed over the chit from my company commander, explaining that I had to be back at my unit within the week. He nodded and promised to see to it, shook hands, and said he was glad to have me on the strength. Then he glanced at the note, frowned, turned it over, and said:

"That's strange . . . no, your company commander doesn't seem to have mentioned it . . . I wonder why? Still, you can tell me." He looked at me, clear-eyed and rational: "Are you a lurkin' firkin or a peepin' gremlin?"

Just when I'd started believing he was all there. I glanced at Jones, but he was gazing stolidly at the wall.

"I beg your pardon, sir?" I said, and Grief repeated the question, with just a hint of suspicion.

"I'm afraid I don't know, sir."

"You – don't – know?" He seemed stunned. "Well," he said severely, "you'll have to find out by tomorrow, you know! Oh, yes! Dammit all, d'you think you can just walk in here off the street, without proper classification or even a note from Miss Tempest the games mistress? We have to know who we're dealing with, for heaven's sake! You find out, *jildi,** or there'll be fire and sword along Banana Ridge, I can tell you! Understand? Right, fall out!"

He sat down abruptly, seized a map, gave me a dirty look, peered at the map intently, and gave a violent start: "'Here be dragons', by God! But stay – can it be a minute shred of mosquito dung? Let us read on . . ."

When we were safely outside I turned helplessly to Jones: "Which are you – a lurkin' firkin or a peepin' gremlin?" He gave me a look.

"Me? I'm a tricksy pixie. An' that's not all, boyo. Soon's he found out I was Welsh he wanted me to sing the Hallelujah Chorus. I told 'im I can't sing a note, an' 'e says: 'You're no more Welsh than I am. You're prob'ly a bloody spy. Spell Llandudno, or it'll be the worse for you!' Straight up, it's what 'e said. Oh, aye, some mothers do 'ave 'em."

"But . . . it's just an act – isn't it? I mean, for a minute he sounded perfectly normal. Or is he really cocoa?"

"Don't look at me, boy," said Jones wearily. "Oh, 'e's all right, like . . . well, 'e's daft as a badger, but 'e knows what 'e's doin' – most o' the time. Between you an' me, I reckon 'e's due for leave, know what I mean? Aye, about two years' leave. Come on, an' we'll get you settled."

He had a little hut of his own, and I dumped my gear while he brewed up and got out the bully and biscuits and put me in the picture. The unit, which was only of platoon strength, was composed entirely of Shan scouts, friendly hillmen from beyond the Salween; it was one of those little temporary groups which

* quickly

spring up on the fringes of most armies in the field and fade away when no longer needed. This one, Jones believed, was Grief's personal creation.

"'E's an I-man, see – an Intelligence wallah – well, you can tell from 'is patter, can't you? – but 'e was with the Bombay Sappers an' Miners, accordin' to what 'e told me –"

"I'm not surprised. You're not an Engineer or an I-man, are you?"

"No bloody fears, I'm Signals, me. But I speak Burmese, see, an' Grief doesn't. Boy, you should try translatin' 'is sort o' chat to a bunch o' Shans! Yeah, I been out yere since '37. Puttin' up telegraph lines for the bleedin' elephants to pull down. Aye, well, roll on demob!"

"But what d'you do – the unit, I mean?"

"Watchin' the river, layin' ambushes, at night, mostly, 'cos that's when Jap tries to slip past. 'E 'ad two armies up yonder, you know, 15th an' 33rd –"

"I'm aware."

"Oh, at Meiktila, was you? An' Pyawbwe? Well, you seen 'em for yourself, then. They been swarmin' down this way lately, keepin' as far east as they can, see, but plenty of 'em uses the river, too, an' we've 'ad three or four duffies, an' shot up their boats an' rafts. A lot of 'em got by, mind you –"

"So that's why he was on about boats! God, he *must* be harpic – what does he think a Piat can do against open boats that grenade launchers and two-inch mortars can't?"

"Oh, we got mortars an' launchers, but I s'pose 'e figured a Piat would be more accurate, bein' a tank-buster . . . Look, boyo, if 'e 'eard somebody 'ad invented a gun for firin' Rugby balls under water, 'e'd want it! An' 'e'd find a use for it, an' all. You wait an' see."

The demonstration firing of the Piat took place on a paddy close to the camp. Grief, bursting with excitement, strode up and down before his platoon, sturdy Burmans in khaki shorts and head scarves who listened with no trace of expression on their flat, sinister faces while I named the parts and explained the mechanism with Jones translating. Then I cocked the thing, nipping my fingers in my nervousness, trying to ignore Grief's barks of encouragement. "Take the strain – heave! Bags of action, bags o' swank, Strang the Terrible pits his muscles against the machine, can he do it, can he hell, yes he can! Got it, corporal! Smashing, good show! Spinach wins the day!"

The target chosen was an old Jap bunker, a good solid construction, and I wondered if the Piat would even dent it – assuming I hit it, for never having fired the weapon it was with no confidence that I uncapped a bomb, laid it carefully in place, and took up the firing position.

"Range – eighty yards!" bawled Grief, standing over me. "Well, eighty or eighty-two, we won't niggle!" Silly bastard. "Wind backing nor-nor-east, visibility good, scattered showers in western districts! On your marks, take your time, and may God defend the right!" He flourished his hands and placed his forefingers in his ears. I had adjusted the supporting leg to what I hoped was the correct elevation, took a firm grip, lined up the sight, and pulled. There was an ear-splitting crack, the pad hit me a smashing blow, and as Piat and I were shunted violently back there was a great crump from up ahead. I looked, and approximately halfway to the target a large cloud of smoke was hanging over a tiny crater.

"Jesus McGonigal!" roared Grief. "Ranging shot! Up fifty, direction, spot on, elevation – well, nobody's perfect! Try again, corporal, remember the spider, we're all with you, man and beast! Bags I be number two on the gun!"

He recocked the Piat himself, and by the time I had another bomb ready he was fiddling with the sight, adjusting the elevating leg, and squinting towards the target. "Gravity, muzzle velocity, density, intensity, one for his nob, and bullshit baffles brains! There – into the breach, old Whatsit, and if all else fails we'll fix a bayonet on the bloody thing and charge! Fire at Will, he's hiding in the cellar, the cowardly sod!"

I lined up the sight, held on like grim death, pulled the trigger, and being ready this time for the recoil was able to watch the bomb's flight. It arced slowly up, dipped, and descended, there was a brilliant orange flash and a roar, a billowing black cloud, and beneath it – nothing. The bunker had vanished.

"Take that, you jerry-built abomination! Flaunt your roof at me, would you? I'll huff and I'll puff and you've had your chips!"

Grief was off like an electric hare, with his platoon chattering and laughing at his heels. Well pleased, I followed more slowly, pacing out the range: it was exactly seventy-nine yards.

"He'd measured it, had he?" I said to Jones.

"Don't you believe it, boyo," he said. "He didn't need to."

Grief and his gang were standing round the wreckage-filled pit in which beams and thatch were tangled in the fallen earth of the roof. As we joined him he heaved a deep sigh and looked solemn.

"Alas, poor Will, everybody's target, I fear he's been fired at for the last time. He's down there somewhere with his ears ringing and his arse full of shrapnel." He shook his head and then was off again, sixteen to the dozen. "Not a bad bomb, corporal, not bad at all – and you can tell the manufacturers I said so, you unregenerate gremlin, you! Or was it firkin? Not that I give two hoots, I couldn't care less, but I don't want you wandering about in a state of uncertainty. Right, Sarn't Jones, dismiss the parade, depart and take your ease, and if anyone rings tell 'em the redskins have cut the wires. I'm going for a kip."

He strode off to his basha, humming "Any Old Iron", and I didn't see him again for twenty-four hours, which was a nuisance, because I wanted to suggest that I give two of his scouts a thorough course on the Piat and return to my unit without delay; I felt I'd had just about my ration of Captain Grief. But he had attached his own version of a "Do Not Disturb" sign to his basha door (it read "Wake Me At Your Peril"), so I turned in early and was lulled to sleep by Sergeant Jones, who had the Welsh gift of talking perfect English in a musical monotone, on and on and on. He lay on his charpoy, staring at the roof, telling me how he and his unit had once mounted guard at Caernarvon Castle, or it may have been the Naafi at Catterick, and so help me he did it down to the smallest detail.

"... it was full ceremonial, Jock, see, an' we was fell in in greatcoats with belts an' bay'nets, bags o' bull, an' a luvvly sight we were. 'You're a luvvly sight, lads', says the R.S.M., Williams 'is name was, played in the back row, was it, for Neath, big strong fellow, built like a slag-heap, played a trial once, I think, anyway 'e fell us in an' inspected us, an' then it was 'Atten-shun!, slope

arms, as-you-were, slope arms, that's better, move to the right in
threes, right turn, by the left quick march, 'eft-'ight-'eft-'ight, pick
'em up, bags o' swank . . ."

You have to make allowances for a man who's had nobody but
Grief to talk to for weeks, but I was astonished, on waking some
time towards dawn, to hear a hoarse murmur from the other side
of the hut: ". . . an' then for the last time it was present arms,
one-two-three, an' the general salute, an' all the top brass at attention, see, and the band playin' the Luvvly Ash Grove, an' slope
arms, one-two-three, an' march off by comp'nies, sarn't-major,
an' platoon move to the left in threes, left turn, by the right quick
march, an' we marched off, bags o' swank, 'eft-'ight-'eft-'ight an'
the band playin' Men of Harlech in the hollow, do ye hear like
rushin' billow, an' Williams sayin' keep the dressin', don't go
spoilin' it now . . ."

Grief was absent next morning, and Jones, possibly exhausted
by his nocturnal filibuster, or sulky because I'd dropped off in the
middle of it, was withdrawn and edgy. With his help I got two of
the Shan scouts proficient on the Piat, but firmly refused their
request to be allowed to fire it; with only ten bombs in hand we
couldn't afford it.

It was dusk when Grief reappeared, emerging from the jungly
fringe of the paddy with his long loping stride, two of his Shans
trotting behind. They'd been travelling; Grief's bush-shirt was
badly torn, and all three were caked in mud to the thighs, breathing
hard and soaked in sweat. Grief flourished his carbine and shouted
"Sarn't Jones!", and for the next half-hour the two of them were
in closed conference while I kicked my heels, feeling out of it and
wondering what was up, and how it would concern me. I brewed
up, and presently Jones emerged, issuing instructions to the Shan
sergeant and his section leaders; they scampered away, and Jones
came across to my fire, filled his pialla, and asked how I fancied
night marching.

"Jap's comin' down-river tonight, see, a big bunch. Some of 'em
in boats, mebbe rafts, wi' the main body marchin' on the far bank
to cover 'em. It's paddy that side, see, an' they'll 'ave scouted to
make sure it's clear. But this yere bank's jungly, an' we got West
Yorks an' Gurkhas farther up, an' no sign o' Jap this side o' the

river. 'E'll try to slip past on the water an' the far bank, an' we won't let 'im. Grief wants you on the Piat."

It was no time to suggest that one of the Burmans I'd instructed should take over. I asked how far.

"Near eight miles to the ambush point, an' gotta be there by midnight." That was less than four hours away.

"Over wet paddy and jungle? That's shifting. I'll need two men to take turns with me toting the Piat. And two for the bombs. How many Japanni?"

"Hundred, maybe two, Grief thinks." He shook his head in admiration. "'E's a bugger, 'e is. Been scoutin' em 'alf the day, up to 'is neck in river. Then 'e comes back at the double, bitten rotten with leeches, 'e is. There's a Gurkha platoon rendezvousin' with us at the ambush, so we'll 'ave plenty support. Right." He emptied his pialla on to the fire. "Let's earn our Jap campaign pay."

I'd say that when you've done one night march through scrub and paddy you've done them all, except that this one was a bastard. Three miles an hour on hard level is the Army norm, but you can't do that through ankle-deep water and undergrowth, not by starlight you can't, so we were forced marching whenever the ground permitted. Luckily silence didn't matter, or we'd not have got half-way in time. The Piat was a monster, heavy as sin and snagging on everything, and we had to change carriers every few minutes, except on the open ground, where we could carry it two at a time, one on either end. Jones and another scout carried the bomb cases and our rifles, and since we were at the rear of the little column I cannot report on Captain Grief's deportment at the head. If he had breath enough to natter, even to himself, he was a fitter man than I. Within twenty minutes I was streaming sweat, and the Piat was wearing burning grooves on either shoulder; after two hours I was seriously wondering if I'd make it. My back and leg muscles were one great ache, the skin seemed to have been worn off my shoulders, I'd been whipped stupid by foliage, and I could only hope that the mud which plastered my legs was suffocating the leeches. In the last hour, by the time the whisper for silence came down the line, I was tottering, and too beat to take consolation from the fact that Jones and even the Shans didn't seem any better.

Then we were lying in rank grass among bushes, with the jungly screen behind us, and dimly seen in front the pale sheen of river water. Overhead a few stars were out in the pale night sky, but the far bank was lost in darkness, as if anybody cared by that time. It was positive pleasure just to lie there on the soggy ground, letting the aches drain away, muscles fluttering with tiredness. A couple of yards to my left there was a Shan mortar team in the lee of a bamboo thicket; Jones was to my right with the bomb-cases.

I must have dozed, rotten soldier that I was, for it was with a start that I was aware of movement behind, and heard Grief's voice and another English one: the Gurkha subaltern. There was rustling in the undergrowth, whispering of orders, as the Gurkhas took up their positions along the bank to our right; then the sound of their stealthy movement died away, and there was only the soft jungle chorus of chirps and croaks against the background murmur of the heavy Burmese night, and a voice at my ear inquiring: "Ever had an invite to Viceregal Lodge, corporal? Course you haven't, neither have I, so we can compare notes, tear their characters to pieces, mean bastards. Bugger these night-glasses, show you nothing but war movies, no cartoons, not even an organ interlude . . ."

He was alongside, prone in the grass, and although his face was nothing but a pale blur I could imagine the manic gleam in his eye. He went on, in a conversational whisper:

"Right, this is the form! There's one bloody great boat, sampan type, full of paying passengers, and she'll be as close in under the far bank as she can get – unless some dopey Samurai has run her aground first, in which case we'll demand our money back. Wait for the mortar flares, and then sink me the ship, master gunner, sink her, split her in twain – or thrain, if you feel like it. Don't bother about anything else; she's your bird. The range'll be about eighty yards – is the figure familiar? Spot on! Jones! Jones, are ye there, Morriarity? Slither over here to the mortar – no, never mind his bloody bombs, I'll look after 'em! Come on, *jildi!*"

Jones wriggled past me, and there was more whispering beside the bamboo thicket as Grief issued instructions for the mortar. "Two flares, and then the H.E. *iskers,* as fast as you can – and make sure the buggers put 'em in right way up, or they'll find your bollocks on a nearby tree . . ."

Then he was away into the dark, and the Shan who had been with Jones crawled up beside me, opening a bomb case, and I realised with a shock that I hadn't cocked the Piat. I rolled over, pulled the heavy tube on top of me, heaved until it clicked, checked that the elevating leg was where it had been for the successful practice shot, and took a bomb from the case, fingers over the safety cap. I could hear Jones busy with the little two-inch mortar, and to my right there was the snap of a Bren magazine being pushed home, and the oily sliding click as the gun was cocked. No sound from far out in the darkness ahead; as we lay waiting I became aware for the first time of clouds of voracious mosquitos, but you daren't slap or do anything except keep rubbing your face and cursing inwardly.

A silent, sweating fifteen minutes, and Grief was kneeling beside me again. "There's someone at the door," he whispered. "Two minutes, about." Without being told I uncapped the bomb and laid it in place. "All set, Jones? On the whistle, let there be light, and we'll be able to see for bleeding miles!"

I suppose I must have been on edge with excitement, but I don't remember it. I know I was straining eyes and ears – was there sound or movement far out in the murk, where the far bank must be, or was it my imagination? I cuddled the butt-pad, left hand up and across to grip the barrel, felt in the dark for the trigger, touched it, and took my hand away, which was just as well, for when the whistle came with a piercing unexpected shriek I gave a violent twitch which would certainly have sent the bomb winging away prematurely. Jones's mortar exploded with a metallic whang, echoed twice along the bank, there was a second's pause and then three soft pops far overhead – and the darkness lifted in a great blaze of silver light as the three tiny parachutes with their burning flares hung over the river.

It all registered in an instant: the broad surface of the water shining with the reflected glare, the far bank lined with little dark figures caught like rabbits in headlights, standing, running, drop- ping to earth, a raft halfway across crowded with men, and beyond it, near the far bank, the dark outline of a big unwieldy-looking craft about twice the size of a ship's lifeboat and high out of the water, and even as I took it in the Brens were stuttering along the bank, the rifles cracking in rapid fire, and I lined the barleycorn sight on the gleaming copper nose and pulled the trigger, shuddered with the recoil, rolled on my back dragging the Piat on top of me, and I was counting, one-thousand-two-thousand-three-thousand . . . up to six, waiting for the blast that would mean a hit, but it didn't come. Snarling, I dumped the Piat down, rolled in behind it, and Grief was slipping another bomb into the cradle while all around the rattle of Brens and rifles was deafening, and the air was heavy with cordite smoke, and the scene ahead was changing eerily as the flares drifted down to the water even as other flares broke out overhead, and a crimson Verey light arced away with a trail of smoke, passing over the raft and plumping into the water – an instant's glimpse of the raft suddenly bare as the Brens raked it and ploughed up the bright water in which heads were bobbing. Beyond it the boat was drifting slowly, and now there were men visible on her stern. I lined up the sight, aiming just behind the bow, squeezed, took a terrific glancing blow on the chin from the recoil, and was on my back again, feet slipping on the rest – strange that I should remember that, and the Piat twisting in my grip like a live thing – and then the firing position again, and Grief slipping in another bomb and leaning towards me to shout above the noise:

"Near miss, just short! Keep her as she is!"

Just short . . . I tried to snuggle the butt just that bit lower, squeezed, absorbed the recoil, rolled over dragging at the Piat and thinking, Jesus the things you do for eighteen rupees a week . . . and the next few seconds live in my memory like nothing else in my life. It seems now to have gone on forever, but it can have been only a few heart-beats, a tiny piece of time in which I thought this is the end, china, and you're going to find the Great Perhaps.

The light was beating down on the group by the bamboo thicket, almost close enough to touch – my frantic rollings had brought me right beside them. Jones was lying on the mortar base-plate, one hand steadying the upright tube of the barrel, the other on the firing-wheel. A kneeling Shan was shoving an uncapped high explosive shell into the muzzle, and he was doing what Grief had warned against, what every mortar instructor has nightmares about – inserting the gold-gleaming nose first! Upside bloody down, and when he let it go it would slide down the eighteen-inch tube with that metallic slither which would be the last thing that anyone within ten feet of the mortar would ever hear.

The phrase "my heart stood still" isn't really adequate, because it didn't have time. Even if I hadn't been pinned under the Piat like a blasted beetle I couldn't have done anything, nor could Jones for the simple reason that he hadn't noticed, and why Grief, who should have been watching my bomb's flight, should have glanced aside, God alone knows, instinct, telepathy, search me, but in that split instant he was suddenly hurtling over me in a flat dive, yelling "Jesus!", one hand outflung to drive the mortar barrel sideways, knocking the Shan arse over tip so that he and Grief hit the bamboo stalks in a tangle of limbs – and the bomb rolled gently over the wet grass, stopped, and lay there winking at us.

Grief sat up, adjusted his hat, picked up the bomb, helped Jones to resurrect the mortar, took the goggling Shan gently by the ear, said: "Oh, you clumsy-clumsy!", and carefully showed him how the bomb should go in, fins first. Then he said: "See? No sweat, no panic, *tik hai?*" and patted the Shan on the head before scrambling forward to look at the river. I snapped into action as one is liable to do after a moment's immobilising panic, cocking the Piat and rolling back into a firing position, but Grief wasn't bothering with a bomb, and the Shan scout beside me was pointing and shouting in excitement.

I'd heard no explosion from my last shot, my attention being elsewhere, and it was a moment before I took in the significance of the small black cloud over by the far bank. Half-hidden by it, the boat had swung away from us and was lying at an odd angle, bow submerged, there were men in the water – and suddenly the last flare must have died in the river and there was pitch blackness with the red tracers flying and criss-crossing through it, two streams of them converging where the boat had been. Two more flares went up, in quick succession, illuminating river and far bank, and the boat was gone, heads bobbing in the broken water, the raft had split into chunks of bamboo debris, and shots were whipping overhead – the Japs on the far bank were firing back at the Bren flashes, but after a while the shots became sporadic and then stopped altogether, and Grief came scrambling back. "Cease fire!" sounded along the bank as the flares went out again, and I heard Grief telling Jones to put up another. The mortar whanged, the flare burst, and now the river was empty except for a few shreds of the raft drifting away to the right. Nothing was moving on the far bank; you couldn't see if there was anything hidden in the narrow shadow beneath its overhang, but either Grief or the Gurkha officer was taking no chances, for presently three of the Brens opened up again, raking the shallows and the face of the bank. The flare vanished, the firing stopped, the command came to ease springs, the stench of cordite began to clear, the Gurkhas were getting to their feet, and I pressed the trigger of the empty Piat which clanged resoundingly as the spring was released. Bad practice, I should have released it gradually, but I was too damned tired and shaken by the memory of that mortar bomb.

So, I gathered, was Jones, for he held me spellbound with his description of how that bloody daft Shan, look you, had been puttin' an effin' H.E. down the spout the *WRONG WAY* for Chrissake, an' Jones hadn't seen nuthin', see, till Grief came flyin' an' knocked the silly bugger endways in the nick o' time, see, or we'd all have been blown to buggery, of all the stupid bloody wog tricks it would turn your hair white, bigod. Thanks to him I caught only snatches of what Grief and the Gurkha were saying ... "None got over this side, anyway ... about twenty on the raft ... can't say about the boat ... write 'em off, sick and wounded probably ... God knows about those on the bank ... Baluch'll take care of 'em."

From which I deduced that the fugitives on the far side could expect another ambush farther down, but how many were accounted for, by us or anyone else, I don't know. It was a not untypical operation for that time, fairly messy and of minor importance in military terms. It was the last time I ever heard a shot fired in war. For the rest, I'm not ashamed to admit that my most lasting memory of the night's work is of that dully gleaming bomb-nose poised at the muzzle of Jones's mortar with the thin brown fingers about to let it go – and if, considering what else happened in that faraway forgotten ambush, that seems unreasonably egoistic, I can only quote Macaulay on the folly of supposing that a man cares for his fellow-creatures as much as he cares for himself.

The return journey I hardly remember, except that we reached the camp in broad daylight, knackered to a man, and I steeped my feet in hot salt water before collapsing on my blanket. After that it's vague: I think I was there for another day, possibly two, before being jeeped to the main road and hopping a truck to the battalion, but I certainly recall stripping, cleaning, and reassembling the Piat, handing it over to two grinning Shans and getting a receipt for it and its remaining bombs from Jones, and Grief sitting back in his canvas chair with his hands behind his head, holding forth:

"There's a nasty secretive streak in you, Whatsit, and I take a pretty dim view of it – fact, I can hardly bloody see it, through a glass darkly. You knew dam' well you weren't a peepin' gremlin *or* a lurkin' firkin, didn't you, but did you let on, did you hell, and don't tell me you'd forgotten, either! Good God, one look in the mirror, plain as a pikestaff, even Jones can see it, can't you, Jones? Yes, blush, Whatsit, the murder's out – evil weevil written all over you! Can't think how I didn't spot it, got weevils in my own family, both sides, incestuous business, don't talk about it. So, you're going – well, so long, mind the step, don't lift anything on the way out, and keep an eye open for the roamin' gnomes, the bastards are everywhere! Who knows, we may meet at Philippi . . ."

Thus far, I'm happy to say, we haven't.

"'Ey, Grandarse, 'ear w'at they're sayin' on't wireless? The Yanks 'ave dropped a bomb the size of a pencil on Tokyo an' it's blown the whole fookin' place tae bits!"

"Oh, aye. W'at were they aimin' at – 'Ong Kong?"

"Ah'm tellin' ye! Joost one lal bomb, an' they reckon 'alf Japan's in fookin' flames. That's w'at they're sayin'!"

"W'ee's sayin'?"

"Ivverybody, man! Ah'm tellin' ye, it's on't wireless! 'Ey, they reckon Jap'll pack in. It'll be th' end o' the war!"

"Girraway? Do them yeller-skinned boogers oot theer knaw that?"

"Aw, bloody 'ell! 'Oo can they, ye daft booger! They 'evn't got the fookin' wireless, 'ev they?"

"Awreet, then. Ah's keepin' me 'eid doon until the Yanks've dropped a few more pencils on Tokyo. An' w'en them boogers oot theer 'ev packed in, Ah'll believe ye."

"Aw, Ah's wastin' me time talkin tae you! 'Ey, Foshie, 'ear aboot the Yanks? They've dropped a secret weapon on Tokyo, an' the whole fookin' toon's wiped oot!"

"'Igh bloody time. W'ee's smeukin', then? Awoy, Jock, gi's one o' yer H.Q. Coompany fags, ye mean booger!"

It was a fine sunny morning when the news, in its garbled form, ran round the battalion, and if it changed the world, it didn't change Nine Section. They sat on the floor of the basha, backs to the wall, supping chah and being sceptical. "Secret weapon" was an expression bandied about with cynical humour all through the war; Foshie's socks and Grandarse's flatulence, those were secret weapons, and super-bombs were the stuff of fantasy. I didn't believe it, that first day, although from the talk at company H.Q. it was fairly clear that something big had happened, or was about to happen. And even when it was confirmed, and unheard of expressions like "atomic bomb" and "Hiroshima" (then pronounced Hirosheema) were bandied about, it all seemed very distant and unlikely. Three days after the first rumour, on the very day that the second bomb fell on Nagasaki, one of the battalion's companies was duffying with a Jap force on the Sittang bank and killing 21 of them – *that* was the war, not what was happening hundreds of miles away. As Grandarse so sagely observed: "They want tae drop their fookin' atoms on the Pegu Yomas, then we'll git the bleedin' war ower." Even then, Nick wasn't prepared to bet that we wouldn't be going into Malaya with mules; we would all, he prophesied, get killed.

It took a week, as all the world knows now, for the Japanese government to call it a day, but even after the official surrender of August 14 there was no cease-fire along the Rangoon road; it was almost a fortnight before the Japs in the field started to come in, and the business of rounding up and disarming the remnants began, but by that time I was over the hills and far away, perspiring before a selection board at Chittagong, playing idiotic games of word association, trying to convince psychiatrists that I combined the qualities of Francis of Assisi and Genghiz Khan, that I knew which knife and fork to use, and "actually, sir, the reason I want to be an officer is, honestly, that I'm sure it's how I can best serve the Army, if you know what I mean, sir." "Quite so, corporal – now, when I say the word 'rape' what's the first thought that comes to your mind?" "Sir? Sorry, sir, I didn't quite catch that..."

But that was still in the future. The war ended in mid-August, and even before then Nine Section had decided that the fight, if not necessarily done, had reached a stage where celebration was permissible. I joined them in the makeshift canteen, quantities of beer were shifted, Forster sang "Cumberland Way" and "The Horn of the Hunter" in an excruciating nasal croak with his eyes closed, Wedge wept and was sick, Wattie passed out, Morton became bellicose because, he alleged, Forster had pinched his pint, Parker and Stanley separated them, and harmony of a sort was restored with a thunderous rendering of "John Peel", all verses, from Denton Holme to Scratchmere Scar with Peel's view-halloo awakening the dead – Cumbrians may be among the world's worst

216

vocalists, but they alone can sing that rousing anthem of pursuit as it should be sung, with a wild primitive violence that makes the Horst Wessel sound like a lullaby, Grandarse red-faced and roaring and Nick pounding the time and somehow managing to sing with his pipe clenched in his teeth.

Like everyone else, we were glad it was over, brought to a sudden, devastating stop by those two bombs that fell on Japan. We had no slightest thought of what it would mean for the future, or even what it meant at the time; we did not know what the immediate effect of those bombs had been on their targets, and we didn't much care. We were of a generation to whom Coventry and the London Blitz and Clydebank and Liverpool and Plymouth were more than just names; our country had been hammered mercilessly from the sky, and so had Germany; we had seen the pictures of Belsen and of the frozen horror of the Russian front; part of our higher education had been devoted to techniques of killing and destruction; we were not going to lose sleep because the Japanese homeland had taken its turn. If anything, at the time, remembering the kind of war it had been, and the kind of people we, personally, had been up against, we probably felt that justice had been done. But it was of small importance when weighed against the glorious fact that the war was over at last.

There was certainly no moralising, no feeling at all of the guilt which some thinkers nowadays seem to want to attach to the bombing of Hiroshima and Nagasaki. And because so many myths have been carefully fostered about it, and so much emotion generated, all on one side, with no real thought for those most affected by it on the Allied side, I would like just to look at it, briefly, from our minority point of view. And not only ours, but perhaps yours, too.

Some years ago I heard a man denounce the nuclear bombing of Japan as an obscenity; it was monstrous, barbarous, and no civilised people could even have contemplated it; we should all be thoroughly ashamed of it.

I couldn't argue with him, or deny the obscenity, monstrosity, and barbarism. I could only ask him questions, such as:

"Where were you when the war ended?"

"In Glasgow."

QUARTERED SAFE OUT HERE

"Will you answer a hypothetical question: if it were possible,
would you give your life now, to restore one of the lives of
Hiroshima?"

He wriggled a good deal, said it wasn't relevant, or logical, or
whatever, but in the end, to do him justice, he admitted that he
wouldn't.

So I asked him: "By what right, then, do you say that Allied
lives should have been sacrificed to save the victims of Hiroshima?
Because what you're saying is that, while you're not willing to give
your life, Allied soldiers should have given theirs. Mine for one,
possibly."

It was a bit unfair, perhaps, if only because I am rather heavily
built and he was an elderly philosopher and I was obviously much
moved, which may have flustered him, because he was unwise
enough to say that *that* was the point – we were soldiers, the bomb
victims were civilians. I did not pursue the question whether the
lives of your own soldiers should be sacrificed for the safety of
enemy civilians, because if you get into that particular moral jungle
you'll never come out; but I did point out that we were, in fact,
civilians, too – civilians in uniform, and could he understand our
possible resentment that people whose lives and liberties we had
been fighting to protect (him, in fact) should be ready to expend
us for the sake of Japanese?

He was getting quite alarmed now, because I do have a tendency
to raise my voice in debate. But he stuck to his guns and cried
"Japanese women and children!" I conceded this, and pointed out
that I had three children – but if I'd gone down in Malaya they'd
never have been born; they would, in fact, have been as effectively
deprived of existence as the children of Nagasaki. Was he advocat-
ing that?

He pointed out, fairly, that I might not have gone down in
Malaya, to which I (only too glad to escape from the *argumentum
ad hominem* which I'd introduced, because it makes you sound
like a right moaning "I-was-there" jungle-basher) retorted that
someone would surely have bought his lot in Malaya, and how
about *his* children?

He bolted, predictably, along the only escape route open to him
– and a well-worn one it has become – by saying that the bombs

were unnecessary because Japan was ready to surrender anyway, and it was only done because Truman wanted to use the thing to frighten the Russians, and all this talk that it would have cost 50,000 Allied lives to storm Japan was horse manure, because it would never have come to that.

"You think," I said, "you hope. But you don't *know*."

Yes, he did, and cited authorities.

"All right," I said. "Leave aside that I am arguably in a better position than you are to judge whether Jap was ready to surrender or not, at least at the sharp end, whatever Hirohito and Co were thinking – are you saying that the war would have ended on August 15 if the bombs hadn't been dropped?"

"No, of course not. But not long after . . . a few weeks . . ."

"Months, maybe?"

"Possibly . . . not likely . . ."

"But at any rate, *some* Allied lives would have been lost, after August 15 – lives which in fact were saved by the bombs?" Not mine, because I'd been in India by then, and the war would have had to go on for several months for me to get involved again. I didn't tell him that; it would just have confused the issue.

Yes, he admitted, some additional Allied lives would have been lost; he didn't say they were expendable, but he plainly thought so.

"And that would have been all right with you? British, Indian, American, Australian, Chinese – my God, yes, even Russian – all right for them to die, but not the people of Hiroshima – or you?"

He said something about military casualties being inevitable in war (*he* was telling *me!*), but that the scale of Hiroshima, the devastation, the after-effects, the calculated immolation of a whole city's population . . .

"Look," I said, "I'm not arguing with you. I'm not necessarily disagreeing with you. I just wanted to know where you stood, and to mention some points which you may not have considered, and to have you ask yourself if you are really in a position, morally speaking, to say who should have died and who shouldn't?"

"Well!" he said, looking aggrieved. "Where do *you* stand?"

"None of your goddam business," I said, sweetly reasonable as always, "but wherever it is, or was, it's somewhere you have never been, among people whom you wouldn't understand." Which was a bit over the score, but these armchair philosophers who live in their safe havens of the mind, and take their extensive moral views without ever really *thinking,* or exploring those unpleasant dark corners of debate which they don't like to think are there – they can, as Grandarse would have said, get on my wick.

As to where I stand – oh, in so many different places. They change with time, and my view is coloured by many different considerations. These are some of them.

The dropping of the bombs was a hideous thing, and I do not wonder that some of those who bore a part in it have been haunted by it all their lives. If it was not barbaric, the word has no meaning.

I led Nine Section for a time; leading or not, I was part of it. They were my mates, and to them I was bound by ties of duty, loyalty, and honour. Now, take Nine Section as representing those Allied soldiers who would certainly have died if the bombs had not been dropped (and remember that Nine Section might well have been not representatives, but the men themselves). Could I say, yes, Grandarse or Nick or Forster were expendable, and should have died rather than the victims of Hiroshima? No, never. And that goes for every Indian, American, Australian, African, Chinese and other soldier whose life was on the line in August, 1945. So drop the bomb.

And it was not only their lives, as I pointed out to my antibomb disputant. To reduce it to a selfish, personal level . . . if the bombs had been withheld, and the war had continued on conventional lines, then even if I'd failed my board and gone with the battalion into Malaya, the odds are that I'd have survived: 4 to 1 actuarially speaking, on the section's Burma fatalities. But I *might* have been that one, in which case my three children and six grandchildren would never have been born. And that, I'm afraid, is where all discussion of pros and cons evaporates and becomes meaningless, because for those nine lives I would pull the plug on the whole Japanese nation and never even blink. And so, I dare suggest, would you. And if you wouldn't, you may be nearer to the divine than I am but you sure as hell aren't fit to be parents or grandparents.

It comes to this, then, that I think the bombing was right? On those two counts, without a doubt. If it wasn't, what were we fighting for? And then I have another thought.

You see, I have a feeling that if – and I know it's an impossible if – but if, on that sunny August morning, Nine Section had known all that we know now of Hiroshima and Nagasaki, and could have been shown the effect of that bombing, and if some voice from on high had said: "There – that can end the war for you, if you want. But it doesn't have to happen; the alternative is that the war, as you've known it, goes on to a normal victorious conclusion, which may take some time, and if the past is anything to go by, some of you won't reach the end of the road. Anyway, Malaya's down that way . . . it's up to you", I think I know what would have happened. They would have cried "Aw, fook that!" with one voice, and then they would have sat about, snarling, and lapsed into silence, and then someone would have said heavily, "Aye, weel," and got to his feet, and been asked "W'eer th' 'ell you gan, then?" and given no reply, and at last the rest would have got up, too, gathering their gear with moaning and foul language and ill-tempered harking back to the long dirty bloody miles from the Imphal boxes to the Sittang Bend and the iniquity of having to do it again, slinging their rifles and bickering about who was to go on point, and "Ah's aboot 'ed it, me!" and "You, ye bugger, ye're knackered afower ye start, you!" and "We'll a' git killed!", and then they would have been moving south. Because that is the kind of men they were. And that is why I have written this book.

Perhaps that image of them is imprinted so strongly on my mind because that is how I last saw them, on one of those dusty, languid summer afternoons, on my last day in Fourteenth Army. What am I talking about? My last day in Fourteenth Army will be the day they shovel me under. But it was the day on which I was summoned to the company basha and handed my pay-book by the O.C., with a travel warrant to Meiktila and on to Chittagong where the selection board were crouched to spring.

"Well, let's hope we're seeing the last of you," he said, grinning. "Wonder where they'll send you, if you pass? There are four officer training schools for the Indian Army, you know – Dehra Dun for gentlemen, Bangalore for soldiers, Mhow for schoolboys, and Belgaum – can't remember what it's for, head-cases, maybe. Well, good luck, and remember not to scratch your arse or giggle – they can't stand gigglers."

I went out practising my expression of grim resolve, and with unsteady hands leafed through my pay-book to the vital entry which Long John had written – but he had been kinder than I deserved; it wouldn't be his fault if I failed. Then I got my kit together, big pack, small pack, blanket and groundsheet, rifle and bayonet and kukri. I charged my magazine out of sheer habit, and then took my bandolier with its remaining rounds and my two grenades to the Q.M. store. There was about half an hour before the 15cwt truck came to ferry me and other travellers north – it would be odd, going back through Penwegon and Pyawbwe and Meiktila again; they would be busier, in one way, with support troops and establishments, but much quieter in another. And there wouldn't be a thing stirring in the temple wood, or in the little village with the high banks where I'd nearly done for Nick, or on the sandy ground where I'd talked geometry with the Duke. It was all past and done with.

I can't say those thoughts were in my mind, then; I was probably too excited and anxious about going before the selection board. But they occur naturally now, nearly half a century after, and I wonder what I think about it all.

Glad I was there; I wouldn't have missed it for anything. A good thing to have done, and to have been, as Samuel Johnson so wisely observed. No regrets about it, and much gratitude. I can almost hear an interviewer saying: "What about guilt?", to which I could only reply: "What's to be guilty about? I didn't ask for the bloody war." He might speculate, because it seems to be the fashion nowadays, on guilt for having survived where others did not – which is one of the silliest notions I have ever heard. If you feel someone got killed because you let them down, that's a reason for guilt, no question – but to feel guilty because the man next to you caught it when you didn't, that's pointless. Remember him, revere him, but don't feel guilty.

It's terribly trite, no doubt, but like most trite things it's absolutely true: the best comment on infantry war, the best philosophy, and above all the best advice, was written in four lines by Rudyard Kipling. It isn't jingoistic, it's realistic; it has nothing to do with the higher questions of morality, but it has deep meaning for anyone who finds himself, as so many have done and will continue to do, facing the moment.

> When first under fire and you're wishful to duck,
> Don't look nor take heed at the man that is struck,
> Be thankful you're living, and trust to your luck,
> And march to your front like a soldier.

There was just time to walk the hundred yards to Nine Section's billet to say good-bye – after all, I might pass the examiners and never see Burma again. But the basha was empty, except for a young fellow sweeping the floor; from the newness of his jungle-green trousers and the fact that the dye hadn't soaked out of his vest, he was obviously a newcomer.

I asked where they were, and he said they'd gone out the day before to a village not far away, and were due back today, but he didn't know when. "Trouble?" I asked, but he didn't think so, just routine. He himself had arrived yesterday, and seen them only briefly before they set out.

"Ah wish they'd took us wid them," he added wistfully, "but corp'ral told us tae settle in, like."

Something about him made me feel terribly old. I asked where he was from.

"Ah came oop f'ae Rangoon, but –"

"No, I mean where in Cumberland."

He brightened. "Brampton. Ye knaw it, it's aboot ten mile –"

"Yes, the Howard Arms. What's your name?"

"Storey, corp'ral."

Well, that figured. "You'll be at home, then. They're a good bunch."

"Aye?" There was a shade of doubt in his voice. "Ah dunno . . . some o' them's foony boogers." I made an inquiring noise. "They were on aboot the coostard gun."

"The custard gun? That's a new one. Go on."

"Weel, the big stoot feller, dunno 'is name –"

"Grandarse."

"Aw, aye – weel, 'e wes tellin' us, that of a' the weapons the Japs 'ev got, the coostard gun's the woorst, because it fires coostard pies, an' if one o' them boorsts near ye –" he began to laugh "– an' the coostard splashes ye, ye've 'ed it!"

"That sounds like Grandarse."

"An' the lal feller they ca'd Nick, 'e sez the coostard's bad enoof, but if the croost 'its yer, an' rings yer neck, it'll tak' yer 'eid off!" He held on to his broom, heaving with mirth. "They aren't 'alf a daft boonch, eh?"

"Too true. Well, look, will you tell them Jock was in, just to say so long? I'm flying out to India."

"Reet, corp. Ah'll tell 'em tarra-well."

"Thanks." Tarra-well. "And good luck."

I was in the back of the 15cwt, and the driver was heaving up the tailboard, when they hove in view, the dusty file swinging up the dirt road, and I heard Forster's raucous voice raised in Parker's signature tune. There wasn't a chance to get out, for the engine was idling, the driver was going round to his seat, and their corporal, who must have been a real regimental idiot, was actually calling the step – left-right, dear God, when they'd been on patrol. Change and decay, I thought, and then one of them spotted me and let out a yell.

"'Ey, look at yon! 'Ey, Jock, w'eer ye gan, lad?"

"Going out to India!" I shouted, as the truck began to move.

"Ye w'at? By God, it's awreet for soom, eh?"

"Boogerin' off w'en oor back's turned, an' a' –"

"I came to the billet," I shouted, "but you weren't –"

"Bloody 'ell! 'E's bin gan through oor kit for fags! We'll be smeukin' grass an' goat-shit!"

"Shoot the booger, 'e's desertin'!"

"Sharrup!" cried the corporal. "Keep the step!"

"Aw, fook off, you! So long, Jock lad!"

"Wiv my permish you'll get a commish!"

"'Ey, Jock! Git stoofed!" (God bless, Foshie.)

"Tarra, son!"

"'Bye, Jock!"

I wanted to shout back, but I couldn't. I could only wave, as the truck gathered speed, and for some daft reason – it must have been Forster's raucous singing when they first came into view – the only sound I could make was a whisper to myself of the words running through my head:

> Wrap up all my care and woe,
> Here I go, swinging low,
> Bye-bye, Shanghai.
> Won't somebody wait for me,
> Please get in a state for me,
> Bye-bye, Shanghai . . .

But if I couldn't call good-bye, there was something else I could do. It came to me as I looked back, the thought: you must never forget this moment. Fix it in your mind forever, because it's the ending to a chapter of your life, and you'll never see anything like it again. Salt it away in your memory, so that you'll always be able to close your eyes and see the single file of dark green figures in the dusty sunlight, marching at ease, the bush-hats tilted, the rifles slung. That's something you must always remember.

> Up before the colonel in the morning
> He gave me a rocket and a warning:

And I have remembered.

> "You've been out with Sun-yat-sen,
> You won't go out with him again!"
> Shanghai!
> Bye-bye!

EPILOGUE
Fifty Years On

On the fiftieth anniversary of VJ-Day I made a special trip to Carlisle for the Cathedral service, wearing my medals for the first and probably the last time. I hadn't intended to go. I'm not one for formal reunions, with British Legion standards and intonations of Laurence Binyon, and never felt comfortable watching the big Burma bash in the Albert Hall on tv (or the Remembrance Sunday show, for that matter, with its energetic Sea Scouts climbing poles and artillery teams assembling guns to the cheer-leading of a commentator, before the petals shower down). I don't know why this kind of thing doesn't attract me. I think it's because it has bugger-all to do with Tich Little (no, give him his real name now, Ike Blakeley) going down before Kinde Wood, or John Luke (Gale in the book) dropping in the bunker entrance, or going in under the guns at Pyawbwe. I don't need a reunion to remember them; they'll be with me always. But of course their kinsfolk weren't at Kinde or Pyawbwe, and must take their memories from the last time they saw them, and I guess the Remembrance ceremonies are a comfort to them.

The annual 9th Border service at the Cathedral, and the booze and sandwiches at the Castle later, are different. There are never that many of us, forty maybe, and it's good to gossip and be jolly. Camaraderie, that's what they are about, and old times, and seeing Sam Wilson and Dalgleish and Jimmy Gibson well and hearty. None of 9 Section survives, so far as I know, and Tommy Martin, whose voice (pure Denton Holme gravel) was always in my ears when I wrote the dialogue passages, died a couple of years back. But, as I say, that kind of occasion is different, or was, for now we've held the last of them.

VJ-50 was something else. I had supposed, in advance, that it would be used as a great propaganda occasion by the anti-bomb

227

brigade, who would have a field day about the obscenity, inhumanity, etc., of Hiroshima and Nagasaki. After all, the VE-Day 50th anniversary had been marred, for me, by the great outcry not long before over Dresden, with a member of the Royal Family being dragooned, no doubt unwillingly, into apologizing for that bombing. As if it was his damned business; he wasn't even born. To think of our air crews, people like Bill Hetherington, my wife Kathy's Canadian cousin, killed in action, and Bob Fowler with his parachute on fire, and contrast that with a British Royal having to humble himself before the nation who started it all, and gave Hitler their full backing. But I must be calm. Anyway, it wasn't a good augury for VJ-50.

In the event, it was a terrific success. The sun shone in London, and the old buffers turned out, and Prince Philip took part in the march past, and it was all glorious. XIVth Army were the country's darlings—"no longer forgotten", as the pundits kept saying. (Quite honestly, I never thought we were.) Hiroshima and Nagasaki never got a look-in, probably because our case had been stated, unanswerably, in the tv programmes in the run up to the day itself. The P.O.W.s had a good airing, the horrors of the railway were described, and at last the message got home that if it hadn't been for the bombs the prisoners would probably have been massacred, and Allied casualties would have been horrific. Anyway, the country was in no mood to be sorry for the Japs.

I had taken part in two or three tv programmes, about the war, and the Japs, and "guilt", and was able to say on the air what I've said in this book. I hope I put it fairly; I noticed that most of those interviewed said the same thing; we were not forgiving. The man I was most pleased to hear was Bishop Montefiore, whom no one could accuse of being a blood-lusting reactionary; no one listening to him could doubt that the bombing was right.

Anyway, I had decided to give the Carlisle Cathedral service a miss. I declined an invitation to read the Kohima Epitaph at the service (the thought of Lance-corporal Fraser doing that on national tv, when there were so many worthier people available, was unbearable), but at the last minute I decided I'd like to be there. Long John Petty had died just a couple of weeks earlier, I hadn't been able to get to his funeral, and for some reason that helped to make up my mind. I bummed an eleventh-hour invitation, and went over the day before, staying at the Crown and Mitre, next door to the Cathedral.

In the morning I put on my good suit, regimental tie, and the gongs, and loafed out in good time to have a walk round the old city before the service. They already had the barriers up, but there weren't many folk about, only a couple of young policemen outside the hotel. They noticed the gongs—and saluted! I must say that took me flat aback; I mumbled something and took off, thinking, how nice of them. I tooled about Scotch Street and Fisher Street and Long Lane and the Cathedral grounds, and then went in when the crowds started to arrive.

There were a lot of grey heads and Burma Stars in the pews, naturally, with the VIPs down in the nave, but I had one of the choir stalls (Canon 11) which heave you out if you go to sleep—or so they used to tell us when we attended the old Grammar School's service on Ascension Day. Some port-wine-faced berk tried to pinch my seat, but I looked at him and he faded.

I didn't care for the sermon. The preacher struck me as rather trendy, and I got the impression that he was a bit of a reconciler and forgiver. The hell with that. Also, they had some ghastly new version of "Who would true valour see?"—imagine, someone, some appalling brute that perishes, actually thought he could write better verse than Bunyan! Well, the hell with him, too; I sang the old words, hobgoblins, foul fiends, and all. Likewise in the National Anthem, while the rest were singing the unutterable, sanctimonious, politically correct pap of the new third verse, I'm glad to say I was confounding their politics and frustrating their knavish tricks at full belt.

The chap who spoke the sort of layman's part of the service felt he had to say something about forgiveness, too, but I'm sure he didn't mean it. I thought of Oliver Cromwell standing in the Cathedral 350 years earlier, giving orders for the stabling of his cavalry mounts in the nave (a bit gross, but that's Old Noll for you), and thought to myself that he wouldn't have had much time for forgiving the Huns and Japs, either.

The whole performance being on national tv, I was delighted when Long John's picture came up on the screen, and Johnny Burgess's, and I thought: "Ah's wid tha, marras."

Afterwards, the "veterans", as they call us (in my youth a veteran was a 30-year service man), fell in outside to march to the Town Hall. I had determined that I was not going to make a spectacle of

229

myself by shambling in the ranks at my time of life, but when I saw
them forming up I thought, what the hell, it's the last time, and fell
in, too. There were King's Own behind me (they amalgamated with
the Borders years ago), and of course they were belly-aching about
how it was all Border Regiment today, and why hadn't the service
been held in Lancaster? For the very good reason that the Border
Regiment had three battalions in Burma, and no regiment better
typified XIVth Army infantry.

They marched us to the Town Hall, a couple of hundred of us,
old as sin and not two pounds of us hanging straight. The people
behind the barriers began clapping, which I confess took me by
surprise, and I found my eyes stinging. I thought we'd stop at the
Town Hall, but damned if they didn't march us back along Castle
Street, and the people still clapping and cheering, and I heard a little girl's voice piping: "'Ey, theer's gran'pa! 'Ey, gran'pa!" Lucky
gran'pa, whoever he was.

It was blazing sunshine, and by the time we got abreast of Tullie
House there was a fair amount of wheezing and gasping audible in
the ranks, and more than one exclamation of "Booger me!" God
knows what the band was playing, but as we staggered up the
causeway and under the Castle gateway, they struck up "John
Peel", and I thought, by God, you're privileged, for this is the last
march of the old Border Regiment, Lucas's Foot, founded 1702
(Richard Steele of essay fame was one of its junior officers), the old
34th of Arroyo and China and the frontier and God knows where
else, the inheritors of the men who garrisoned this Castle and held
this border eight hundred years ago, and after those three regimental
centuries we're coming off parade for the very last time, and there'll
be no more Border Regiment ever again. Oh, I know there's the
amalgamated KORB, but we're the last of the real Border.

They halted us in the square, and there were Army boys on a big
tank, with an enormous gun, taking pictures of us as we dismissed.
A voice somewhere in the parade bellowed: "'Ey, 'ev ye got a pullthrough for that goon? There's a lal feller 'ere needs pullin'
through, 'is legs is bad!"

It might have been Grandarse, and the lal feller might have been
Nick, but since he didn't cry "We'll all git killed!" I guess it must
have been two other chaps.

I didn't stay for the VIP lunch afterwards. I had a notion that not many of those who had marched would have been invited, and I had no wish to sit down with the good and great, worthy folk though I know they were. I walked along Castle Street and English Street to the station, having divested myself of my gongs in the Crown and Mitre bogs, and caught the train, thinking: wrap up all my care and woe, so long, lads, and thanks. How the years go by, and how changed everything is, and how much you see around you today that you didn't fight for, and sometimes you can feel betrayed and pretty fed up. But think of the Carlisle people clapping and "'Ey, gran'pa!" Aye, it was worth it. By God, it was worth it.

Watching the evening celebrations of VJ-50 on tv that night, the rockets and the floodlights, the Queen and the huge crowds, the music and the cheering, and the amber streaks in the western sky, I thought to myself: the sun set on the British Empire a long time ago, irrevocably, and inevitably, but what you're seeing now, this night of VJ-50, is the last reflection of that imperial sun, gone beneath the horizon, but reminding generations who never knew the Empire and its heartland, of what once was. The British were happy that night of VJ-50, with a sense of something well done, not just in 1945, but for centuries before.

My daughter Caro and her husband (his father was a prisoner of the Japanese) took their children to see the fireworks on the Thames, and amidst all the noise and merrymaking our little granddaughter, Genny, aged six, who is English-Scottish-Welsh, raised her paper cup of lemonade and cried: "A toast—to victory!" And the people laughed and cheered.

GLOSSARY

Foreign words are Hindustani unless otherwise stated.

admi	man
bait	food, snack
basha	native house, hut
bibi, bint	girl
bidi	native cheroot
bund	embankment
bundook	rifle
burgoo	porridge (Turkish, *burghal*)
bus	finished, the end
chaggle	canvas water-bag
chah	tea
charpoy	native rope bed
chaung	river gully, watercourse (Burmese)
cheeny	sugar
chota wallah	little fellow
coggage	paper (*kaguz*)
connor	food (*khana*)
dah	machete (Burmese)
dekko	look, see
Denton Holme	a district of Carlisle
dersi	tailor
dhobi	laundryman
dhoti	loincloth
dood	milk
doolally	mad (from Deolali, Indian transit camp famous for sunstroke)
durwan	porter, doorkeeper
duser	other
ek	one (numeral)
glasshouse	military prison (from the glass roof at Aldershot)

gongs	war medals
goolie	ball (*gola*)
ham	I (personal pronoun)
havildar	sergeant
housewife	hold-all for needle, thread, etc.
idderao!	come here!
indaba	affair, concern (Swahili, council)
isker	thing (Arabic)
jao	go
jawan	soldier
jildi	quickly
khud	jungle hill
klifty	steal
kukri	Gurkha short sword
lathi	policeman's staff
maidan	plain, exercise ground
mallum	understand
marra	(lit. "marrow"), comrade, pal
mera	my
naik	corporal
nappy-wallah	barber
nullah	gully, dry watercourse
pani	water
pialla	enamelled mug
punji	poisoned stake, booby-trap
sarf karo	to clean (up), hence, to kill
shabash!	bravo!
stag	guard, sentry-go
sub-cheese	everything, the lot (also "sub-muckin")
tairo	wait, hold on
tum	thou
tik hai	all right, good

COMMON READER EDITIONS

As booksellers since 1986, we have been stocking the pages of our monthly catalogue, A COMMON READER, with "Books for Readers with Imagination." Now as publishers, the same motto guides our work. Simply put, the titles we issue as COMMON READER EDITIONS are volumes of uncommon merit which we have enjoyed, and which we think other imaginative readers will enjoy as well. While our selections are as personal as the act of reading itself, what's common to our enterprise is the sense of shared experience a good book brings to solitary readers. We invite you to sample the wide range of COMMON READER EDITIONS, and welcome your comments.

www.commonreader.com